Future of Tourism Marketing

Marketing in the tourism and hospitality industry has transformed with the development of digital marketing tools and the evolution of social culture. Recently, the advent of new technologies such as smartphones, artificial intelligence, virtual reality, robots, and new Geographic Information System (GIS) systems has created more possibilities for marketing innovations. Advancements in information technology are leading to changes in business processes, service standards, and management mindsets. Meanwhile, consumers are also adapting to the new marketing paradigm. Researchers are interested in studying this newly emerging and unpredictable business environment, customer decision-making, new management tactics, and business analytic strategies.

Future of Tourism Marketing aims to assess the role of modern technologies in marketing tourism destinations and their effects on potential visitors. This book will provide an update on research into the new marketing paradigm that is developing as a result of new technologies in a post-modern era.

The chapters in this book were originally published in *Journal of Travel & Tourism Marketing*.

Seongseop (Sam) Kim is Professor at the School of Hotel and Tourism Management at The Hong Kong Polytechnic University, China. He is a prolific author in the field of tourism and hospitality, and is on the editorial board of multiple international journals.

Dan Wang is Associate Professor at the School of Hotel and Tourism Management at The Hong Kong Polytechnic University, China. She is interested in the impact of information technology on tourist's behaviour and organizational changes from the sociological and management lens.

Future of Tourism Marketing

Edited by
Seongseop (Sam) Kim and Dan Wang

LONDON AND NEW YORK

First published 2021
by Routledge
2 Park Square, Milton Park, Abingdon, Oxon, OX14 4RN

and by Routledge
605 Third Avenue, New York, NY 10158

Routledge is an imprint of the Taylor & Francis Group, an informa business

British Library Cataloguing-in-Publication Data
A catalogue record for this book is available from the British Library

ISBN13: 978-1-032-00834-9 (hbk)
ISBN13: 978-1-032-00838-7 (pbk)
ISBN13: 978-1-003-17603-9 (ebk)

Typeset in Myriad Pro
by codeMantra

Publisher's Note
The publisher accepts responsibility for any inconsistencies that may have arisen during the conversion of this book from journal articles to book chapters, namely the inclusion of journal terminology.

Disclaimer
Every effort has been made to contact copyright holders for their permission to reprint material in this book. The publishers would be grateful to hear from any copyright holder who is not here acknowledged and will undertake to rectify any errors or omissions in future editions of this book.

Contents

Citation Information   vi
Notes on Contributors   viii

Preface: future of tourism marketing   1
Seongseop (Sam) Kim and Dan Wang

1   Consumer adoption of the Uber mobile application: Insights from diffusion of innovation
    theory and technology acceptance model   2
    Somang Min, Kevin Kam Fung So and Miyoung Jeong

2   Marketing robot services in hospitality and tourism: the role of anthropomorphism   16
    Jamie Murphy, Ulrike Gretzel and Juho Pesonen

3   Classifying technological innovation attributes for hotels: an application of the Kano model   28
    Chun-Fang Chiang, Wen-Yu Chen and Chia-Yuan Hsu

4   The view from above: the relevance of shared aerial drone videos for destination marketing   40
    Uglješa Stankov, James Kennell, Alastair M. Morrison and Miroslav D. Vujičić

5   Using tracking technology to improve marketing: insights from a historic town in
    Tasmania, Australia   55
    Bob Mckercher, Anne Hardy and Jagannath Aryal

6   Consequences of psychological benefits of using eco-friendly services in the context of
    drone food delivery services   67
    Jinsoo Hwang, Sun-Bai Cho and Woohyoung Kim

7   Integrating virtual reality devices into the body: effects of technological embodiment on
    customer engagement and behavioral intentions toward the destination   79
    Carlos Flavián, Sergio Ibáñez-Sánchez and Carlos Orús

8   Tourists as Mobile Gamers: Gamification for Tourism Marketing   96
    Feifei Xu, Feng Tian, Dimitrios Buhalis, Jessica Weber and Hongmei Zhang

Index   115

Citation Information

The chapters in this book, except Chapter 8, were originally published in the *Journal of Travel & Tourism Marketing*, volume 36, issue 7 (2019). Chapter 8 was originally published in volume 33, issue 8 of the same journal. When citing this material, please use the original page numbering for each article, as follows:

Preface
Preface to journal of travel & tourism marketing special issue on future of tourism marketing
Seongseop (Sam) Kim and Dan Wang
Journal of Travel & Tourism Marketing, volume 36, issue 7 (2019), pp. 769

Chapter 1
Consumer adoption of the Uber mobile application: Insights from diffusion of innovation theory and technology acceptance model
Somang Min, Kevin Kam Fung So and Miyoung Jeong
Journal of Travel & Tourism Marketing, volume 36, issue 7 (2019), pp. 770–783

Chapter 2
Marketing robot services in hospitality and tourism: the role of anthropomorphism
Jamie Murphy, Ulrike Gretzel and Juho Pesonen
Journal of Travel & Tourism Marketing, volume 36, issue 7 (2019), pp. 784–795

Chapter 3
Classifying technological innovation attributes for hotels: an application of the Kano model
Chun-Fang Chiang, Wen-Yu Chen and Chia-Yuan Hsu
Journal of Travel & Tourism Marketing, volume 36, issue 7 (2019), pp. 796–807

Chapter 4
The view from above: the relevance of shared aerial drone videos for destination marketing
Uglješa Stankov, James Kennell, Alastair M. Morrison and Miroslav D. Vujičić
Journal of Travel & Tourism Marketing, volume 36, issue 7 (2019), pp. 808–822

Chapter 5
Using tracking technology to improve marketing: insights from a historic town in Tasmania, Australia
Bob Mckercher, Anne Hardy and Jagannath Aryal
Journal of Travel & Tourism Marketing, volume 36, issue 7 (2019), pp. 823–834

Chapter 6
Consequences of psychological benefits of using eco-friendly services in the context of drone food delivery services
Jinsoo Hwang, Sun-Bai Cho and Woohyoung Kim
Journal of Travel & Tourism Marketing, volume 36, issue 7 (2019) pp. 835–846

Chapter 7

Integrating virtual reality devices into the body: effects of technological embodiment on customer engagement and behavioral intentions toward the destination
Carlos Flavián, Sergio Ibáñez-Sánchez and Carlos Orús
Journal of Travel & Tourism Marketing, volume 36, issue 7 (2019), pp. 847–863

Chapter 8

Tourists as Mobile Gamers: Gamification for Tourism Marketing
Feifei Xu, Feng Tian, Dimitrios Buhalis, Jessica Weber and Hongmei Zhang
Journal of Travel & Tourism Marketing, volume 33, issue 8 (2016) pp. 1124–1142

For any permission-related enquiries please visit:
http://www.tandfonline.com/page/help/permissions

Contributors

Jagannath Aryal Surveying and Spatial Sciences Group, University of Tasmania, Hobart, Australia.

Dimitrios Buhalis School of Tourism, Bournemouth University, UK.

Wen-Yu Chen Department of Leisure Management, National Pingtung University, Taiwan.

Chun-Fang Chiang Department of Tourism Management, Chinese Culture University, Taipei, Taiwan.

Sun-Bai Cho The Department of Hotel Management, Cheongju University, Cheongju-si, South Korea.

Carlos Flavián Department of Marketing Management and Market Research, University of Zaragoza, Spain.

Ulrike Gretzel Annenberg School for Communication and Journalism, University of Southern California, Los Angeles, USA.

Anne Hardy Tasmanian School of Business and Economics, University of Tasmania, Hobart, Australia.

Chia-Yuan Hsu Department of Tourism Management, Chinese Culture University, Taipei, Taiwan.

Jinsoo Hwang College of Hospitality and Tourism Management, Sejong University, Seoul, South Korea.

Sergio Ibáñez-Sánchez Department of Marketing Management and Market Research, University of Zaragoza, Spain.

Miyoung Jeong School of Hotel, Restaurant and Tourism Management; College of Hospitality, Retail and Sport Management; University of South Carolina, Columbia, USA.

James Kennell Faculty of Business; Department of Marketing, Events and Tourism; Old Royal Naval College; University of Greenwich; London; UK.

Seongseop (Sam) Kim School of Hotel and Tourism Management, The Hong Kong Polytechnic University, China.

Woohyoung Kim Graduate School of Technology Management, Kyunghee University, Yongin, South Korea.

Bob Mckercher School of Hotel and Tourism Management, The Hong Kong Polytechnic University, China.

Somang Min School of Hotel, Restaurant and Tourism Management; Center of Economic Excellence in Tourism and Economic Development; College of Hospitality, Retail and Sport Management; University of South Carolina; Columbia; USA.

Alastair M. Morrison Graduate Institute of Tourism, National Kaohsiung University of Hospitality and Tourism, Taiwan.

Jamie Murphy Centre for Tourism Studies, University of Eastern Finland, Joensuu, Finland.

Carlos Orús Department of Marketing Management and Market Research, University of Zaragoza, Spain.

Juho Pesonen Centre for Tourism Studies, University of Eastern Finland, Joensuu, Finland.

Kevin Kam Fung So School of Hotel, Restaurant and Tourism Management; Center of Economic Excellence in Tourism and Economic Development; College of Hospitality, Retail and Sport Management; University of South Carolina; Columbia; USA.

Uglješa Stankov Faculty of Sciences; Department of Geography, Tourism and Hotel Management; University of Novi Sad; Serbia.

Feng Tian Centre of Creative Technology, Bournemouth University, UK.

Miroslav D. Vujičić Faculty of Sciences; Department of Geography, Tourism and Hotel Management; University of Novi Sad; Serbia.

Dan Wang School of Hotel and Tourism Management, The Hong Kong Polytechnic University, China.

Jessica Weber School of Tourism, Bournemouth University, UK.

Feifei Xu School of Humanities, Southeast University, Nanjing, China.

Hongmei Zhang is College of Territorial Resources and Tourism, Anhui Normal University, Wuhu, China.

Preface: future of tourism marketing

Marketing in the tourism and hospitality industry has been transformed with the development of digital marketing tools and the evolution of social culture. Recently, the advent of new technologies, such as smartphones, artificial intelligence, virtual reality (VR), robots, and new GIS, has created added possibilities for marketing innovations. Advancements in information technology have resulted in changes in business processes, service standards, and management mindsets. Meanwhile, consumers have adapted the new marketing paradigm. Researchers are interested in studying the newly emerging and unpredictable business environment, customer decision-making, new management tactics, and business analytic strategies. Accordingly, this volume aims to assess the role of modern technologies in marketing tourism destinations and their effects on potential visitors.

In this book, diverse future technological channels are introduced: mobile applications, technological facilities, and services in hotels, robots, aerial drone videos, tracking applications, VR devices, and drone food delivery. Eight articles are introduced in the following paragraphs. Capitalizing on innovation theory and technology acceptance model, Min, So, and Jeong attempted to examine Uber's mobile application. Accordingly, they found that the model's compatibility, complexity, relative advantage, observability, and social influence significantly affect perceived usefulness and perceived ease of use. They concluded that the two traditional models explain consumers' adoption of Uber's mobile application.

Chiang, Chen, and Hsu classified technological innovation attributes of hotels by using the Kano model. The results of their empirical testing demonstrate the contribution of four technological innovation factors to hotel businesses, namely, the Internet and its application use, smartphone usage as a room key and for payment, e-housekeeping, and use of electronic self-service systems.

Murphy, Gretzwl, and Pesonen assessed the role of robots in offering hospitality and tourism services. Their research identified the robotic service (rService) model with expounding 11 robot capabilities that facilitate anthropomorphism. This paper sheds diverse managerial implications on how to accommodate industrial robots and understand rService experience. The research of Stankov, Kennell, Morrison, and Vujicic enlighten us on the use of drones for destination marketing. As research methods, YouTube metadata and spatial overlay analysis of shared aerial drone videos were applied. They found that shared aerial drone videos provide unique user-generated content features and show more spatial distribution in populated districts.

Similar with Stankov et al.'s study, Hwang, Cho, and Kim investigated the possibility of drone food delivery. Their study assessed psychological benefits using the eco-friendly delivery service and expected emotions accrued from drone delivery. This study has a value in view of anticipated future trends and customers' responses. McKercher, Hardy, and Aryal analyzed the movement patterns of different market segments in a historic town using visitor surveys. The technology informs us of preferred destinations, movement time, movement duration, and routes. Consequently, the tracking technology facilitates the development of the tourist route, congestion control, and tourism attraction development plan. Flavian, Ibanez-Sanchez, and Orus adopted a lab experiment method to investigate the usefulness of VR devices. VR head-mounted displays offer more engagement and high behavioral intention through their immersive experiences and sensory stimuli. Therefore, VR technology can be utilized to the handicapped or underprivileged who have limited accessibility because the devices cater to the alternate satisfaction.

In the next chapter, Xu, Tian, Buhalis, Weber and Zhang adopted gaming or gamification to identify its potential to facilitate tourism demand according to an increase in gaming population.

Overall, the eight articles presented in this special issue have a well-balanced combination in terms of new technological realms (mobile applications, robots, drone videos, tracking technology, and VR), methodologies (lab experiments, surveys, and descriptive), and study regions (US, Taiwan, Korea, Spain, UK, and Australia). We anticipate and trust you will love reading this volume and spread the content to other readers.

Seongseop (Sam) Kim
School of Hotel and Tourism Management, The Hong Kong Polytechnic University
✉ sam.kim@polyu.edu.hk
ⓘ http://orcid.org/0000-0002-9213-6540

Dan Wang
School of Hotel and Tourism Management, The Hong Kong Polytechnic University
✉ d.wang@polyu.edu.hk

Consumer adoption of the Uber mobile application: Insights from diffusion of innovation theory and technology acceptance model

Somang Min, Kevin Kam Fung So and Miyoung Jeong

ABSTRACT

The sharing economy literature has largely concentrated on the examination of peer-to-peer accommodation platforms such as Airbnb, with little attention paid on other innovations in collaborative consumption. This study investigates consumer adoption of the Uber mobile application through lenses of two theoretical models – Diffusion of Innovation Theory and Technology Acceptance Model. The results suggest that relative advantage, compatibility, complexity, observability, and social influence have a significant influence on both perceived usefulness and perceived ease of use, which in turn lead to subsequent consumer attitudes and adoption intentions. This study demonstrates the integration of the two classic adoption theories.

Introduction

The sharing economy is a trending business concept, which has recently emerged as an innovative business model where people collaboratively make use of under-utilized resources in innovative ways (Cohen & Kietzmann, 2014). This new consumption model, described as "disruptive innovation", has challenged the traditional business concept by altering the modes of business as well as shifting the concept of consumption – what to consume and how to consume (Botsman & Rogers, 2011). Most notably, consumers are getting the option to share or rent resources such as cars and rooms from each other rather than from traditional businesses such as taxi companies and hotels (Satama, 2014).

One of the most typical representatives of collaborative consumption adopted in the tourism industry is Uber. Uber utilizes a mobile application that provides an online network for people to share rides by connecting independent drivers and customers (Hall, Kendrick, & Nosko, 2015). It has taken a role of a traditional taxi and is becoming more and more popular, reaching up to 40 million monthly active riders worldwide in 2016 (Kokalitcheva, 2016). Also, its popularity can be seen from the ranking of free download applications both in Apple and Android market, where Uber was ranked top 20 as of 2017 (iTunes; Google Play). In fact, the idea of sharing rides would not have been possible without the development of smartphones as a new technology. Since smartphones are now embedded in people's daily lives (Wang, So, & Sparks, 2014), it has changed the way people live, communicate, and conduct transactions (De Ridder, 2016). The unique characteristics of a smartphone include diversifying the input capability, Internet access, and location awareness functions (Want, 2009). These unique functions enable drivers and consumers to receive real-time information of users' location, which makes their sharing possible. As such, smartphones make it easier for travelers to access the Uber mobile application anytime and anywhere, when they need to take an Uber.

However, despite the increasing adoption of such new technology by travelers, as well as the thriving sharing economy as a whole, few studies have examined the factors affecting the adoption of the Uber mobile application. While a significant body of the literature on the sharing economy is developing, most recent studies have concentrated on the business or governmental perspective, such as impact of Airbnb on the tourism industry (Oskam & Boswijk, 2016), local regulations of Uber (Rauch & Schleicher, 2015), how to overcome regulations as a barrier (Cannon & Summers, 2014), impacts on global sustainability (Cohen & Kietzmann, 2014), rather than focusing on the consumers' perspective. A review of the literature suggests that very limited studies have examined consumers' perspective, with the exception of several recent studies. For example, Zhu, So, and Hudson (2017) examined consumers' motivations behind the adoption of mobile applications of the sharing economy, Liu and Mattila (2017) studied consumer decisions on Airbnb, So, Oh, and Min (2018) modeled motivations and constraints of Airbnb consumers, and Tussyadiah and Pesonen (2016) examined the impact of peer-to-peer accommodation on travelers' behavior. Despite the rapid growth of the sharing economy, the literature still lacks empirical research addressing a critical research question of this phenomenon from the consumer's perspective: What are the main factors that affect consumers to adopt the Uber mobile application (both from the aspect of the business concept and the technological aspect)? As such, this study sets forth to examine factors influencing consumer utilization of the Uber mobile application by integrating diffusion of innovation theory (DIT) and technology acceptance model (TAM).

The new theoretical model introduced in this study contributes to the literature by advancing our current understanding of consumers' adoption behavior through the lens of TAM and DIT, and by providing important practical insights to enhance industry practices. The ensuing section presents the theoretical foundation upon which this investigation is based, followed by a theoretical framework that integrates TAM and DIT. The research hypotheses are developed based on previous relevant literature. Next, the research methodology is discussed along with the results. Finally, this paper concludes with discussions of theoretical and practical implications, as well as the limitations and suggestions for future research.

Theoretical background

In examining factors affecting the adoption of the Uber mobile application, this study takes an innovative approach by integrating diffusion of innovation theory (DIT) and the technology acceptance model (TAM). DIT is known to be useful in understanding specific innovation characteristics (Rogers & Shoemaker, 1983) and TAM recognizes the key factors that affect the acceptance of a new innovation (Venkatesh & Davis, 2000). Integrating the two theories can not only explain consumers' general perception toward adopting the Uber mobile application (by using TAM) but also the specific characteristics that attract consumers to adopt the application (by using DIT).

Technology acceptance model (TAM)

The technology acceptance model (TAM) (Davis, 1989) is the most influential and widely used theory for explaining an individual's acceptance of information technology (Lee, Hsieh, & Hsu, 2011). TAM determines user attitude (Davis, 1989) and recognizes the role of perceived ease of use (PEOU) and perceived usefulness (PU) in understanding user acceptance in information systems (Taylor & Todd, 1995; Venkatesh & Davis, 2000). However, while extensive research has adopted TAM, it has been criticized for not fully reflecting the nature of consumer adoption.

Some studies (i.e., Kim, 2016; Lee et al., 2011; Morosan & DeFranco, 2014; Yang, 2005) have extended the TAM framework by adding more antecedents to obtain a better explanatory power (Kim, 2016; Lee et al., 2011; Morosan & DeFranco, 2014; Yang, 2005). Kim (2016), for example, incorporated subjective norm and perceived credibility into the model as antecedents to examine their effects on customers' behavioral intention toward hotel tablet apps. The study of Morosan and DeFranco (2014) showed that subjective norm, PU, and PEOU were key factors determining club members' intention to use mobile devices in clubs.

In TAM, PU and PEOU are the two key exogenous constructs, and attitude and intention to use are the key endogenous factors. PU is defined as "the degree to which a person believes using a particular system would enhance his or her job performance" (Van der Heijden, 2003, p. 542), while PEOU is defined as "the degree to which a person believes that using a particular system would be free of effort" (Van der Heijden, 2003, p. 542). Attitude refers to a person forming favorable or unfavorable feelings toward adopting a certain technology (Kim, 2016), which leads to the intention to use a particular technology and determines the adoption of such technology (Wang, Wu, Lin, Wang, & He, 2012). Past studies found that PU and PEOU positively affect users' intention to adopt systems (Chin & Todd, 1995). On this basis, we propose that

H1: Users' perceived usefulness is positively related to their attitude toward the Uber mobile application.

H2: Users' perceived ease of use is positively related to their attitude toward the Uber mobile application.

H3: Users' attitude is positively related to their future usage intention the Uber mobile application.

Diffusion of innovation theory (DIT)

While previous studies have commonly adopted TAM to explain the user acceptance of technologies, it is uncertain if TAM sufficiently explains the adoption of different types of technology. Several studies have recommended integrating TAM with other theories, most notably DIT, to better understand the rapid changes in information technology and to achieve a better explanatory power (Hardgrave, Davis, & Riemenschneider, 2003; Lee et al., 2011; Legris, Ingham, & Collerette, 2003). DIT is an extensive social and psychological theory that aims to help predicting how people make decisions to adopt a new innovation by finding their adoption patterns and understanding its structure (Rogers, 1995; Rogers & Shoemaker, 1983). Specifically, DIT presents five innovation characteristics that are antecedents to any adoption: 1) relative advantages (economic gains or perceived convenience), 2) complexity (relatively free of effort to use or try), 3) compatibility (being consistent with the existing values, needs, and past experiences of potential adopters), 4) observability (assessment of implication), and 5) trialability (experimented with before adoption) (Rogers, 1995, pp. 212–251).

In contrast to TAM, DIT encapsulates more specific characteristics of an innovation, which are useful in explaining why users adopt the innovation or how they make a decision when adopting it (Rogers, 1995). Consequently, such characteristics are conceptualized as antecedents of TAM, especially for explaining consumers' adoption of new innovation, such as information technology (Wang et al., 2012).

Moreover, Rogers (2002) described diffusion as a social process that spreads an innovation by people talking to other people about the adoption of an innovation. As such, the adoption of an innovation cannot be fully understood without taking the social system into consideration. However, the five innovation characteristics of DIT do not consider the potential effects of any social factors. The social factor is considered particularly important when explaining individuals' mobile technology adoption (Sarker & Wells, 2003). Therefore, in this study, in addition to the five innovation characteristics, we included social influence as an antecedent to better understand the users' adoption behavior toward the Uber mobile application. To measure PU and PEOU, only respondents who have used the Uber mobile application can answer the questions, whereas the inclusion of trialability, one of the characteristics of innovation from the original DIT, is only appropriate when respondents have not had any adoption in the past. Thus, on this basis, this study only focuses on adopters, resulting in the removal of trialability from this study. The ensuing section discusses the relationships between DIT factors (i.e., relative advantage, compatibility, complexity, observability, and social influence) and TAM factors (i.e., PU and PEOU), leading to attitude and future usage intention.

Relative advantage

Relative advantage (RA) is one of the main factors in DIT. RA is defined as a degree to which an innovation is perceived as providing more benefits than its predecessor (Rogers & Shoemaker, 1983). People adopt new innovations when it is believed to be more useful, such as increasing efficiency and effectiveness (Lin & Chen, 2012). Consumers determine the overall evaluation of a mobile application's relative advantages by comparing it to the previous technologies that they have been using, leading to PU and PEOU. Lee et al. (2011) confirmed that relative advantage predicts both PU and PEOU in the context of the e-learning system. Similarly, Shih and Fang (2004) found relative advantage positively affects attitude toward adopting Internet banking.

In this study, relative advantages of the Uber mobile application are evaluated by consumers by comparing to that of requesting a regular taxi, given that is a previous method that has been used before the Uber mobile application was introduced. By comparing it to the previous methods that the users have been utilizing, the overall evaluation of mobile applications' relative advantages is assessed, resulting in PU and PEOU. Thus, we hypothesize that

> H4: RA is positively related to PU of the Uber mobile application.

> H5: RA is positively related to PEOU of the Uber mobile application.

Compatibility

Compatibility refers to the degree to which a service is perceived as consistent with users' existing values, beliefs, habits, and present and previous experiences (Rogers, 1995). Compatibility plays a key role in examining how the users' previous experience with similar technologies can affect PU and PEOU. Previous studies found that there is a positive relationship between compatibility and people's adoption of new information technology (Agarwal & Prasad, 1999; Zhang, Guo, & Chen, 2008). However, Agarwal and Prasad (1999) found that compatibility is not significant in explaining PU, but it is significantly related to PEOU, while the study of Hardgrave et al. (2003) showed again that compatibility affects PU positively. Similar findings are also reported by other scholars (Chang & Tung, 2008; Tung, Lee, Chen, & Hsu, 2009; Wu & Wang, 2005). Thus, we hypothesize that:

> H6: Compatibility is positively related to PU of the Uber mobile application.

> H7: Compatibility is positively related to PEOU of the Uber mobile application.

Complexity

Complexity is defined as the extent to which an innovation can be considered relatively difficult to understand and use (Rogers & Shoemaker, 1983). Complexity may lead users to misunderstand the function of the technology (Holak & Lehmann, 1990). Theoretically, complexity from DIT and PEOU from TAM are similar constructs, although the direction of the constructs is different (Moore & Benbasat, 1991). Complexity is included to capture one of the five innovation characteristics and PEOU is included to assess one of the two salient beliefs (PU and PEOU) when adopting a new technology. Complexity in this study is included to examine the functional aspect of the Uber mobile application as one of the independent variables, whereas PEOU is included to understand how consumers perceived the idea of using the Uber mobile application. In fact, Lee et al. (2011) have tested the two constructs and verified the discriminant validity between them, and also showed that complexity has a negative effect on PEOU when applied to employees' use of E-learning system, suggesting that complexity and PEOU are two separate concepts.

In this study, mobile applications for requesting a transportation can be misunderstood by consumers if they fail to clearly deliver the advantages of using it due to complexity. The Uber mobile application may be perceived to require complex procedures, such as input of user's personal and location information: Method of payment, phone number, email address, and pick-up location and address. It would be a potential hassle that makes customers feel the Uber mobile application useless and difficult to use and they rather make a phone call to request a taxi. The study by Hardgrave et al. (2003) revealed that complexity had a significantly negative influence on PU when the software developers had to adopt formalized methodologies, while Hasan (2007) confirmed that complexity has significant direct effects on both PU and PEOU. Thus, we propose that

H8: Complexity is negatively related to PU of the Uber mobile application.

H9: Complexity is negatively related to PEOU of the Uber mobile application.

Observability

The fourth DIT factor is observability. Observability is the extent to which an innovation is visible to the members of a social system and the benefits can be easily observed and communicated (Rogers, 2003). When integrating DIT factors with TAM, a previous study proposed that when the employees could easily observe the system, it had a positive effect on PU and PEOU (Lee et al., 2011). Consumers are more likely to adopt new innovations when their effects or benefits are visible to them. Park and Chen (2007) demonstrated

that observability positively affects user attitude. As a new innovation, the Uber mobile application provides various benefits to its users prior to their selection of the Uber. For the sake of user observability, the Uber mobile application provides the information about the requested service such as estimated time of arrival, cost for the trip, the Uber information (plate number, type of the car, color, driver information, etc.), and transaction history, which further heightened the relevance of observability. In addition, the Uber mobile application offers customers' trip history, frequent destination, and help center. Based on the argument advanced in the prior literature (Lee et al., 2011), these observable features are considered to have a positive effect on PU and PEOU. Thus, we propose the following hypotheses:

H10: Observability is positively related to PU of the Uber mobile application.

H11: Observability is positively related to PEOU of the Uber mobile application.

Social influence

The last factor included as an antecedent of PU and PEOU is social influence. Social influence represents the extent to which members of a reference group influence one another's behavior (Kelman, 1958). The impacts of influential others are important in individuals' adoption decision process because people consider their social context when positioning their attitudes, behaviors, and beliefs (Salancik & Pfeffer, 1978). As such, social influence has been recognized as an essential factor in previous innovation diffusion literature (e.g., Cooper & Zmud, 1990; Young, 2009). Thus, we claim that understanding the effect of social influence is critical when investigating consumers' adoption of an innovation.

Social influence is defined as people adopting an innovation in a conformity motive, which occurs when enough number of influential others have adopted the innovation (Young, 2009). Social influence is impactful in people's adoption decision process, because it reduces the uncertainty and provides opportunities for individuals to have informational and normative social influences (Lu, Yao, & Yu, 2005). Thus, in this study, we hypothesize that social influence, that is caused by close social groups by seeing one's close social groups using the Uber mobile application, will affect consumers' adoption of the mobile application. Consumers are exposed to a social system of their friends, families, members, and other connections, who can potentially influence one's decisions and behaviors toward the innovation. Accordingly, consumers evaluate an innovation by seeing and learning from other people using the innovation and decide if the innovation is worth adopting (Young, 2009). This influence can affect consumers' evaluation of the usefulness of an innovation. Also, social influence may affect individuals' internal aspects in shaping the decision of using an innovation, such as one's confidence in using an innovation or ability to use an innovation well (Lu et al., 2005). Furthermore, in line with previous studies (López-Nicolás, Molina-Castillo, & Bouwman, 2008; Lu et al., 2005), how influential others view and evaluate an innovation could also affect consumers' perceived usefulness of the innovation as well as its ease of use. Therefore, we propose that

> H12: Social influence is positively related to PU of the Uber mobile application.
>
> H13: Social influence is positively related to PEOU of the Uber mobile application.

Based on the extensive review of the literature presented above, a conceptual model is proposed, as Figure 1 shows.

Methodology

In order to test the research hypotheses, a quantitative method that included a survey questionnaire was used to measure the constructs included in the model. An online survey was utilized to gather data from respondents who had used the Uber mobile application before. We conducted the survey in two phases, with a pilot study using a convenience sample of college students, followed by a main study through Amazon's Mechanical Turk (MTurk).

Pilot study

A pilot study was conducted to identify potential issues and to check the measurement items. A convenience sample of 220 college students was drawn in the Midwest of

the United States. In the pilot study, we used a different study context (i.e., food ordering innovation) and included items to measure the five innovation characteristics (relative advantage, compatibility, complexity, observability, and social influence), PU, PEOU, attitude, and future usage intention. Based on the results of the analysis, several refinements, including rewording items and finding additional measurement scales, were made to the survey instrument.

Sample

The Uber users were recruited through Amazon's Mechanical Turk (MTurk), an online crowdsourcing system. To address the issues of respondents from MTurk, we followed the four categories of screening techniques from Goodman, Cryder, and Cheema (2013). First, we limited the time to the minimum required time for taking a survey of 100 s. Since the survey contained a total of 57 questions, it was considered inadequate when a respondent took less than 100 s to complete the survey. Second, we included a pre-screening question, which required the respondents to have adopted the Uber mobile application in the past 12 months. At the beginning of the survey, we specifically asked a screening question (i.e., How many times have you used the Uber mobile application for requesting transportation in the last 12 months?) to check if respondents had used the Uber mobile application. The respondents who indicated that they had never used the Uber mobile application before were eliminated from the sample. Third, each respondent was compensated US$0.50 for successfully completing the survey, leading to a better response rate that could enhance the validity and generalizability of the data. Lastly, three attention check questions were included to effectively identify and remove "poor" participants from the data.

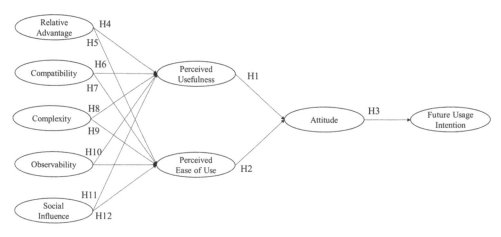

Figure 1. Conceptual framework.

The adoption of this systematic process and procedure helped in minimizing the validity issues of MTurk data.

The survey was developed on Qualtrics in January 2017. To ensure the sample is appropriate for this study, we specifically targeted those who had used the Uber mobile application in the past 12 months. Thus, only respondents had used the Uber mobile application for requesting transportation in the past 12 months were qualified to participate in this study. In addition, we had another screening question at the beginning of the survey to check again if respondents have used the Uber mobile application. The question was "How many times have you used the Uber mobile application for requesting transportation in the last 12 months?" and the respondents who answered "not at all" were eliminated from the sample. A total of 404 surveys were collected, of which 336 were considered valid. In our survey, we used a forced response option to avoid missing values. All respondents could move on to the next question only when they have made responses to the all the questions that are shown on the page. Incomplete surveys and surveys with incorrect answers to the attention check questions (i.e., to show that you are reading all questions, please select the response corresponding to strongly disagree for this statement) were removed from further analysis.

Measurement items

A survey instrument was developed based on an extensive literature review. A total of 57 questions modified to suit the context of mobile application usage were asked, including demographic characteristics, the DIT factors, perceived usefulness, perceived ease of use, attitude, and future usage intention the Uber mobile application. Specifically, six items measuring relative advantages were adapted from Moore and Benbasat (1991). Four items measuring compatibility were adapted from Taylor and Todd (1995) and Sundarraj and Manochehri (2013), three complexity items were borrowed from Tan and Teo (2000) and Cruz, Laukkanen, and Muñoz (2009), two observability items were adapted from Moore and Benbasat (1991) and Al-Jabri and Sohail (2012), and three items were adapted from Moore and Benbasat (1991) to measure social influence. Five items were used to measure PU, of which three were adapted from Kim, Mirusmonov, and Lee (2010), and the other two were created for this study on the basis of the literature. Furthermore, three items from Kim (2016) and one item created for this study were used to measure PEOU, and three items from Taylor and Todd (1995) and one item written for this study were used to measure attitude. Finally, two items adapted from Karahanna and Straub (1999) were used to measure future usage intention. In sum, a large majority of the scales used in this study was adapted from existing literature, thus the validity and reliability of the measurement were ensured. All constructs were measured on a seven-point Likert scale ranging from 1 (strongly disagree) to 7 (strongly agree).

Results

Demographic profile

Table 1 presents the demographic profile of the sample of this study. Male respondents represented 60.1% of the sample, while female respondents accounted for 39.9%. The majority of respondents were between 18 and 35 years old (51.2%), 27.1% were aged between 36 and 45, 11.3% were between the ages of 46 and 55, with 7.7% between 56 and 65 years old, and 2.7% over the age of 65. In terms of annual household income, approximately 26% of the respondents earned less than $20,000, 21.7% earned between $20,000 and $40,000, 21.4% earned between $40,000 and $60,000, 18.8% earned between $60,000 and $80,000, 11.1% earned more than $80,000, and 1.2% did not want to disclose their annual income. With respect to education levels,

Table 1. Demographic profile.

Demographic profile	N	%
Gender		
Male	202	60.1
Female	134	39.9
Total	336	100.0
Age		
18–35 years	172	51.2
36–45 years	91	27.1
46–55 years	38	11.3
56–65 years	26	7.7
66 years or older	9	2.7
Total	336	100.0
Income		
Less than $20,000	87	25.9
$20,000-$39,999	73	21.7
$40,000-$59,999	72	21.4
$60,000-$79,999	63	18.8
$80,000-$99,999	21	6.3
$100,000 or above	16	4.8
I do not want to disclose	4	1.2
Total	336	100.0
Education		
Less than high school	1	0.3
High school graduate	22	6.5
Some college	46	13.7
Associate degree	24	7.1
Bachelor's degree	156	46.4
Master's degree	85	25.3
Doctorate degree	2	0.6
Total	336	100.0
Smartphone operation system		
Apple iOS	97	28.9
Android	226	67.3
Windows	13	3.8
Total	336	100.0

6.8% had high school degree or lower, 20.8% had some college or associate degree, and more than 72% had bachelor's degree or higher. In terms of the smartphone operation system, 67.3% used Android, 28.9% used Apple iOS, and 3.8% used Windows.

Partial Least Squares Path Modeling (PLS-PM) was used to test the hypotheses in the proposed model. PLS-PM is considered to be the most appropriate analytical technique for analyzing the data, as the focus of this study is to understand the predictive relationships among the constructs, rather than theory conformation or testing (Chin & Newsted, 1999; Sarstedt, Ringle, & Hair, 2014). In contrast to the Covariance Based Structural Equation Modeling (CB-SEM), PLS-PM is a soft modeling approach, which does not require a large sample size and is not based on the assumption of normal distribution of the data (Arnett, Laverie, & Meiers, 2003). PLS-PM has received increased recognition in the tourism literature (Ahrholdt, Gudergan, & Ringle, 2017; Kim, Lee, Petrick, & Hahn, 2018). Given that this study requires the examination factors that affect consumers' adoption behavior of the Uber mobile application, the predictive relationships are the focus of this investigation, rather than theory testing, PLS-PM was considered more appropriate for the analysis. The analysis followed a two-stage process, which includes separate evaluations of the outer model and inner model (Hair, Hult, Ringle, & Sarstedt, 2016).

To check nonresponse bias, the early respondents (top 5%) were compared with late respondents (bottom 5%) on the demographic variables (e.g., gender, age, and income) and the measurement items (Armstrong & Overton, 1977). We conducted chi-square tests to examine the respondents' demographic characteristics and the result showed no significant differences ($\alpha = .05$) between early and late respondents. Also, t-tests were conducted to assess the measurement items, and the result showed that there were no significant differences ($\alpha = .05$) between early and late respondents. Thus, nonresponse bias was not a major concern for this study.

Test of the outer model

The outer model was assessed through the validity and reliability of the measurement scales to ensure their sound psychometric properties. Validity was examined based on convergent validity and discriminant validity (Hulland, 1999). Convergent validity was evaluated through the strength and significance of the loadings. The results of the initial measurement model show that three items (COMP3, RA5, and OBS2) were problematic due to their low factor loadings. After careful examination of the items together with the definition of their

respective construct, they were removed for subsequent analysis. The results of the final outer model indicate that, all the 30 remaining indicators had loadings exceeding the satisfactory level of >0.7 (Gerbing & Anderson, 1988). In addition, the bootstrap critical ratios indicate that all indicators are statistically significant $p < .001$, and all AVEs were greater than .50 (Fornell & Bookstein, 1982), providing evidence for convergent validity (see Table 2).

Discriminant validity was examined by employing two classical approaches (Hair et al., 2016). First, cross-loadings were assessed. All of the indicators' outer loading on the associated constructs are greater than any of the loadings on other constructs (Hair et al., 2016), supporting discriminant validity. Second, we compared the square root of the AVE to the inter-correlations between constructs. With the exception of one, the square root of the AVE of all constructs was greater than the inter-construct correlations (see Table 3), providing evidence of discriminant validity (Chin, 1998; Fornell & Larcker, 1981). We further tested whether the correlation between constructs is significantly less than one (Anderson & Gerbing, 1988; Bagozzi & Heatherton, 1994). Discriminant validity is evidenced if the value of one is not contained within 2 standard errors of the correlation. All the associated confidence intervals did not capture the value of one. Therefore, on the basis of the three analysis tests, discriminant validity was supported for all pairs of constructs.

The reliability of the scales was examined through average variance extracted (AVE), composite reliability (CR), and Cronbach's Alpha (Chin, 1998; Fornell & Larcker, 1981; Hair et al., 2016). The results showed that for all the measured constructs, all AVEs were greater than 0.5, and the estimates of CR and Cronbach's Alpha were greater than 0.7 (Fornell & Larcker, 1981), thus indicating reliability (see Table 2).

Since this study used the same method (i.e., self-administered online surveys) and gathered data on all the constructs from the same respondents, it has a potential for introducing common method bias (Podsakoff & Organ, 1986). We used Harman's one-factor test to examine if a single factor can account for all of the variances in the data (e.g., Mossholder, Bennett, Kemery, & Wesolowski, 1998), and the factor analysis of the dependent and independent variables resulted in a solution that accounts for 60.80% of the total variance, with the first factor explaining 45.97%, the second factor 6.51%, and the third factor 4.49%. This analysis suggested that there was no significant common method bias in our dataset. Furthermore, we also controlled the common method variance by adopting

Table 2. Results of measurement model.

Construct	Items	Mean[a]	Factor Loading	AVE	CR	Cronbach's Alpha
Relative Advantage (RA)	RA1	6.02	0.850	0.681	0.914	0.883
	RA2	6.13	0.831			
	RA3	6.07	0.827			
	RA4	6.13	0.813			
	RA6	5.96	0.804			
Compatibility (COMP)	COMP1	6.03	0.871	0.788	0.918	0.866
	COMP2	6.08	0.889			
	COMP4	6.03	0.903			
Complexity (CPLEX)	CPLEX1	3.13	0.790	0.735	0.892	0.828
	CPLEX2	2.56	0.896			
	CPLEX3	2.54	0.882			
Observability (OBS)	OBS1	5.87	1.000	1.000	1.000	1.000
Social Influence (SI)	SI1	5.63	0.865	0.809	0.927	0.882
	SI2	5.52	0.924			
	SI3	5.39	0.909			
Perceived Usefulness (PU)	PU1	6.10	0.860	0.714	0.926	0.900
	PU2	6.18	0.861			
	PU3	6.23	0.815			
	PU4	6.05	0.858			
	PU5	5.98	0.832			
Perceived Ease of Use (PEOU)	PEOU1	6.11	0.863	0.739	0.919	0.882
	PEOU2	6.06	0.858			
	PEOU3	6.22	0.870			
	PEOU4	6.23	0.847			
Attitude (ATT)	ATT1	6.05	0.900	0.775	0.932	0.903
	ATT2	6.16	0.864			
	ATT3	6.07	0.871			
	ATT4	6.12	0.887			
Future Usage Intention (FUI)	FUI1	5.73	0.958	0.923	0.960	0.917
	FUI2	5.70	0.963			

[a]Items measured on a 7-point Likert scale (1 = strongly disagree; 7 = strongly agree); AVE = Average Variance Extracted; CR = Composite Reliability.

Table 3. Discriminant validity analysis based on Fornell-Larcker criterion.

	ATT	COMP	CPLEX	FUI	OBS	PEOU	PU	RA	SI
ATT	0.881								
COMP	0.784	0.888							
CPLEX	−0.355	−0.303	0.857						
FUI	0.551	0.577	−0.181	0.961					
OBS	0.614	0.513	−0.232	0.284	1.000				
PEOU	0.830	0.724	−0.411	0.473	0.635	0.859			
PU	0.866	0.770	−0.393	0.534	0.597	0.808	0.845		
RA	0.805	0.763	−0.363	0.461	0.591	0.760	0.837	0.825	
SI	0.428	0.410	−0.108	0.439	0.354	0.420	0.421	0.371	0.899

Lower left diagonal is correlation matrix of latent variables; Diagonal elements are the square root of AVE; RA = Relative Advantage; COMP = Compatibility; CPLEX = Complexity; OBS = Observability; SI = Social Influence; PU = Perceived Usefulness; PEOU = Perceived Ease of Use; ATT = Attitude; FUI = Future Usage Intention.

Podsakoff et al. (2012)'s procedural remedy to avoid common scale attributes. Therefore, common method bias is unlikely to be a major issue in this study.

Test of the inner model

The proposed inner model was assessed through a systematic examination of indices, including path coefficients between the exogenous and endogenous, bootstrap critical ratios coefficient of determination R^2, f^2 effect size, and predictive relevance Q^2 (Hair et al., 2016). The results are shown in Table 4. The hypothesized model was estimated based on bootstrapping with 5,000 subsamples. All 13 hypotheses were supported. Of the 13

relationships tested, 8 were found to be significant at $p < .001$, 2 were found to be significant at $p < .01$, and 3 to be significant at $p < .05$. Specifically, relative advantage had a positive effect on both PU ($\beta = .50$, $p < 0.001$) and PEOU ($\beta = .32$, $p < 0.001$). Compatibility also had a positive effect on PU and PEOU, with $\beta = .27$, $p < 0.01$, and $\beta = .28$, $p < 0.001$, respectively. However, complexity had a negative influence on PU and PEOU, with $\beta = -.01$, $p < 0.01$, and $\beta = -.15$, $p < 0.001$, respectively. Also, observability had a positive impact on both PU and PEOU, with $\beta = .11$, $p < 0.05$, and $\beta = .24$, $p < 0.001$, respectively. In addition, social influence had a positive impact on PU and PEOU, with $\beta = .07$, $p < 0.05$, and $\beta = .09$, $p < 0.05$, respectively. PU and PEOU were both significantly related to attitude,

Table 4. Results of the hypothesized structural model.

	Hypotheses	Path Coefficient	Standard Error	T Statistics	P Values	Hypothesis Testing Result
H1:	Relative Advantage -> PU	0.492	0.080	6.299	0.000	Supported
H2:	Relative Advantage -> PEOU	0.317	0.078	4.140	0.000	Supported
H3:	Compatibility -> PU	0.280	0.078	3.447	0.001	Supported
H4:	Compatibility -> PEOU	0.285	0.079	3.487	0.000	Supported
H5:	Complexity -> PU	−0.094	0.033	2.902	0.004	Supported
H6:	Complexity -> PEOU	−0.144	0.035	4.096	0.000	Supported
H7:	Observability -> PU	0.113	0.046	2.470	0.014	Supported
H8:	Observability -> PEOU	0.234	0.056	4.227	0.000	Supported
H9:	Social Influence -> PU	0.073	0.034	2.145	0.032	Supported
H10:	Social Influence -> PEOU	0.086	0.037	2.360	0.018	Supported
H11:	PU -> Attitude	0.560	0.070	7.999	0.000	Supported
H12:	PEOU -> Attitude	0.378	0.068	5.515	0.000	Supported
H13:	Attitude -> FUI	0.550	0.063	8.702	0.000	Supported

All estimates were produced based on bootstrapping with 5000 subsamples; PU = Perceived Usefulness; PEOU = Perceived Ease of Use, FUI = Future Usage Intention.

with $\beta = .56$, $p < 0.001$, and $\beta = .38$, $p < 0.001$, respectively, and, in turn, attitude positively influenced future usage intention, with $\beta = .55$, $p < 0.001$.

Second, since the goal of PLS-PM is to predict key target constructs, it is important to assess the structural model by evaluating the coefficient of determination (R^2 value) (Hair et al., 2016). As Figure 2 indicates, the R^2 values for all endogenous variables surpassed the .26 values suggested by Cohen (1988), indicating reliable predictive power of the model. In addition, the effect size of f^2 was also evaluated in order to access the PLS-PM structural model. With values of about 0.02, 0.15, or 0.35 indicating that the exogenous latent variable has a small, medium, or large effect on the endogenous latent variable, respectively (Hair et al., 2016). In this study attitude had a large effect on future usage intention ($f^2 = 0.436$), PU had a large effect on attitude ($f^2 = 0.549$), and relative advantage had a large effect on PU ($f^2 = 0.373$); whereas PEOU had a medium effect on attitude ($f^2 = 0.243$). All the other significant paths had a small effect on their dependent latent variables.

Lastly, we used the blindfolding procedure to generate the cross-validated redundancy measure Q^2 (Stone–Geisser test) (Geisser, 1974; Stone, 1974), which provides evidence that the proposed model has the predictive validity of the exogenous latent variables. All predictive relevance Q^2 values well exceeded zero, indicating the results provide strong evidence signifying the predictive ability of the hypothesized theoretical model.

Discussion and conclusions

Theoretical implications

Our study employed two theories – DIT and TAM – to investigate the factors that affect consumers' adoption of the Uber mobile application. By combining the two theories, this study has made several important theoretical contributions. DIT is a well-established theory for explaining how innovation spreads throughout the population (Wang et al., 2012), while TAM has been widely used within the hospitality and tourism industry to investigate how people accept new technologies (Kim, 2016; Morosan & DeFranco, 2014). However, even though the similarities of the two theories have been recognized and the literature has linked the two to understand consumers' adoption behavior (Lee et al., 2011) and developed measurement scales by

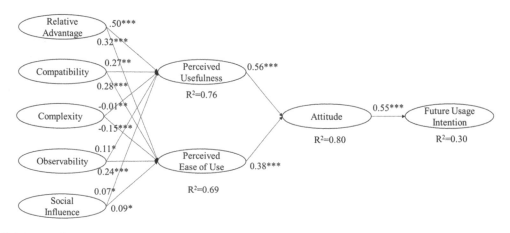

Figure 2. The PLS-PM results.
***$p < 0.001$; **$p < 0.01$; *$p < 0.05$.

integrating the two theories (Moore & Benbasat, 1991), few empirical studies that incorporated these two theories, have been conducted from the consumer's perspective. This study has filled this knowledge gap by focusing on the adoption of the Uber mobile application.

Findings of this study indicate that when consumers notice that there are relative advantage, compatibility, observability, and social influence in using the Uber mobile application, they positively affect PU and PEOU of the mobile application. On the other hand, when consumers feel the complexity in using the Uber mobile application, it negatively influences toward PU and PEOU of the application. The results show that high in PU and PEOU contributes significantly to consumer attitude toward adopting the Uber mobile application. Also, this study contributes to prior literature by adding social factor – social influence, to existing DIT factors. While DIT is originated to explain the diffusion of innovations throughout a population or social system (Rogers & Shoemaker, 1983), which fundamentally contains the concept of "social influence" within the theory, it has not directly examined the social context within DIT. Furthermore, the term "social" used in this study differs from majority of previous studies. Social influence has been defined that it has a close meaning to subjective norm or social pressure, which examines the degree of which people desire to be in their social group. However, this study features social influence as an influential factor that examines how many people are influenced by close social groups by seeing them using the Uber mobile application. As such, this study contributes to the original DIT by adding social influence factor to complement its insufficiency in the social context.

Our results show that all DIT factors proposed in this study – relative advantage, compatibility, complexity, observability, and social influence- were significantly related to TAM factors – PU and PEOU. Since the key idea of the Uber mobile application is on "sharing" with others, and because of the business model of the Uber mobile application (i.e., sharing economy), the diffusion of the idea being shared across the population is inevitable. Accordingly, this study incorporated the key elements of diffusion of innovation to better understand the adoption of the Uber mobile application. The result supported that DIT factors can be used to measure consumers' perception on technology adoption as an independent variable. Especially among the variables, relative advantage had a strong influence on PU and PEOU, confirming a previous study (Lee et al., 2011). However, even though many studies have extended the TAM to examine external factors that influence on PU

and PEOU (Kim, 2016; Kim et al., 2010; Lee et al., 2011; Morosan & DeFranco, 2014; Yang, 2005), much less work exists that clearly defines the factors affecting people's perception of new technology adoption, specifically mobile application. Even though the context of mobile application might be different, when focused on the concept of behavior of adoption itself, it can be concurred into several common factors that explain what factors affect PU and PEOU. This study is successful in adopting DIT factors and supporting that these factors had direct influence on PU and PEOU of mobile application.

Practical implications

Several practical implications can be highlighted for the tourism and hospitality industry. The results suggest that mobile application adoption can be enhanced by improving its features. Relative advantage of the Uber mobile application compared to requesting a regular taxi has a significant influence on PU and PEOU. It implies that adding the unique features into the Uber mobile application, such as providing more accurate GPS location information on the map would help to enhance users' perceived advantages of using the Uber mobile application. Also, by providing a filter option, such as refining Uber, who can pick up the passenger within certain period-of-time (3 min/5 min/10 min) could help to increase the users' perceived advantages. However, considering the significant effect of relative advantage, Uber should not only strengthen its advantages compared to previous method of requesting transportation, namely regular taxi, but also should consider its competitors in the overall transportation market, by continuing to focus on building its strengths and advantages to keep the existing consumers and attract new consumers. Such interpretations are equally relevant to hospitality organizations such as restaurants and hotels when evaluating consumer usage of their mobile applications.

The significant influence of compatibility on both PU and PEOU suggests that practitioners need to focus on understanding consumers' lifestyle and incorporate their preferences into the Uber mobile application to ensure that consumers consider the application is compatible. Gathering the data of user information and find their common characteristics may help Uber to provide services that customers need. Negative relationships between complexity and PU and PEOU suggest that the Uber mobile application needs to design the functions less complex and more convenient for all users to utilize the application. Even though the usage of smartphone is becoming more common and many people are exposed in the situation of using various mobile applications, complexity of the technology is still an issue determining consumer adoptions (Kim et al., 2010). In addition, the findings suggest that adding observable features, such as ride history and estimated time of arrival, positively influences PU and PEOU, which lead to people's intention to adopt the Uber mobile application. The significant effects of social influence also suggest that the Uber mobile application can positively influence the perception of using the mobile application (i.e., PU and PEOU), when people can see others around them using the application. Based on the findings, some marketing tactics to expose the application could be used to influence potential users. For example, Uber may consider providing one free ride to an existing customer when requesting two cars through Uber, one for him/herself and one for a friend. Providing a situation that the current user can show their friends what Uber is and how easily and usefully it can be adopted may help in attracting more users. Overall this study makes a unique and important contribution to the body of literature in adoption of mobile technology within the sharing economy.

Limitations and suggestions for future research

This study has some limitations that could be addressed for future research. First, the survey was conducted by using M-Turk, which may lead to the sample bias. People who participated in M-Turk implies that they are likely to be more familiar with using technologies, which may result in a less representative sample. The measurement of complexity, one of the constructs, may be violated because the sample of this study only included those who were registered in M-Turk. As such, they may be already familiar with the technology, compared to the general population. Future studies may need to encompass a wider sampling frame and also utilize various methods for conducting a survey.

A future study can focus on social influence in its definition and by categorizing different types of social influence. This study particularly focused on social influence in terms of how people are influenced by seeing other people who are in the same social group using the mobile application, whereas past studies have focused on subjective norms or peer pressure. According to the research conducted by Google (Tiongson, 2015), 1 in 4 application users discover an application through searching, which could be interpreted as similar to seeing other people using the application. However, the term "other people" is more likely from anonymous people, not from one's own social group. In this case, it implies that consumers could also be affected by people with whom they do not have a connection. Approaching from different point of views may generate interesting findings that could expand and detail the term "social influence".

In addition, there are some limitations in examining all the features of Uber, since the Uber mobile application is kept developing and adding new features. The questions covered in the survey may not have encompassed all the features of the Uber mobile application, and thus may not have fully covered consumers' perceptions of the Uber mobile application in general. Survey questions could be better designed in the future to be more accurate, detailed, and thoroughly addressing the features of the Uber mobile application.

Another limitation of this study may result from the potential effects of various demographic characteristics of the respondents on the results. For example, generation could be a conceptually relevant factor which was not formally examined in this study. More than half of the respondents were aged between 18 and 35. Such sample may not completely represent the wider population. Younger generation may have different characteristics or prior experience with mobile technologies from older generation. They might be more familiar with new technologies or have different perceptions of new business models. However, mixed findings from the past studies have shown that the age effect in adopting a new innovation is inconsistent (see Kim, 2016). To comprehensively understand consumer adoption of the Uber mobile application, future research could be undertaken to further understand different generations' perceptions affect their adoption attitude and behavior differently. Other equally plausible and relevant factors may include age, gender, and cultural background.

Our findings provide a basis for several research avenues. First, future research could investigate individuals' characteristics in their readiness of using technology. As more people are using smartphones, the mobile application is also widely used in our daily lives. It is becoming a common technology and thus, using a mobile application is already familiar for many consumers. However, some people are still at the stage of adopting mobile applications and not familiar with the technology. As such, mobile application adoption may differ depending upon individuals' own characteristics, particularly their levels of technology readiness. Therefore, future research may examine how individuals could have different adoption perceptions and behaviors based on their own technology readiness.

Additionally, given that the measurement of the constructs in this study required respondents to have direct usage experience with the Uber mobile application, the sample of our study included only people who have already used the Uber mobile application. However, to attract non-users' adoption of the Uber mobile application, it is also important to investigate what factors may prevent non-users from utilizing the application. As such, future research could explore barriers to adoption of the Uber mobile application in order to provide a more complete understanding of consumer adoption behaviors.

Survey Items

Relative Advantage (RA)

RA1: Compared to requesting a regular taxi, Uber mobile application improves the quality of my task for requesting transportation.

RA2: Compared to requesting a regular taxi, Uber mobile application gives me greater control over my task for requesting transportation.

RA3: Compared to requesting a regular taxi, Uber mobile application makes it more convenient to access transportation.

RA4: Compared to taking a regular taxi, Uber mobile application enables me to make a payment in a more convenient way.

RA5: Uber mobile application saves me money compared to taking a regular taxi (DELETED).

RA6: Compared to taking a regular taxi, Uber mobile application enhances my overall transportation experience.

Compatibility (COMP)

COMP1: Uber mobile application fits well with the way I like to request transportation.

COMP2: Uber mobile application is compatible with my lifestyle.

COMP3: Uber mobile application does not fit with my preferences (reversed coded) (DELETED).

COMP4: Uber mobile application fits with my service needs.

Complexity (CPLEX)

CPLEX1: Uber mobile application requires technical skills.

CPLEX2: Uber mobile application requires a lot of mental effort.

CPLEX3: Uber mobile application can be frustrating.

Observability (OBS)

OBS1: I can see the benefits of using Uber mobile application immediately.

OBS2: I have seen what others can do using their Uber mobile application (DELETED).

Social Influence (SI)

SI1: I have seen others using Uber mobile application.

SI2: In my social group, I see Uber mobile application on many people's smartphones.

SI3: It is easy for me to observe others using Uber mobile application in my social group.

Perceived Usefulness (PU)

PU1: Using Uber mobile application would enable me to access transportation more quickly.

PU2: Using Uber mobile application makes it easier for me to request transportation.

PU3: I would find Uber mobile application a useful option for getting transportation.

PU4: Using Uber mobile application makes me save time.

PU5: Using Uber mobile application improves my efficiency.

Perceived Ease of Use (PEOU)

PEOU1: My interaction with Uber mobile application is clear and understandable.

PEOU2: It is easy for me to get Uber mobile application to do what I want it to do.

PEOU3: Overall, Uber mobile application is easy for me to use.

PEOU4: Learning to use the Uber mobile application is easy for me.

Attitude (ATT)

ATT1: I am positive about requesting transportation through Uber mobile application.

ATT2: Using Uber mobile application for requesting transportation is a good idea.

ATT3: I like the idea of using Uber mobile application for requesting transportation.

ATT4: Using Uber mobile application for requesting transportation is favorable.

Future Usage Intention (FUI)

FUI1: I intend to use Uber mobile application the next time I travel.

FUI2: The next time I travel I am likely to use Uber mobile application.

Disclosure statement

No potential conflict of interest was reported by the authors.

References

Agarwal, R., & Prasad, J. (1999). Are individual differences germane to the acceptance of new information technologies? *Decision Sciences*, *30*(2), 361–391.

Ahrholdt, D. C., Gudergan, S. P., & Ringle, C. M. (2017). Enhancing service loyalty: The roles of delight, satisfaction, and service quality. *Journal of Travel Research*, *56*(4), 436–450.

Al-Jabri, I. M., & Sohail, M. S. (2012). Mobile banking adoption: Application of diffusion of innovation theory. *Journal of Electronic Commerce Research*, *13*(4), 379–391.

Anderson, J. C., & Gerbing, D. W. (1988). Structural equation modeling in practice: A review and recommended two-step approach. *Psychological Bulletin*, *103*(3), 411.

Armstrong, J. S., & Overton, T. S. (1977). Estimating nonresponse bias in mail surveys. *Journal of Marketing Research*, *14*(3), 396–402.

Arnett, D. B., Laverie, D. A., & Meiers, A. (2003). Developing parsimonious retailer equity indexes using partial least squares analysis: A method and applications. *Journal of Retailing*, *79*(3), 161–170.

Bagozzi, R. P., & Heatherton, T. F. (1994). A general approach to representing multifaceted personality constructs: Application to state self-esteem. *Structural Equation Modeling: A Multidisciplinary Journal*, *1*(1), 35–67.

Botsman, R., & Rogers, R. (2011). *What's mine is yours: How collaborative consumption is changing the way we live*. New York, NY: Harper Collins.

Cannon, S., & Summers, L. H. (2014). How Uber and the sharing economy can win over regulators. *Harvard Business Review*, *13*(10), 24–28.

Chang, S. C., & Tung, F. C. (2008). An empirical investigation of students' behavioural intentions to use the online learning course websites. *British Journal of Educational Technology*, *39*(1), 71–83.

Chin, W. W. (1998). The partial least squares approach to structural equation modeling. *Modern Methods for Business Research, 295*(2), 295–336.

Chin, W. W., & Newsted, P. R. (1999). *Structural equation modeling analysis with small samples using partial least squares, statistical strategies for small sample research*. Thousand Oaks, CA: Sage Public.

Chin, W. W., & Todd, P. A. (1995). On the use, usefulness, and ease of use of structural equation modeling in MIS research: A note of caution. *MIS Quarterly, 19*(2), 237–246.

Cohen, B., & Kietzmann, J. (2014). Ride on! Mobility business models for the sharing economy. *Organization & Environment, 27*(3), 279–296.

Cohen, J. (1988). *Statistical power analysis for the behavioral sciences*. Hilsdale, NJ: Lawrence Earlbaum Associates.

Cooper, R. B., & Zmud, R. W. (1990). Information technology implementation research: A technological diffusion approach. *Management Science, 36*(2), 123–139.

Cruz, P., Laukkanen, T., & Muñoz, P. (2009). Exploring the factors behind the resistance to mobile banking in Portugal. *International Journal of E-Services and Mobile Applications, 1*(4), 16–35.

Davis, F. D. (1989). Perceived usefulness, perceived ease of use, and user acceptance of information technology. *MIS Quarterly, 13*(3), 319–340.

De Ridder, V. (2016). *How mobile and the internet of things can increase revenue and guest satisfactory in the hospitality industry* (Unpublished manuscript).

Fornell, C., & Bookstein, F. L. (1982). Two structural equation models: LISREL and PLS applied to consumer exit-voice theory. *Journal of Marketing Research, 19*(4), 440–452.

Fornell, C., & Larcker, D. F. (1981). Structural equation models with unobservable variables and measurement error: Algebra and statistics. *Journal of Marketing Research, 18*(3), 382–388.

Geisser, S. (1974). A predictive approach to the random effect model. *Biometrika, 61*(1), 101–107.

Gerbing, D. W., & Anderson, J. C. (1988). An updated paradigm for scale development incorporating unidimensionality and its assessment. *Journal of Marketing Research, 25*(2), 186–192.

Goodman, J. K., Cryder, C. E., & Cheema, A. (2013). Data collection in a flat world: The strengths and weaknesses of Mechanical Turk samples. *Journal of Behavioral Decision Making, 26*(3), 213–224.

Google Play. *Free popular Android application*. Retrieved from https://play.google.com/store/apps/collection/topselling_free

Hair, J. F., Hult, G. T. M., Ringle, C., & Sarstedt, M. (2016). *A primer on partial least squares structural equation modeling (PLS-SEM)*. Thousand Oaks, CA: Sage.

Hall, J., Kendrick, C., & Nosko, C. (2015). *The effects of Uber's surge pricing: A case study*. The University of Chicago Booth School of Business.

Hardgrave, B. C., Davis, F. D., & Riemenschneider, C. K. (2003). Investigating determinants of software developers' intentions to follow methodologies. *Journal of Management Information Systems, 20*(1), 123–151.

Hasan, B. (2007). Examining the effects of computer self-efficacy and system complexity on technology acceptance. *Information Resources Management Journal, 20*(3), 76–88.

Holak, S. L., & Lehmann, D. R. (1990). Purchase intentions and the dimensions of innovation: An exploratory model. *Journal of Product Innovation Management, 7*(1), 59–73.

Hulland, J. (1999). Use of partial least squares (PLS) in strategic management research: A review of four recent studies. *Strategic Management Journal, 20*(2), 195–204.

iTunes. *iTunes chart*. Retrieved from https://www.apple.com/itunes/charts/

Karahanna, E., & Straub, D. W. (1999). The psychological origins of perceived usefulness and ease-of-use. *Information & Management, 35*(4), 237–250.

Kelman, H. C. (1958). Compliance, identification, and internalization three processes of attitude change. *Journal of Conflict Resolution, 2*(1), 51–60.

Kim, C., Mirusmonov, M., & Lee, I. (2010). An empirical examination of factors influencing the intention to use mobile payment. *Computers in Human Behavior, 26*(3), 310–322.

Kim, J. (2016). An extended technology acceptance model in behavioral intention toward hotel tablet apps with moderating effects of gender and age. *International Journal of Contemporary Hospitality Management, 28*(8), 1535–1553.

Kim, M. J., Lee, C.-K., Petrick, J. F., & Hahn, S. S. (2018). Factors affecting international event visitors' behavioral intentions: The moderating role of attachment avoidance. *Journal of Travel & Tourism Marketing*, 1–16. doi.org/10.1080/10548408.2018.1468855

Kokalitcheva, K. (2016). *Uber now has 40 million monthly riders worldwide*. Retrieved from http://fortune.com/2016/10/20/uber-app-riders/

Lee, Y. H., Hsieh, Y. C., & Hsu, C. N. (2011). Adding innovation diffusion theory to the technology acceptance model: Supporting employees' intentions to use e-learning systems. *Journal of Educational Technology & Society, 14*(4), 124–137.

Legris, P., Ingham, J., & Collerette, P. (2003). Why do people use information technology? A critical review of the technology acceptance model. *Information & Management, 40*(3), 191–204.

Lin, A., & Chen, N.-C. (2012). Cloud computing as an innovation: Percepetion, attitude, and adoption. *International Journal of Information Management, 32*(6), 533–540.

Liu, S. Q., & Mattila, A. S. (2017). Airbnb: Online targeted advertising, sense of power, and consumer decisions. *International Journal of Hospitality Management, 60*, 33–41.

López-Nicolás, C., Molina-Castillo, F. J., & Bouwman, H. (2008). An assessment of advanced mobile services acceptance: Contributions from TAM and diffusion theory models. *Information & Management, 45*(6), 359–364.

Lu, J., Yao, J. E., & Yu, C.-S. (2005). Personal innovativeness, social influences and adoption of wireless Internet services via mobile technology. *The Journal of Strategic Information Systems, 14*(3), 245–268.

Moore, G. C., & Benbasat, I. (1991). Development of an instrument to measure the perceptions of adopting an information technology innovation. *Information Systems Research, 2*(3), 192–222.

Morosan, C., & DeFranco, A. (2014). When tradition meets the new technology: An examination of the antecedents of attitudes and intentions to use mobile devices in private clubs. *International Journal of Hospitality Management, 42*, 126–136.

Mossholder, K. W., Bennett, N., Kemery, E. R., & Wesolowski, M. A. (1998). Relationships between bases of power and work reactions: The mediational role of procedural justice. *Journal of Management, 24*(4), 533–552.

Oskam, J., & Boswijk, A. (2016). Airbnb: The future of net-worked hospitality businesses. *Journal of Tourism Futures*, *2*(1), 22–42.

Park, Y., & Chen, J. V. (2007). Acceptance and adoption of the innovative use of smartphone. *Industrial Management & Data Systems*, *107*(9), 1349–1365.

Podsakoff, P. M., & Organ, D. W. (1986). Self-reports in organizational research: Problems and prospects. *Journal of Management*, *12*(4), 531–544.

Podsakoff, P. M., MacKenzie, S. B. & Podsakoff, N. P. (2012). Sources of method bias in social science research and recommendations on how to control it. *Annual Review of Psychology*, *63*, 539–569.

Rauch, D. E., & Schleicher, D. (2015). Like Uber, but for local government law: The future of local regulation of the sharing economy. *George Mason Law & Economics Research Paper*, *15–01*, 1–61.

Rogers, E. M. (1995). *Diffusion of innovations*. New York, NY: Free Press.

Rogers, E. M. (2002). Diffusion of preventive innovations. *Addictive Behaviors*, *27*(6), 989–993.

Rogers, E. M. (2003). *Diffusion of innovations*. New York, NY: Free Press.

Rogers, E. M., & Shoemaker, F. (1983). *Diffusion of innovation: A cross-cultural approach*. New York, NY: Free Press.

Salancik, G. R., & Pfeffer, J. (1978). A social information processing approach to job attitudes and task design. *Administrative Science Quarterly*, *23*(2), 224–253.

Sarker, S., & Wells, J. D. (2003). Understanding mobile handheld device use and adoption. *Communications of the ACM*, *46*(12), 35–40.

Sarstedt, M., Ringle, C. M., & Hair, J. F. (2014). PLS-SEM: Looking back and moving forward. *Long Range Planning*, *47*(3), 132–137.

Satama, S. (2014). *Consumer adoption of access-based consumption services-Case AirBnB* (Unpublished manuscript). Aalto University, Helsinki, Finland.

Shih, Y. Y., & Fang, K. (2004). The use of a decomposed theory of planned behavior to study Internet banking in Taiwan. *Internet Research*, *14*(3), 213–223.

So, K. K. F., Oh, H., & Min, S. (2018). Motivations and constraints of Airbnb consumers: Findings from a mixed-methods approach. Tourism Management, *67*, 224–236.

Stone, M. (1974). Cross-validatory choice and assessment of statistical predictions. *Journal of the Royal Statistical Society. Series B (Methodological)*, *36*(2), 111–147.

Sundarraj, R., & Manochehri, N. (2013). Application of an extended TAM model for online banking adoption: A study at a Gulf-region university. *Information Resources Management Journal*, *24*(1), 1–13.

Tan, M., & Teo, T. S. (2000). Factors influencing the adoption of Internet banking. *Journal of the AIS*, *1*(5), 1–42.

Taylor, S., & Todd, P. (1995). Assessing IT usage: The role of prior experience. *MIS Quarterly*, *19*(4), 561–570.

Tiongson, J. (2015). *Mobile app marketing insights: How consumers really find and use your apps*. Retrieved from https://www.thinkwithgoogle.com/consumer-insights/mobile-app-marketing-insights/

Tung, F. C., Lee, M. S., Chen, C. C., & Hsu, Y. S. (2009). An extension of financial cost and TAM model with IDT for exploring users' behavioral intentions to use the CRM information system. *Social Behavior and Personality: an Internaional Journal*, *37*(5), 621–626.

Tussyadiah, I. P., & Pesonen, J. (2016). Impacts of peer-to-peer accommodation use on travel patterns. *Journal of Travel Research*, *55*(8), 1022–1040.

Van der Heijden, H. (2003). Factors influencing the usage of websites: The case of a generic portal in the Netherlands. *Information & Management*, *40*(6), 541–549.

Venkatesh, V., & Davis, F. D. (2000). A theoretical extension of the technology acceptance model: Four longitudinal field studies. *Management Science*, *46*(2), 186–204.

Wang, Y., So, K. K. F., & Sparks, B. A. (2014). What technology-enabled services do air travelers value? Investigating the role of technology readiness. *Journal of Hospitality & Tourism Research*, *41*(7), 771–796.

Wang, Y. S., Wu, S. C., Lin, H. H., Wang, Y. M., & He, T. R. (2012). Determinants of user adoption of web "Automatic Teller Machines": An integrated model of 'Transaction Cost Theory' and 'Innovation Diffusion Theory'. *The Service Industries Journal*, *32*(9), 1505–1525.

Want, R. (2009). When cell phones become computers. *IEEE Pervasive Computing*, *8*(2), 2–5.

Wu, J. H., & Wang, S. C. (2005). What drives mobile commerce?: An empirical evaluation of the revised technology acceptance model. *Information & Management*, *42*(5), 719–729.

Yang, K. C. C. (2005). Exploring factors affecting the adoption of mobile commerce in Singapore. *Telematics and Informatics*, *22*(3), 257–277.

Young, H. P. (2009). Innovation diffusion in heterogeneous populations: Contagion, social influence, and social learning. *American Economic Review*, *99*(5), 1899–1924.

Zhang, N., Guo, X., & Chen, G. (2008). IDT-TAM integrated model for IT adoption. *Tsinghua Science & Technology*, *13*(3), 306–311.

Zhu, G., So, K. K. F., & Hudson, S. (2017). Inside the sharing economy: Understanding consumer motivations behind the adoption of mobile applications. *International Journal of Contemporary Hospitality Management*, *29*(9), 2218–2239.

Marketing robot services in hospitality and tourism: the role of anthropomorphism

Jamie Murphy ⓘ, Ulrike Gretzel and Juho Pesonen ⓘ

ABSTRACT

Humanoid robots should play an increasing role in hospitality and tourism services. Anthropomorphic – human like – characteristics seem critical component to consumers accepting robotic service (rService). This conceptual manuscript advances rService research by drawing on services marketing, Human Robot Interaction (HRI) and the Uncanny Valley Theory to explore anthropomorphic characteristics' range, role and impact on rService experiences. The paper proposes eleven robot capabilities that influence anthropomorphism and consequently shape HRI, three Uncanny Valley marketing outcomes, theoretical concepts, and a rich future research agenda. Hospitality and tourism literature and examples highlight the service context's importance when researching, adopting, implementing and marketing rServices.

Introduction

Scholars have written extensively about technology and tourism's intricate relationship (e.g. Werthner & Klein, 1999). Technology's central role in shaping tourism continues as new technological developments disrupt tourism and hospitality paradigms. Many technologies that impact tourism and hospitality are back-office or business-to-business systems and applications. Many other technologies fundamentally change the business and consumer interface, creating or modifying important consumer-marketer touch points across the customer experience.

Consumer acceptance of these technologies drives their use and ultimately, success in facilitating marketing goals. Thus, investigating technology adoption and implementation from a consumer perspective has become a recurrent tourism- and hospitality-marketing theme (Ukpabi & Karjaluoto, 2017). One of the latest technologies entering the tourism and hospitality realm is robots (Ivanov, Webster, & Garenko, 2018; Murphy, Hofacker, & Gretzel, 2017). Given their complex interaction potential, addressing robot diffusion in tourism and hospitality settings and its potential marketing implications is essential.

Robots may have stolen the show at one of the world's largest trade shows of the latest consumer technologies, the Consumer Electronics Show (CES). The January 2017 CES in Las Vegas attracted 177,393 attendees – 68,331 senior level executives, 200 government officials and 7,545 media representatives – from 180 countries (ces. tech/Why-CES/CES-by-the-Numbers). One representative, Jefferson Graham with USA Today, noted the impressive robots and at times, their human likeness.

> "The one, coolest thing from this year's 2017 CES is an easy pick – those amazing robots. We saw robots to make your morning coffee, pour candy, fold your clothes, turn on and off your lights, project a movie on the wall, handle your daily chores and most impressively, look just like a human, or in this case, legendary scientist Albert Einstein, with facial expressions and movement" (Graham, 2017).

Robot presence grew at the 2018 CES, as did skepticism. Although lauded as cute and promising (Gebhart, 2018; Song, 2018), critics noted gimmickry, robotic failures and creepiness (Baraniuk, 2018; Peake, 2018; Song, 2018) – important issues for potential consumer acceptance of, and experiences with, service robots. The Uncanny Valley theory, almost a half-century old, helps explain the creepiness that arises from perceptions of humanoid robots (Mori, 1970; Mori, MacDorman, & Kageki, 2012). This theory posits that as robots become more human-like, i.e. anthropomorphic, acceptance increases up to a point and then this acceptance falls markedly as consumers perceive the robot as bizarre, weird or creepy.

This article has been republished with minor changes. These changes do not impact the academic content of the article.

Acceptance grows again as robots become almost lifelike.

Sophia, one of the most talked about 2018 CES robots, exemplified the Uncanny Valley because of her hyper-realistic facial features and ability to express emotions (Song, 2018). This paper helps understand the importance of service robot design, the drawbacks of the Uncanny Valley and derive implications for designing hospitality and tourism robotic service experiences. It does so by conceptualizing antecedents of anthropomorphism in service robots and introducing the rService paradigm. Consequently, the paper provides important insights for marketing future rService offerings in hospitality and tourism, and navigating the delicate balance between human-likeness and customer acceptance of these service robots.

Literature review

Robot development

While the term robot originated in a 1921 Czech play, *Rossum's Universal Robots* (Čapek, 2001), the concept of humanoid machines goes "back at least to Homer, Plato, and Ovid's tales of statues coming to life" (Belk, 2016, p. 2). This paper defines robots, neither a new nor narrow concept (Belk, 2016; Broadbent, 2017), in the service industry context as a "relatively autonomous physical device capable of motion and performing a service" (Murphy et al., 2017, p. 106).

Assuming Moore's Law and related advancements remain in force, the software capabilities in today's simple robots will double, and double again, while costs will do just the opposite – comparable to micro-processors and computing three decades ago (Brynjolfsson, McAfee, & Cummings, 2014; Touretzky, 2010). Wired Magazine (Wired.com, 2017) explains that the recent bump in robot development is primarily due to cost decreases in sensor technology and actuators that move robotic joints, as well as the shrinking size and increasingly energy-efficient computer chips.

Recent artificial intelligence (AI) advances further encourage robot development. Robots are navigating complex service-scapes due to improved image recognition and processing techniques, and having sophisticated interactions with humans due to increased natural language processing capabilities. Therefore, along with microprocessor developments, resulting computing power increases and AI progress, robots will impact markets and the workforce for centuries (Broadbent, 2017; Brynjolfsson et al., 2014; Frey & Osborne, 2017; van Doorn et al., 2017).

Robots generally fall into one of three categories – industrial, professional service and personal service (Thrun, 2004; Vaussard et al., 2014). The capabilities and design of personal service robots, also known as companion or social robots, generated the CES buzz and the recent tourism and hospitality research interest (Ivanov, Webster, & Berezina, 2018; Pan, Okada, Uchiyama, & Suzuki, 2015; Tung & Law, 2017).

Robots in hospitality and tourism

This manuscript focuses on personal service robots, which have the most autonomy and social interaction potential of the three robot categories, because of their relevance and expected impact on tourism and hospitality service provision and consumption (Ivanov et al., 2018; Murphy et al., 2017; Tung & Law, 2017; Tussyadiah & Park, 2018). Emerging hospitality and tourism robotic applications include service robots as waiters in southeast Asia, bellboys in the USA and staff in a Japanese hotel, and industrial robots that clean, flip hamburgers or make drinks (Belk, 2016; Collins, 2015; Godwin, 2018; Pan et al., 2015; van Doorn et al., 2017).

Current tourism and hospitality robotic research tends to be conceptual because a limited range of robots is operational within a few tourism and hospitality businesses. Three such conceptual studies proposed research agendas (Ivanov & Webster, 2017; Murphy et al., 2017; Tung & Law, 2017); another two studies examined the adoption of service robots (Ivanov et al., 2018; Kuo, Chen, & Tseng, 2017).

Four empirical papers, the only empirical studies to date to the authors' knowledge, examined consumer evaluations of human robot interaction (HRI) with hotel service robots. The first paper illustrated the importance of robotic head movements and direct greetings (Pan et al., 2015). The second paper, a survey of 260 Russians from 18 to 30 years old, reported that Muscovites, males, and those favorable towards service robots were significantly amenable to robotic hotel service (Ivanov et al., 2018). The respondents were indifferent to the robots appearing machine- or human-like.

The final two papers explored robot appearances and used robots from Hen-Na, the world's first robot hotel. One study compared 233 hotel guests' reactions to photos of smiling human or robotic staff, with various degrees of head tilt (Yu 2018). Depending on their age group, male and female guests differed in their visiting intentions and perceptions of perceived staff reliability and assurance.

The other study, an online survey and a laboratory experiment, found that HRI dimensions of perceived intelligence, perceived security and anthropomorphism related to adoption. The results underline anthropomorphism's importance in understanding hospitality and tourism guest-robot interactions (Tussyadiah & Park, 2018). While research recognizes its importance, anthropomorphism's role for marketing robotic services in tourism and hospitality remains under-conceptualized.

rService

Marketing thought – especially i service industries – is moving towards experience design and customer value co-creation (Balmer & Greyser, 2006; Gummesson, 2014). Customer experience has also become a central concept in tourism marketing and tourism scholars are paying increasing attention to service experience elements (Campos, Mendes, Do Valle, & Scott, 2016; Kastenholz, Carneiro, Marques, & Loureiro, 2018). The tourist is seen as a co-creator of the experience (Campos, Mendes, Valle, & Scott, 2018), where the number and quality of interactions between the tourist and service-scape define the experience.

The rise of social media and the resulting review economy further illustrate that tourism and hospitality marketing must increase its focus on the experience itself (Xiang, Magnini, & Fesenmaier, 2015). As service robots become more commonplace, their role in mediating customer experience co-creation grows. Consequently, HRI design should fundamentally shape future customer experiences and be integral to tourism and hospitality experience design and marketing efforts.

In relationship marketing as well, robots create new opportunities. Companies seek to create long and stable customer relationships, which deliver favorable word of mouth, reduce employee training costs, lower staff turnover and justify premium prices (Yim, Tse, & Chan, 2008). Customer-staff relationships are important for business operations (Yim et al., 2008), and the field is now open for exploiting potential customer- and staff-robot relationship benefits (van Doorn et al., 2017).

Customer relationship management databases, online big data and artificial intelligence could enable robots to know customers better than any human, and utilize this knowledge to create relationships that increase customer loyalty and commitment towards a firm during the service delivery process. For instance, room service delivery robots could greet customers with their actual name and ask whether a service preference should be added to their profile.

Service robots are thus moving away from being standalone machines to networked entities that generate collective intelligence, enabling these entities to process, synthesize and learn from large amounts of data (Huang & Rust, 2017). From a marketing perspective, companies with the requisite technology to collect and analyze extensive customer data could improve relationships through human-like robots automating marketing in situ in the service-scape.

Services marketing is concerned with technology adoption and technology's subsequent customer impacts (see Kim, Wang, & Malthouse, 2015; Lam & Shankar, 2014 for recent examples). This concern helps bridge the gap between general service research and HRI. Services scholars developed the eService paradigm – providing service over electronic networks (Rust & Kannan, 2003, p. 38) – to conceptualize the impact on customers (e.g. Collier & Bienstock, 2006; Fassnacht & Koese, 2006; Parasuraman, Zeithaml, & Malhotra, 2005).

Almost all eService studies, innovation adoption or implementation, focus on software that runs on an inert device such as a desktop computer or a mobile phone. Therefore, a robotic service – rService – paradigm is critical for driving service robot research and practice forward. rService implies that the service delivery channel is a robot and therefore examining and potentially re-conceptualizing all assumptions regarding every aspect of service, such as service quality, service failure, service cost, and service recovery.

Articles that examine rService often draw on HRI principles (Tung & Law, 2017; Tussyadiah & Park, 2018). For example, an experimental study in Japan tested different interaction formats for hotel lobby robots (Pan et al., 2015). Another article introduced the automated social presence (ASP) concept, developed a typology of different automated and human social presence with customers and conceptualized relationships between ASP and key service and customer outcomes (van Doorn et al., 2017). The authors noted that a major study limitation was ignoring the Uncanny Valley theory (Belk, 2016; Broadbent, 2017; Mori, 1970; Mori et al., 2012).

In tourism and hospitality, customers may evaluate service robots more directly than in other industries, comparing these robots to the experience human service staff would have delivered. Understanding how the human-likeness of a robot influences this experience is therefore an important antecedent for investigating HRI within the rService paradigm.

Human Robot Interaction (HRI)

Broad academic literature noting that robots have leapt from science fiction into hospitality and tourism is gaining traction and often mentions HRI as a key area to investigate (Andrews, 1984; Belk, 2016; Fan, Wu, & Mattila, 2016; Pan et al., 2015; van Doorn et al., 2017). Dautenhahn (2013: n.p.) explains that:

"HRI is the science of studying people's behaviour and attitudes towards robots in relationship to the physical, technological and interactive features of the robots, with the goal to develop robots that facilitate the emergence of human-robot interactions that are at the same time efficient (according to the original requirements of their envisaged area of use), but are also acceptable to people, and meet the social and emotional needs of their individual users as well as respecting human values."

HRI is an important consideration when robots provide services because of the encounter's dynamic, unstructured and personal nature. Robot communication capabilities – e.g. voice, haptic, visual and programming – and other anthropomorphic features embedded in robot form and mobility shape HRI (Belk, 2016).

Anthropomorphism – how robots look, move and communicate similar to humans – helps "predict the degree of moral care and concern afforded to an agent, the amount of responsibility and trust placed on an agent, and the extent to which an agent serves as a source of social influence" (Waytz, Cacioppo, & Epley, 2014, p. 1). For example, a robot's head tilt or gaze can affect user perceptions of that robot and underscore the importance of non-verbal cues in robot design (Mara & Appel, 2015; Pan et al., 2015).

How anthropomorphic characteristics and communication capabilities relate to HRI and service robot success seems critical for tourism and hospitality enterprises, as well as for theory development. Tourism and hospitality constitute contexts in which robots replace or support staff that perform complex tasks or provide emotional labor. Ensuring the acceptance of robots and designing successful interactions is far from trivial in these contexts (Murphy et al., 2017; Pan et al., 2015; Tung & Law, 2017; Tussyadiah & Park, 2018). For example, as hospitality and tourism service interactions are often cross-cultural, marketers must consider establishing robot characteristics and interaction routines based on likeness with the service provider/host or with the customer.

Robot autonomy, capabilities and design

Anthropomorphism is the extent to which a character has the appearance or behavioral attributes of a human being (Koda, 1996). Anthropomorphism related to tourism and hospitality technologies includes the context of Facebook pages (Perez-Vega, Taheri, Farrington, & O'Gorman, 2018), self-service interfaces (Fan et al., 2016), mobile phones (Tussyadiah, 2014) and virtual agents in recommender systems (Yoo & Gretzel, 2009). Anthropomorphism influences the believability of robots and thus is instrumental in shaping HRI (Simmons et al., 2011). Concepts that inform anthropomorphism include *autonomy*, *robot*

capabilities and *robot design*. As engineering achievements will condition the consumer or demand side of the robot story, it makes sense to examine how consumer encounters shape rService delivery and outcomes.

Autonomy, critical to the notion of any intelligent system and therefore of a robot (Gretzel, 2011), helps distinguish among devices that make decisions with or without human input. Rather than a dichotomy, robot autonomy ranges from basic levels of manual teleoperation to full autonomy (Beer, Fisk, & Rogers, 2012).

In addition to considering autonomy, the proposed robot capability hierarchy in Table 1 below has two interpretations. First, robots vary in their capabilities; there are and will be many specialized robot types with different capabilities. Second, with the addition of each row, robots become more adept and capable (Brynjolfsson et al., 2014; Touretzky, 2010).

Design relates to how robots move and interact. Fong, Nourbakhsh, and Dautenhahn (2003) posit that "any truly social intelligence must have an embodiment that is structurally and functionally similar to the human sensorimotor system" (p.33). Consequently, designing for human (or at least creature) likeness has been a major robot design issue. For example, robots' arm/leg-like subsystems vary in the degrees of freedom of translation and rotation (Kavic, 2004), i.e. their degree of humanness. Robots also vary in their surface composition. Designers may use plastic or metal, or create a skin-like look such as using "frubber" for Sophia in CES 2018 (Gebhart, 2018). Another important design aspect is including human features such as head dimensions, faces and elements essential for facial expressions like eyebrows and ears (DiSalvo, Gemperle, Forlizzi, & Kiesler, 2002).

Not all robots, however aim for human-likeness; robots may be much smaller or larger than human-scale. Many CES 2017 service robots tended to be short, white, round and smooth, albeit one robot resembled Albert Einstein's head (Ackerman, 2017; Graham, 2017). While smaller sizes and bigger heads

Table 1. Proposed robot capability hierarchy.

Capability	Examples
General Mobility	Stationary, Mobile, Swimming, Flying
Task Mobility	Lifting, Carrying, Pushing, Opening
Memory	Storing, Retaining and Retrieving Information
Sensory Processing	Sensing, Perceiving, Identifying
Communication: Robot-Human	Voice, Gestures, Touch, Emotions, Display
Communication: Human-Robot	Voice, Gestures, Touch, Emotions, Remote Control, Sensors
Communication: Robot-Robot	Swarming, Coordinating
Sociality: Human-Robot	Understanding, Empathizing, Learning
Sociality: Robot-Human	Explaining, Advising, Conveying Affect
Symbolic Processing	Understanding, Thinking, Reasoning
Creation	Innovating, Spawning, Originating, Conceiving

can trigger "baby schema" and therefore create cuteness perceptions, such design features could seriously attenuate ascriptions of intelligence and capability. Human likeness influences the wish to affiliate with robots and is a significant driver of forming social relationships (Simmons et al., 2011). Yet designing robots *not* to resemble humans can avoid Uncanny Valley effects.

The Uncanny Valley

Robot autonomy, capabilities and anthropomorphic cues embedded in robot design, as well as the context and humans themselves, may lead to non-linear human responses to robots. As Table 1 above illustrates, many of the eleven robot capabilities imply physical forms. Mobility, for example, can involve life-like robot morphology (e.g. legged robots) and thus imitate a biological organism. In contrast, robots can be wheeled or spherical (rolling ball robots) and imitate machines like automobiles. The Robot-Human Communication capability category suggests that some robots can express emotions with human-like voices. This blurring of the living and the mechanical gives robots their dominant perceptual characteristics but also makes it difficult for humans to classify robots into the machine/object category.

A popular theory, the Uncanny Valley Theory (Belk, 2016; Broadbent, 2017; Mori, 1970; Mori et al., 2012) suggests that a robot's degree of human likeness relates to feeling comfortable with the robot. Rather than a linear relationship though, feelings become eerie as robots almost resemble humans – leading to the Uncanny Valley. Figure 1 below shows that as the human likeness increases, the emotional response increases up to the "Uncanny Valley" in gray. Emotion then turns negative, below the horizontal black line, and then increases again as the likeness becomes almost human. At least one study extends this

Uncanny Valley to monkeys' visual behavior towards monkey faces (Steckenfinger & Ghazanfar, 2009), suggesting that the Uncanny Valley is a fundamental principle guiding social interactions.

Uncanny Valley research often draws on perceptual, cognitive, and social mechanisms and predominantly studies human faces. For example, manipulating computer generated human facial proportions, skin texture, and facial detail suggested that complex factors and interactions vary the level of eeriness (MacDorman, Green, Ho, & Koch, 2009). Furthermore, an experiment drawing on subjective ratings of video clips of 13 different robots and one human found no single Uncanny Valley for a particular range of human likeness. Appearance is one of many factors influencing perceptions of a robot as strange or eerie (MacDorman, 2006). Finally, ample evidence suggests that a robot user's culture affects how they perceive robots (Bartneck, Suzuki, Kanda, & Nomura, 2007; Kaplan, 2004; Rau, Li, & Li, 2009). The Uncanny Valley seems personal depending on various background factors such as culture, which is important in tourism and hospitality rService contexts.

Other robotic factors include touch, movement (including approach), materials and speech (Mori et al., 2012; Pan et al., 2015; Tung & Law, 2017). For example, participants reacted favorably when a nursing robot touched them (Chen, King, Thomaz, & Kemp, 2014). The robot's perceived intent however, showed a more favorable response for cleaning participants' arms than for comforting participants. Furthermore, a verbal warning decreased the favorability.

And although not a robot per se, an experimental study tested the impact of a self-service technology (SST) machine's voice on consumer intentions to switch to traditional interpersonal customer service (Fan et al., 2016). A human-like rather than robotic voice reduced switching intentions. This research highlights the consumer's role in HRI, as the consumer's sense of power and the presence of other customers attenuated the switching intentions for powerful customers (Fan et al., 2016). Similarly, a type of technological readiness, using the Internet via a smartphone, showed a strong interaction effect on perceived human likeness and service robot adoption (Goudey & Bonnin, 2016).

In addition to human likeness, which can vary from machine- to creature- to human-like, the study context and the study participants can attenuate or amplify perceived human likeness effects (Goudey & Bonnin, 2016; Read & Belpaeme, 2014; Rosenthal-von der Pütten, Krämer, Hoffmann, Sobieraj, & Eimler, 2013). van Doorn et al. (2017) suggest that in addition to technology readiness, relationship orientation (social- vs. exchange-orientation) and the tendency to

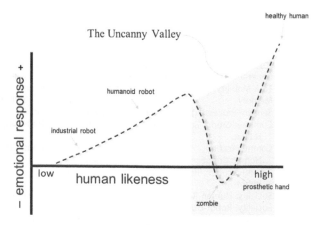

Figure 1. Uncanny Valley theory (adopted from Mori, 1970).

anthropomorphize are important individual characteristics to consider when examining reactions to service robots. In summary, teasing out the Uncanny Valley is a difficult, complicated and ongoing quest (Belk, 2016; Broadbent, 2017; van Doorn et al., 2017; Waytz et al., 2014). Understanding the Uncanny Valley's particular shapes and drivers across various tourism and hospitality service encounters is a critical step towards facilitating rService adoption and success.

Tourism and hospitality marketing considerations

The robotic continuum from machine- to human-likeness has marketing implications that require careful consideration by tourism and hospitality service providers. As noted, anthropomorphism can predict care, concern, responsibility and trust afforded by a robot and the robot's social influence on customers (Tussyadiah & Park, 2018; Waytz et al., 2014). The above literature review leads to conceptualizing how the Uncanny Valley may translate into three important and possible marketing outcomes (Figure 2).

Figure 2's bottom panel shows Uncanny Valley *affective reactions* (Belk, 2016; Broadbent, 2017; Mori, 1970; Mori et al., 2012). While the literature emphasizes eeriness, immediate reactions at the edges of the Uncanny Valley might support novelty effects. For example, recent industry reports suggest that robots have become hotel attractions, bringing customers curious to experience such robots on the hotel premises (Travelweekly.com, 2018).

The middle panel in Figure 2 focuses on a long-term outcome, namely *acceptance*, a standard innovation adoption metric (Rogers, 2003). Human likeness at low levels should have little influence on the acceptance of robotic service delivery (van Doorn et al., 2017). Yet, once human likeness reaches a certain threshold, individuals and organizations may completely stop accepting robots, potentially leading to a significant temporal gap in service robot implementation until reaching acceptable levels of human-likeness. Robot acceptance determines whether robots can deliver services and facilitate experience co-creation. As acceptable human-likeness seems unlikely in the near future, marketers should consider carefully whether abstract robot forms might deliver a higher rService quality. Comparisons of reactions to and engagement with humanoid versus non-humanoid robots are currently unavailable for rService settings.

Finally, Figure 2's top panel shows the third outcome and a proposed new construct: *anthropomorphic loyalty*. Anthropomorphic loyalty merges consumer loyalty to an inanimate brand, and the loyalty traditionally reserved for a human companion. Anthropomorphic

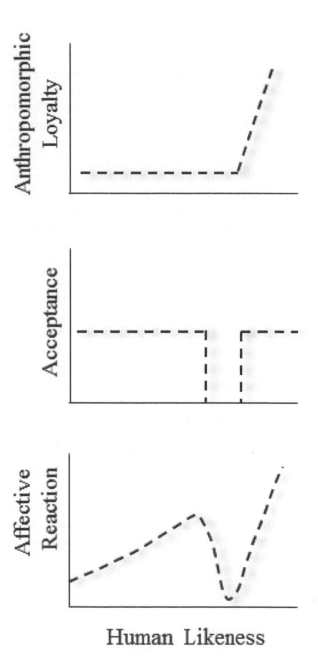

Figure 2. Marketing implications of the Uncanny Valley.

loyalty comes into play when the robot is sufficiently human like. Such anthropomorphic loyalty seems a key outcome as service marketers have long shown various entities to which a relationship, and hence loyalty, can attach. As Reynolds and Beatty (1999) posit, customer-firm and customer-salesperson relationships differ. In the e-commerce sphere, customers may develop interface loyalty (Murray & Häubl, 2003). Given the full force of anthropomorphism and how potent it can be in practice (e.g. Moon, 2003), loyalty could attach to robots in stronger ways than to other interfaces or the brand itself as a result of robots' anthropomorphic qualities.

Robots and tourist experience

Where and how a tourist interacts with a robot will influence the tourist experience. How tourists experience a destination, a tourism business, or a service provider has major marketing implications. How well the service provider has understood customer needs and preferences and designed the robots, robot interactions and experiences can weaken or strengthen customer value perceptions and lead to positive or negative word-of-mouth (Wasko & Faraj, 2005).

As product preferences can relate to anthropomorphization (Maeng & Aggarwal, 2017), a robot's design – and the Uncanny Valley – should influence customer preferences. Such design goes beyond physical appearance and includes behavioral and psychological responses, such as programming robotic pets to display attachment behaviors similar to real animals (Broadbent, 2017). This approach requires dissecting tourism and hospitality services into small enough elements that can translate into robot design. For instance, hotels should determine what constitutes an extraordinary check-in experience as something for service robots to model. Furthermore, an increased conceptualization of service aspects should reach beyond robot capabilities, such as empathy, in order to determine when and how humans should complement rServices.

A robot's functions and appearance, good or bad, could relate to the robot's owner (Moon, 2003) and therefore critically influence a tourism and hospitality organization's brand. Customer interactions in various touchpoints connect directly to branding (Baxendale, Macdonald, & Wilson, 2015). Thus, HRI can be analyzed and designed from a branding perspective (Hogan, Almquist, & Glynn, 2005) and become a critical branding element.

The extent that tourists/guests can customize a service robot (e.g. its voice or personality) and therefore support co-creation activities is another consideration. Customization can enhance customers' sense of control and ultimately their desire to revisit the service experience (van Doorn et al., 2017). Yet personalization imposed by marketers and insufficiently transparent could make robots appear to "know too much" and resemble a creepy stalker. Using too much data might alienate customers, especially publicly available data sets unknown by customers and seem to invade their privacy (Saravanan & Ramakrishnan, 2016).

Lastly, the service robot could be an agent rather than staff, making purchase decisions and representing the customer to the firm such as a physical rather than virtual shopbot (Ivanov & Webster, 2017; Kumar, Dixit, Javalgi, & Dass, 2016). In this case, psychological ownership of the robot driven by the robot's perceived receptiveness, attractiveness and manipulability, as conceptualized by van Doorn et al. (2017), could moderate service outcomes.

Managing robots

By definition of autonomy, managing robotic products will be unlike managing tangible goods that do not exhibit agency. How robots, other robots, staff and customers interact is an important future consideration for tourism and hospitality managers. Both robot capabilities and appearance will be critical with consumers due to problems stemming from the Uncanny Valley. Another aspect is how robot design fits into, and changes, the service culture that forms the core of many tourism and hospitality brands. For example, should service robots wear service uniforms?

The Uncanny Valley in developing and diffusing tourism and hospitality robotics service is a factor that managers should consider from both a customer and human relations perspective. The most technologically advanced and anthropomorphically developed robot may yield a sub-optimal investment compared to older models or to humans. This robot development issue is not yet topical.

The intersection of ownership and anthropomorphism provides two additional areas of interest – legal implications and consumer discomfort. While consumers and organizations have no problems owning objects, most individuals would reject the idea of owning people. "Although the morality of robots is a somewhat philosophical topic, it does have real-world implications for a future in which robots in the real world cause accidents. Who is to blame? The robot? The developer? The owner?" (Broadbent, 2017, p. 643). Perhaps anthropomorphism relates positively to feelings of care and negatively to responsibility for robot actions if it communicates intelligence and autonomy.

Future research

A burgeoning research stream this century has applied SERVQUAL to electronic service quality, or eService (e.g. Fassnacht & Koese, 2006). The automated nature of websites and many email replies, however, renders off-line service quality measures inappropriate for measuring eService (Parasuraman et al., 2005). Albeit, some studies extend SERVQUAL to websites and email (Murphy, Schegg, & Olaru, 2007). Extending SERVQUAL to service robots merits research from two aspects, robots as an employee and as a self-service technology.

Developing r-SERVQUAL would require rewording the questions and a systematic test of the applicability of the current dimensions, thus requiring in-depth qualitative research in addition to theoretical conceptualization. For instance, human-likeness and non-creepiness merit consideration given their centrality in HRI research. A complementary approach to SERVQUAL could compare service robots and humans on two key dimensions – affect and cognition – that drive marketing outcomes (Cronin, Brady, & Hult, 2000).

As indicated in the beginning of this paper, most technology-focused tourism literature deals with technology acceptance. Engagement, critical for HRI and ultimately customer service, goes beyond acceptance and is therefore an important dependent measure for future research. A recent experimental study confirmed and provided evidence that HRI engagement models should consider user attitudes and personality traits in addition to robot qualities (Ivaldi et al., 2016). Extroversion related positively to talking with the robot and a negative attitude towards robots led to looking less at a robot's face and more at the robot's hands. Research of engagement also carries over to revisiting Table 1's proposed hierarchy, particularly communication among robots and humans.

Robot personality and human interaction/communication modes (being embarrassed, spontaneous, funny, moody, flirty, etc.) is another underexplored area. Anthropomorphism-related marketing literature (e.g. Maeng & Aggarwal, 2017; Veer, 1993) has shown that brands successfully use anthropomorphism to stimulate attachment. Applying human-to-human interaction principles to human-machine interactions (Reeves & Nass, 1996) seems applicable if the machines look, act and interact like humans. In accordance with this assumption, Fong et al. (2003) suggest that personality is an important design aspect of social robots. Conversational styles similar to those explored for recommender systems (Ricci, Rokach, & Shapira, 2011) could also help design robots for better rService quality. It is therefore essential to understand which dimensions and levels of anthropomorphism most likely trigger a human-interaction schema that encourages engagement. The extent and quality of engagement are also important factors in the experience co-creation literature (Campos et al., 2016).

The extent that HRI supports intimacy may also play a role, as owners developing intimacy with their Roomba – a robotic vacuum cleaner – had more pleasure cleaning, often adapted their homes to their Roomba, encouraged pet-Roomba interaction and named their Roomba (Gutmann, Culp, Munich, & Pirjanian, 2012; Sung, Grinter, Christensen, & Guo, 2008). Thus, future research should extend customer engagement on social media literature to the HRI context, with emphasis on how to encourage/initiate and sustain engagement and how to measure engagement quality and outcomes effectively.

Future research should also focus on users and the Uncanny Valley. Tourism and hospitality markets are extremely heterogeneous, serving customers from all over the world and in different contexts. Understanding how personal factors such as culture affect service robot perceptions (Bartneck et al., 2007; Kaplan, 2004; Rau et al., 2009) should provide important service marketing insights. Guest personality might be an additional factor worth considering. For instance, extroversion and emotional stability may relate positively to anthropomorphizing a robot (Salem, Lakatos, Amirabdollahian, & Dautenhahn, 2015) and therefore shape HRI.

Data is critical for business competitiveness. Service robots can be Internet-of-Things (IoT) devices, able to collect various kinds of data and feed it into different systems/applications. The data collection capabilities of human-like robots merit further research. How people perceive robots should affect how they interact with them (Maeng & Aggarwal, 2017), which in turn leads to the extent and quality of data these devices could collect from customers.

At the Uncanny Valley's far right, the android/gynoid (male/female) is a personal service robot that is anthropomorphic in both appearance and behavior (Belk, 2016; Broadbent, 2017). Anthropomorphic robots could provide a platform for various new services and business models, such as sex tourism, and raise societal issue about adopting and using human-like robots (Yeoman & Mars, 2012). Researching this end of the spectrum remains a challenge, as the technological development has not advanced enough to create such robots. Future research could examine rService via androids, using scenarios and computer generated images.

Conclusion

That robots will evolve and alter the workforce and marketplace is clear; unclear is the extent of this evolution and the magnitude and reach of its impacts (Broadbent, 2017; Brynjolfsson et al., 2014; Collins, 2015; Frey & Osborne, 2017; van Doorn et al., 2017). HRI is a central issue in this context. Customer-owned robots that function in the house and yard are becoming commonplace (Murphy et al., 2017); personal service/companion/care/butler robots were popular at CES 2017 and 2018 (Ackerman, 2017; Baraniuk, 2018; Gebhart, 2018; Graham, 2017; Peake, 2018; Song, 2018). Firm-owned robots, however, are still uncommon and HRI in an rService environment remains under-researched.

This paper conceptualized anthropomorphism as a critical factor influencing customer-robot service interactions. While existing literature focuses on frequent/regular interactions, the tourism and hospitality field usually does not afford overcoming the Uncanny Valley through learning and habituation. Yet hospitality and tourism can serve as an important context in which to build knowledge and first impressions of robots through short-term interactions. Understanding HRI in this context is important beyond the immediate field.

Limitations

Conceptualizing HRI in tourism and hospitality settings is difficult. Despite the recent hype regarding robots, they remain a comparatively rare phenomenon in these environments. Many assumptions in this paper stem from research in different contexts. Understanding the peculiarities of tourism and hospitality HRI clearly needs empirical research. In addition, this study treated robots as a physical device owned by the tourism and hospitality company, ignoring Robots-As-A-Service (RaaS) concepts where the owner and the user of the service robot are different entities (Remy & Blake, 2011). Both tourists and tourism and hospitality businesses could subscribe to various robotic services for a certain purpose or certain time-period, thus adding additional layers of complexity.

Acknowledgments

This paper is a markedly revised, expanded and updated version of a manuscript presented at the APacCHRIE 2017 conference.

Disclosure statement

No potential conflict of interest was reported by the authors.

ORCID

Jamie Murphy ⓘ http://orcid.org/0000-0002-3935-4303
Juho Pesonen ⓘ http://orcid.org/0000-0003-0167-9142

References

Ackerman, E. (2017). *CES 2017: Why every social robot at CES looks alike*. Retrieved from http://spectrum.ieee.org/tech-talk/robotics/home-robots/ces-2017-why-every-social-robot-at-ces-looks-alike

Andrew, W. P. (1984). Hospitality education and the technological revolution. *Journal of Hospitality & Tourism Research*, 8(2), 15–21.

Balmer, J. M., & Greyser, S. A. (2006). Corporate marketing: Integrating corporate identity, corporate branding, corporate communications, corporate image and corporate reputation. *European Journal of Marketing*, 40(7/8), 730–741.

Baraniuk, C. (2018). CES 2018: Were robots more than a gimmick at the tech show? *BBC.com*. Retrieved from http://www.bbc.com/news/technology-42657607.

Bartneck, C., Suzuki, T., Kanda, T., & Nomura, T. (2007). The influence of people's culture and prior experiences with Aibo on their attitude towards robots. *Ai & Society*, 21(1–2), 217–230.

Baxendale, S., Macdonald, E. K., & Wilson, H. N. (2015). The impact of different touchpoints on brand consideration. *Journal of Retailing*, 91(2), 235–253.

Beer, J. M., Fisk, A. D., & Rogers, W. A. (2012). Toward a psychological framework for levels of robot autonomy in human-robot interaction. *Human Factors and Aging Laboratory Technical Reports*. Atlanta, GA: Georgia Institute of Technology, School of Psychology – Human Factors and Aging Laboratory.

Belk, R. (2016). Understanding the robot: Comments on Goudey and Bonnin (2016). *Recherche Et Applications En Marketing (English Edition)*, 31(4), 83–90.

Broadbent, E. (2017). Interactions with robots: The truths we reveal about ourselves. *Annual Review of Psychology*, 68(1), 627–652.

Brynjolfsson, E., McAfee, A., & Cummings, J. (2014). *The second machine age: Work, progress, and prosperity in a time of brilliant technologies*. New York, NY: W. W. Norton & Company.

Campos, A. C., Mendes, J., Do Valle, P. O., & Scott, N. (2016). Co-creation experiences: Attention and memorability. *Journal of Travel & Tourism Marketing*, 33(9), 1309–1336.

Campos, A. C., Mendes, J., Valle, P. O. D., & Scott, N. (2018). Co-creation of tourist experiences: A literature review. *Current Issues in Tourism*, 21(4), 369–400.

Čapek, K. (2001). *Rossum´s Universal Robots*. (P. Selver & N. Playfair, Trans.). Mineola, NY: Dover Publications.

Chen, T. L., King, C. H. A., Thomaz, A. L., & Kemp, C. C. (2014). An investigation of responses to robot-initiated touch in a nursing context. *International Journal of Social Robotics*, 6(1), 141–161.

Collier, J. E., & Bienstock, C. C. (2006). Measuring service quality in e-retailing. *Journal of Service Research*, 8(3), Retrieved from, 260–275.

Collins, G. (2015). The rise of robotics in hospitality. In *HiTech 2015 special report* (pp. 22–23). https://www.hotel-yearbook.com/article/4072928/the-rise-of-robotics-in-hospitality.html

Cronin, J. J., Brady, M. K., & Hult, G. T. M. (2000). Assessing the effects of quality, value, and customer satisfaction on consumer behavioral intentions in service environments. *Journal of Retailing*, 76(2), 193–218.

Dautenhahn, K. (2013). Human-Robot Interaction. In M. Soegaard & R. F. Dam (Eds.), *The encyclopedia of human-computer interaction* (2nd ed.). The Interaction Design Foundation. Retrieved March 18, 2018, from https://www.interaction-design.org/literature/book/the-encyclopedia-of-human-computer-interaction-2nd-ed/human-robot-interaction

DiSalvo, C. F., Gemperle, F., Forlizzi, J., & Kiesler, S. (2002, June 25–28). *All robots are not created equal: The design and perception of humanoid robot heads. Proceedings of the 4th conference on Designing interactive systems: processes, practices, methods, and techniques* (pp. 321–326). London, England: ACM.

Fan, A., Wu, L., & Mattila, A. S. (2016). Does anthropomorphism influence customers' switching intentions in the self-service technology failure context? *Journal of Services Marketing, 30* (7), 713–723.

Fassnacht, M., & Koese, I. (2006). Quality of electronic services. *Journal of Service Research, 9*(1), 19–37.

Fong, T., Nourbakhsh, I., & Dautenhahn, K. (2003). A survey of socially interactive robots. *Robotics and Autonomous Systems, 42*(3–4), 143–166.

Frey, C. B., & Osborne, M. A. (2017). The future of employment: How susceptible are jobs to computerisation?. *Technological Forecasting and Social Change, 114*(January), 254–280.

Gebhart, A. (2018). The robots of CES 2018: Cuteness reigns supreme. *C|Net News.* Retrieved from https://www.cnet.com/news/the-robots-of-ces-2018-cuteness-reigns-supreme/

Godwin, C. (2018). Burger-flipping robot begins first shift. *BBC News.* Retrieved from http://www.bbc.com/news/av/technology-43292047/burger-flipping-robot-begins-first-shift.

Goudey, A., & Bonnin, G. (2016). Must smart objects look human? Study of the impact of anthropomorphism on the acceptance of companion robots. *Recherche Et Applications En Marketing (English Edition), 31*(2), 2–20.

Graham, J. (2017, January 7). CES 2017: Robots steal show at this year's event. *USA Today.* Retrieved from http://usatoday.com/story/tech/talkingtech/2017/01/07/coolest-thing-ces-2017-robots-steal-show/96241420/

Gretzel, U. (2011). Intelligent systems in tourism: A social science perspective. *Annals of Tourism Research, 38*(3), 757–779.

Gummesson, E. (2014). Productivity, quality and relationship marketing in service operations: A revisit in a new service paradigm. *International Journal of Contemporary Hospitality Management, 26*(5), 656–662.

Gutmann, J. S., Culp, K., Munich, M. E., & Pirjanian, P. (2012). *The social impact of a systematic floor cleaner. Advanced Robotics and its Social Impacts (ARSO), 2012 IEEE Workshop on* (pp. 50–53), Munich, Germany.

Hogan, S., Almquist, E., & Glynn, S. E. (2005). Brand-building: Finding the touchpoints that count. *Journal of Business Strategy, 26*(2), 11–18.

Huang, M. H., & Rust, R. T. (2017). Artificial intelligence in service. *Journal of Service Research, 21*(2), 155–172. 1094670517752459.

Ivaldi, S., Lefort, S., Peters, J., Chetouani, M., Provasi, J., & Zibetti, E. (2016). Towards engagement models that consider individual factors in HRI: On the relation of extroversion and negative attitude towards robots to gaze and speech during a human–robot assembly task. *International Journal of Social Robotics, 9*(1), 1–24.

Ivanov, S., Webster, C., & Garenko, A. (2018). Young Russian adults' attitudes towards the potential use of robots in hotels. In *Technology in Society 55*, 24–32.

Ivanov, S. H., & Webster, C. (2017, June 29–30). *The robot as a consumer: A research agenda (2017). "Marketing: experience and perspectives" Conference*, University of Economics-Varna, Bulgaria.

Ivanov, S. H., Webster, C., & Berezina, K. (2018). Adoption of robots and service automation by tourism and hospitality companies. *Revista Turismo & Desenvolvimento, 1*(27/28), 1501–1517.

Kaplan, F. (2004). Who is afraid of the humanoid? Investigating cultural differences in the acceptance of robots. *International Journal of Humanoid Robotics, 1*(03), 465–480.

Kastenholz, E., Carneiro, M. J., Marques, C. P., & Loureiro, S. M. C. (2018). The dimensions of rural tourism experience: Impacts on arousal, memory, and satisfaction. *Journal of Travel & Tourism Marketing, 35*(2), 189–201.

Kavic, M. S. (2004). Robotics, technology, and the future of surgery. *Journal of the Society of Laparoendoscopic Surgeons, 4*(4), 277–279.

Kim, S. J., Wang, R. J.-H., & Malthouse, E. C. (2015). The effects of adopting and using a brand's mobile application on customers' subsequent purchase behavior. *Journal of Interactive Marketing, 31*(August), 28–41.

Koda, T. (1996). *Agents with faces: A study on the effects of personification of software agents* (Master's Thesis). Massachusetts Institute of Technology, Boston, MA, USA.

Kumar, V., Dixit, A., Javalgi, R. R. G., & Dass, M. (2016). Research framework, strategies, and applications of intelligent agent technologies (IATs) in marketing. *Journal of the Academy of Marketing Science, 44*(1), 24–45.

Kuo, C. M., Chen, L. C., & Tseng, C. Y. (2017). Investigating an innovative service with hospitality robots. *International Journal of Contemporary Hospitality Management, 29*(5), 1305–1321.

Lam, S. Y., & Shankar, V. (2014). Asymmetries in the effects of drivers of brand loyalty between early and late adopters and across technology generations. *Journal of Interactive Marketing, 28*(1), 26–42.

MacDorman, K. F. (2006, July). *Subjective ratings of robot video clips for human likeness, familiarity, and eeriness: An exploration of the uncanny valley. ICCS/CogSci-2006 long symposium: Toward social mechanisms of android science* (pp. 26–29), Vancouver, Canada.

MacDorman, K. F., Green, R. D., Ho, C. C., & Koch, C. T. (2009). Too real for comfort? Uncanny responses to computer generated faces. *Computers in Human Behavior, 25*(3), 695–710.

Maeng, A., & Aggarwal, P. (2017). Facing dominance: Anthropomorphism and the effect of product face ratio on consumer preference. *Journal of Consumer Research, 44* (5), 1104–1122.

Mara, M., & Appel, M. (2015). Effects of lateral head tilt on user perceptions of humanoid and android robots. *Computers in Human Behavior, 44*(March), 326–334.

Moon, Y. (2003). Don't blame the computer: When self-disclosure moderates the self-serving bias. *Journal of Consumer Psychology, 13*(1/2), 125–137.

Mori, M. (1970). The Uncanny Valley. *Energy, 7*(4), 33–35. Retrieved from http://www.movingimages.info/digitalmedia/wp-content/uploads/2010/06/MorUnc.pdf

Mori, M., MacDorman, K. F., & Kageki, N. (2012). The uncanny valley [from the field]. *IEEE Robotics & Automation Magazine, 19*(2), 98–100.

Murphy, J., Hofacker, C., & Gretzel, U. (2017). Dawning of the age of robots in hospitality and tourism: Challenges for teaching and research. *European Journal of Tourism Research, 11*, 104–111.

Murphy, J., Schegg, R., & Olaru, D. (2007). Quality clusters: Dimensions of email responses by luxury hotels. *International Journal of Hospitality Management, 26*(3), 743–747.

Murray, K. B., & Häubl, G. (2003). A human capital perspective of skill acquisition and interface loyalty. *Communications of the ACM, 46*(12), 272–278.

Pan, Y., Okada, H., Uchiyama, T., & Suzuki, K. (2015). On the reaction to robot's speech in a hotel public space. *International Journal of Social Robotics, 7*(5), 911–920.

Parasuraman, A., Zeithaml, V. A., & Malhotra, A. (2005). E-S-QUAL: A multiple-item scale for assessing electronic service quality. *Journal of Service Research, 7*(3), 213–233.

Peake, E. (2018). At CES 2018, the robot uprising is falling flat on its face. *Wired Magazine*. Retrieved from https://www.wired.co.uk/article/ces-2018-robots-lg-cloi.

Perez-Vega, R., Taheri, B., Farrington, T., & O'Gorman, K. (2018). On being attractive, social and visually appealing in social media: The effects of anthropomorphic tourism brands on Facebook fan pages. *Tourism Management, 66*(June), 339–347.

Rau, P. P., Li, Y., & Li, D. (2009). Effects of communication style and culture on ability to accept recommendations from robots. *Computers in Human Behavior, 25*(2), 587–595.

Read, R., & Belpaeme, T. (2014, March). *Situational context directs how people affectively interpret robotic non-linguistic utterances. Proceedings of the 2014 ACM/IEEE international conference on human-robot interaction* (pp. 41–48). Bielefeld, Germany, ACM.

Reeves, B., & Nass, C. (1996). *The media equation: How people treat computers, television and new media like real people and places*. Stanford, CA: CSLI Publishing.

Remy, S. L., & Blake, M. B. (2011). Distributed service-oriented robotics. *IEEE Internet Computing, 15*(2), 70–74.

Reynolds, K. E., & Beatty, S. E. (1999). Customer benefits and company consequences of customer-salesperson relationships in retailing. *Journal of Retailing, 75*(1), 11–32.

Ricci, F., Rokach, L., & Shapira, B. (2011). Introduction to recommender systems handbook. In F. Ricci, L. Rokach, & B. Shapira (Eds.), *Recommender systems handbook* (pp. 1–35). New York, NY: Springer.

Rogers, E. M. (2003). *Diffusion of innovations* (Fifth ed.). New York, NY: Simon & Schuster.

Rosenthal-von der Pütten, A. M., Krämer, N. C., Hoffmann, L., Sobieraj, S., & Eimler, S. C. (2013). An experimental study on emotional reactions towards a robot. *International Journal of Social Robotics, 5*(1), 17–34.

Rust, R. T., & Kannan, P. K. (2003). E-Service: A new paradigm for business in the electronic environment. *Communications of the ACM, 46*(6), 37–42.

Salem, M., Lakatos, G., Amirabdollahian, F., & Dautenhahn, K. (2015). *Would you trust a (faulty) robot?: Effects of error, task type and personality on human-robot cooperation and trust. Proceedings of the Tenth Annual ACM/IEEE International Conference on Human-Robot Interaction* (pp. 141–148), Portland, Oregon, USA.

Saravanan, S., & Ramakrishnan, B. S. (2016). Preserving privacy in the context of location based services through location hider in mobile-tourism. *Information Technology & Tourism, 16*(2), 229–248.

Simmons, R., Makatchev, M., Kirby, R., Lee, M. K., Fanaswala, I., Browning, B., … Sakr, M. (2011). Believable robot characters. *AI Magazine, 32*(4), 39–52.

Song, V. (2018). The adorable, helpful, and creepy robots of CES 2018. *PC Magazine*. Retrieved from https://www.pcmag.com/feature/358509/the-adorable-helpful-and-creepy-robots-of-ces-2018.

Steckenfinger, S. A., & Ghazanfar, A. A. (2009). Monkey visual behavior falls into the uncanny valley. *Proceedings of the National Academy of Sciences, 106*(43), 18362–18366.

Sung, J. Y., Grinter, R. E., Christensen, H. I., & Guo, L. (2008). *Housewives or technophiles?: Understanding domestic robot owners. Proceedings of the 3rd ACM/IEEE international conference on Human robot interaction* (pp. 129–136), Amsterdam, The Netherlands.

Thrun, S. (2004). Toward a Framework for human-robot interaction. *Human–Computer Interaction, 19*(1), 9–24.

Touretzky, D. S. (2010). Preparing computer science students for the robotics revolution. *Communications of the ACM, 53*(8), 27–29.

Travelweekly.com (2018). *Hotel robots do double duty as butlers and featured attractions*. Retrieved March 15, 2018, from http://www.travelweekly.com/Travel-News/Hotel-News/Hotel-robots-do-double-duty-as-butlers-and-featured-attractions

Tung, V. W. S., & Law, R. (2017). The potential for tourism and hospitality experience research in human-robot interactions. *International Journal of Contemporary Hospitality Management, 29*(10), 2498–2513.

Tussyadiah, I., & Park, S. (2018). Consumer evaluation of hotel service robots. In B. Stangl & J. Pesonen (Eds.), *Information and communication technologies in tourism 2018* (pp. 308–320), Jönköping, Sweden, Springer. doi:10.1007/978-3-319-72923-7_24

Tussyadiah, I. P. (2014). Social actor attribution to mobile phones: The case of tourists. *Information Technology & Tourism, 14*(1), 21–47.

Ukpabi, D. C., & Karjaluoto, H. (2017). Consumers' acceptance of information and communications technology in tourism: A review. *Telematics and Informatics, 34*(5), 618–644.

van Doorn, J., Mende, M., Noble, S. M., Hulland, J., Ostrom, A. L., Grewal, D., & Petersen, J. A. (2017). Domo Arigato Mr. Roboto: Emergence of automated social presence in organizational frontlines and customers' service experiences. *Journal of Service Research, 20*(1), 43–58.

Vaussard, F. C., Fink, J., Bauwens, V., Rétornaz, P., Hamel, D., Dillenbourgh, P., & Mondada, F. (2014). Lessons learned from robotic vacuum cleaners entering in the home ecosystem. *Robotics and Autonomous Systems, 62*(3), 376–391.

Veer, E. (1993). Made with real crocodiles: The use of anthropomorphism to promote product kinship in our youngest consumers. *Journal of Marketing Management, 29*(1–2), 195–206.

Wasko, M. M., & Faraj, S. (2005). Why should I share? Examining social capital and knowledge contribution in electronic networks of practice. *MIS Quarterly, 29*(1), 35–57.

Waytz, A., Cacioppo, J., & Epley, N. (2014). Who sees human? The stability and importance of individual differences in anthropomorphism. *Perspectives on Psychological Science : A Journal of the Association for Psychological Science, 5*(3), 219–232.

Werthner, H., & Klein, S. (1999). *Information technology and tourism: A challenging relationship.* Vienna, Austria: Springer-Verlag.

Wired.com (2017). *2017 was the year the robots really, truly arrived.* Retrieved March 21, 2018, from https://www.wired.com/story/2017-was-the-year-the-robots-really-truly-arrived/?mbid=nl_123017_daily_list1_p1.

Xiang, Z., Magnini, V. P., & Fesenmaier, D. R. (2015). Information technology and consumer behavior in travel and tourism: Insights from travel planning using the internet. *Journal of Retailing and Consumer Services, 22* (January), 244–249.

Yeoman, I., & Mars, M. (2012). Robots, men and sex tourism. *Futures, 44*(4), 365–371.

Yim, C. K., Tse, T. K., & Chan, K. W. (2008). Strengthening customer loyalty through intimacy and passion: Roles of customer–firm affection and customer–staff relationships in services. *Journal of Marketing Research, 45*(6), 741–756.

Yoo, K.-H., & Gretzel, U. (2009, August 6–8). *The influence of virtual representatives on recommender system evaluation.* San Francisco, CA: AMCIS.

Yu, C.-E. (2018, March). *Humanlike robot and human staff in service: Age and gender differences in perceiving smiling behaviors.* 7th International Conference on Industrial Technology and Management (ICITM) (pp. 99–103). Oxford, United Kingdom: IEEE.

Classifying technological innovation attributes for hotels: an application of the Kano model

Chun-Fang Chiang ⓘ, Wen-Yu Chen and Chia-Yuan Hsu

ABSTRACT
Technological facilities and services have become attractive features in hotel selection. However, limited research has been conducted on how technological innovation attributes are perceived by hotel tourists. This paper aims to highlight and categorize the technological innovation attributes of hotels based on the Kano model. Empirical testing shows four technological innovation factors: Internet and app usage, smartphone usage as a room key and for payment, E-housekeeping, and the use of electronic self-service systems. Findings provide practical implications for hotel operators planning to introduce technologies into their hotels.

Introduction

Imagine typical hotel accommodations in the future: tourists search for hotels with mobile applications, refer to online reviews of specific hotels, and look at different room types with digitally interactive virtual reality (VR) videos before deciding on hotel reservations. When tourists arrive at the hotel, an automated robot waits politely to take their luggage. Self-service touch screens greet guests and offer check-in, checkout, and accessibility information. Instead of room keys, guests are handed smartphones upon check-in that use digital recognition to navigate guests to their rooms and unlock the door. Bedrooms come equipped with a smartphone, a tablet with apps, or technology walls that allow guests to control the lighting, temperature, curtains, and television to create the perfect ambience. Service automation and built-in infrared sensors alert housekeeping when guests need service, thereby avoiding unwanted encounters. For entertainment, hotels or guest rooms are fitted with a digitally interactive VR and E-entertainment system. These are the trends in technological innovations and are already available at some intelligent hotels at present.

The use of the Internet, online reservation services and online travel agencies (OTA) by hotels has radically changed hotel operations and the hotel business in the past two decades. Moreover, the advent of new technologies such as smartphones, apps, and social media are resulting in significant changes to service processes in the hotel industry. Meanwhile, customers are adapting to new technologies in their decision-making, attitudes and behaviors. Law, Leung, and Buhalis (2009) explained that deploying the latest IT services enhances the competitiveness of hotels because those services help satisfy customers' increasing needs for convenience and immediacy. As more customers begin to expect technological innovations to be provided by hotels, those services and facilities have become attractive attributes in hotel selection. However, is technological innovation the hotel attribute that customers care most about? Understanding customers' needs and expectations as well as their reactions to innovative technologies can enhance the probability of success in hotels' adoption of these innovations. In hospitality research, studies on technology innovation have begun only in recent years; Kokkinoua and Cranage (2013) noted that restaurant operators using self-service technology observed reduced actual waiting times and improved service levels. Wei, Torres, and Hua (2016) assessed self-service check-in and checkout for hotel guests. Kuo, Chen, and Tseng (2017) discussed the use of robotics services to help restaurants handle seasonal employee and labor use. While the use of new technologies is highly valued in the hotel industry, this topic has not been extensively discussed in the field of hospitality research.

The Kano model was proposed by Kano, Seraku, Takahashi, and Tsuji in 1984. The Kano model can be used to categorize different attributes, products, and services, and categorical design of services can be conducted based on the relevance of each attribute. Kano, Seraku, Takahashi, and Tsuji (1984) divided service attributes into five categories: attractive attributes, one-dimensional attributes, must-have attributes, indifferent attributes, and reverse attributes. Service providers must make the greatest effort to improve one-dimensional attributes, whereas attractive quality attributes can be classified as competitive advantages for attracting customers, especially new ones. The Kano model can be used to identify the importance of the individual quality attribute of customer demands, thereby facilitating the construction of better prerequisites and prioritization during product development. Over time, products or services with attractive qualities are transformed into those with must-have qualities (Shen, Tan, & Xie, 2000). The Kano model has already been applied to research on hospitality and tourism (Chen, 2012; Chang & Chen, 2011; Chen & Chen, 2015; Dominici & Palumbo, 2013; Gregory & Parsa, 2013; Kuo, Chen, & Boger, 2016; Lin, Yeh, & Wang, 2015). This study applies the Kano model to identify the types of hotel attributes that are valued by customers during the introduction of technological innovation to hotel operations. It also investigates whether technological innovations and applications are attractive attributes in order to effectively analyze the relative importance of hotel attributes in customers' perceptions and to better understand customers' needs and perceptions.

As hotels change with the times, hotels must understand customer perceptions of changing attributes and customers' classification of these attributes. Past studies on hotel attributes have only pointed out some technological attributes (Lee, Lee, & Tan, 2013; Rhee & Yang, 2014; Shanka & Taylor, 2003), and none have examined the specific technological innovation attributes or how these attributes are perceived by hotel guests. To fill the gap, two research questions are raised in this study: (1) After adding new technological innovation attributes, how do hotel guests perceive the hotel's attributes based on the Kano model classifications? and (2) What are the classifications of hotel attributes, including technological innovation attributes? Therefore, the main purpose of this study is to evaluate hotel attributes using the Kano model and to categorize these attributes by factor analysis. The major attributes perceived by customers reflect the types of technological innovations that hotels should add to their services in the future. This study adds to the theoretical understanding in the technology innovation literature by advancing the connection between hotel technology application and consumer perspectives, while the empirical results provide direction for adopting technological innovation attributes in hotels.

Literature review

Hotel technological innovation

Orfila-Sintesm, Crespí-Cladera, and Martínez-Ros (2005) defined technological innovation as the conversion of technological knowledge into new products, which in turn can lead to the introduction of new products, services, or processes. Law and Jogaratnam (2005) pointed out that some technologies that enhance operational efficiency and service quality while reducing cost have been widely applied in the hotel industry, including online reservations, high-speed Internet, and the regulation of temperatures and lighting in guest rooms, all of which can be classified as technological innovation for hotels. Currently, technological innovation in the service industry is focused on the latest technologies for self-service, which allow customers to serve themselves without direct assistance from employees (Bitner, Ostrom, & Meuter, 2002). Lema (2009) argued that self-service technologies have continuously transformed the hotel industry not only by providing more options for customers but also by changing the staff structure – employees also have to adapt to technological change and new service models (Kucukusta, Heung, & Hui, 2014). Although economy hotels usually invest fewer resources into IT and technological facilities than mid-priced to upscale hotels, Victorino, Verma, Plaschka, and Dev (2005) found that service innovation has a greater impact on customers who opt for economy hotels than on those who opt for mid-to-upscale hotels. In Europe and the U.S., many budget hotels have incorporated technological innovation facilities to attract young tourists. Victorino et al. (2005) also found that, during hotel selection, both business and leisure travelers serve an important role in evaluating innovation, but innovative service amenities have an even greater impact on hotel choices among leisure travelers. Technologically innovative attributes should be considered as important attributes for hotel customers when they are making a decision regarding booking.

Hotel attributes

Hotel attributes have become a long-term and persistent subject in hotel studies (Dolnicar, 2002). Wuest, Tas, and Emenheiser (1996) defined hotel attributes as important services and amenities that satisfy travelers' needs during their stay in a hotel. They exert positive effects on customers' choices and, in turn, develop into determinants for customers' hotel selection and affect their willingness to purchase. Hotel attributes are also considered to be major factors affecting travelers' evaluations of hotel quality. Bowen and Shoemaker (2003) adopted used attributes to determine how hotels should build customer loyalty. Dube and Renaghan (1999) pointed out that hotel attributes including brand name and reputation, employees, guest room design and atmosphere, standard of service quality, tangible assets, and customer marketing are influential to customers' perception of hotels. Chu and Choi (2000), Qu, Ryan, and Chu (2000), and Chu (2002) focused on investigating hotel attributes by grouping them into categories, including employee service quality, business facilities, value, guest rooms and front desk, food and entertainment, and safety. Choi and Chu (2001) studied travelers' perception of and satisfaction with the amenities and services provided by Hong Kong hotels to examine hotel attributes such as employees' service efficiency and multiple language skills, cleanliness and quietness of guest rooms, conference rooms, business facilities, guest rooms, dining services, value for money, and security. Wong and Lam (2002) and Dolnicar (2002) reported that the type of hotel, price of guest rooms, location, brand, and star rating are important hotel attributes. With the prevalence of computers and the Internet, Shanka and Taylor (2003) indicated that Internet connection is a major hotel attribute, and Yavas and Babakus (2005) stated that hotel attributes should include access to computers, modems, and other amenities related to computer networks. Vieregge, Phetkaew, Beldona, Lumsden, and DeMicco (2007) pointed out that the level of comfort and other service amenities – such as comfortable mattresses and pillows, cozy rooms, airport transfers, bellman services, free breakfast, discounts, medical facilities, service centers, and swimming pools – were less important to customers than a centralized room reservation system and a quick check-out service. Fawzy (2010) placed heavy emphasis on the quality of service staff, including empathy, handling of customer complaints, efficiency of check-in/check-out services, politeness, and provision of correct information. Back (2012) summarized 14 attributes into 4 factors to measure customers' evaluation of hotel attributes, consisting of food, atmosphere, service, and value. Tanforda, Raab, and Kim (2012) highlighted the implementation of environmentally friendly measures (e.g., waste recycling procedures, participation in green events, water conservation, use of solar energy as the main energy source, environmental certification, and towel reuse program), a hotel's brand (e.g., reward membership programs, consistency and the reputation of a hotel chain's international brand), and online information, including customer reviews, recommendations, and hotel star ratings, as important hotel attributes. Travelers often rely on online reviews to make purchase decisions; hence, Rhee and Yang (2014) and Lee et al. (2013) recommended that hoteliers gather information regarding customers' preferences based on online ratings and comments on platforms such as online travel agencies. Chen, Wang, Luoh, Shih, and You (2014) examined how hotel facilities geared to the elderly improved the satisfaction of senior customers, indicating that service amenities targeted toward specific customer groups have become important hotel attributes. This study summarizes a list of hotel attributes based on the above studies.

Kano model

Kano et al. (1984) proposed that fulfilling customers' basic requirements alone is inadequate for satisfying customers; rather, customers are satisfied when high expectations are met through services beyond the basics. The Kano model is also known as the two-dimensional quality model. Kano et al. (1984) posited that two aspects of any given attribute should be considered: an objective aspect involving the degree of fulfillment of the quality attribute and a subjective aspect involving the customers' perception of satisfaction. Kano and his colleagues divided service attributes into five categories:

- Attractive attributes: Customers will be satisfied if these attributes are present, but their absence does not cause customer dissatisfaction.
- One-dimensional attributes: Customer satisfaction is positively and linearly related to the performance of these attributes – that is, the greater the degree of fulfillment of these attributes, the greater the degree of customer satisfaction (and vice versa).
- Must-have attributes: The absence of these attributes will result in customer dissatisfaction, but their presence does not significantly contribute to customer satisfaction.
- Indifferent attributes: The presence or absence of these attributes does not cause any substantial satisfaction or dissatisfaction to customers.
- Reverse attributes: The presence of these attributes will cause customer dissatisfaction, and their absence will result in customer satisfaction.

According to the Kano model, must-have attributes are the basic requirements for a product. There is an upper limit for customer satisfaction regardless of how much the product quality improves. Indifferent attributes refer to customers' insensitivity to product quality and satisfaction; in other words, these quality attributes are not valued by customers. One-dimensional qualities are referred to as linear qualities because the higher the quality, the greater the customer satisfaction; conversely, poorer quality leads to customer dissatisfaction. Attractive qualities are quality requirements that possess attractive attributes; the absence of these qualities leads to customer indifference but an increase in these qualities improves customer satisfaction more significantly than an increase in a one-dimensional quality. Hence, attractive qualities are those that are "unexpected" by the customer and can lead to high levels of customer satisfaction. Therefore, the Kano model is an important theoretical model that endorses attractive quality creation.

Matzler and Hinterhuber (1998) and Tan and Pawitra (2001) suggested the Kano model has the following advantages: (1) It builds a better understanding of product requirements not only by improving the must-have attributes of existing products but also by altering their one-dimensional and attractive attributes. (2) It is of great value to product development as it can identify the major attributes affecting customer satisfaction and provide criteria for decision-making. (3) It differentiates between must-have, one-dimensional, and attractive attributes and can be used to identify different customer segments and customize strategies for those segments to fulfill customers' distinctive needs and to improve standards. (4) It can transform the differences among attributes into a strategy – for instance, the revelation of attractive attributes can intensify product differentiation. This study adopts the Kano model for analysis as it attempts to incorporate hotel technological innovation as a new attribute while re-classifying hotel attributes.

Research method

The subjects were travelers who have stayed at four and five-star hotels in Taiwan. A survey was performed to collect data. Four and five-star hotels were selected because these hotels lead the way in technological innovation in the industry. The questionnaire items were reviewed and summarized from the literature on hotel attributes (Choi & Chu, 2001; Chu, 2002; Chu & Choi, 2000; Dolnicar, 2002; Dube & Renaghan, 1999; Fawzy, 2010; Qu et al., 2000; Shanka & Taylor, 2003; Vieregge et al., 2007; Wong & Lam, 2002; Yavas &

Babakus, 2005). The items regarding hotel technological innovation attributes were adopted based on a study from Law and Jogaratnam (2005) and Lema (2009) and were expert-reviewed by hotel managers, OTA operators and professors in the hospitality and tourism academy. After reviewing and removing repeated or semantically similar items, there were 51 items in total, and questionnaire items were translated into Chinese using the back-translation method. A pilot questionnaire was sent out in December 2017, and 44 usable surveys were returned. The questionnaire was revised by correcting and confirming the reliability of the pilot test results, and the survey instrument was finalized.

Respondents were asked about their evaluation of hotel attributes when making hotel reservations. The Kano two-dimensional quality model was then used to measure the attributes, which uses a two-way method with positive and negative statements to inquire about respondents' perceptions in the presence and absence of hotel attributes. The scoring system was based on five options – "I like it that way," "It must be that way," "I am indifferent to it," "I can live with it," and "I dislike it that way." The items were measured using a five-point Likert scale (1 = strongly disagree to 5 = strongly disagree). Convenience sampling was adopted, and researchers distributed the survey in several business districts in Taipei. Gift rewards were also provided to encourage survey participation. After collecting the questionnaires, the authors performed descriptive analysis and exploratory factor analysis using SPSS 21.0. The Kano model was used to assess how guests perceive hotel attributes answering research question 1, and factor analysis categorized hotel attributes and Kano model categories were used to research question 2.

Results and discussion

Demographic background

The survey data were collected from January 2 2018, to January 23 2018, and the participants were customers that had stayed at a four- to five-star hotel in a year. A total of 500 questionnaires were distributed and 454 returned, of which 4 were found to be invalid and were removed. A total of 450 valid completed questionnaires were retained, which resulted in an effective response rate of 90.0%. An analysis of the respondents' demographic background (Table 1) showed the following: 263 (58.4%) of the respondents were female, one-third were between 31 and 40 years old (34.2%), followed by those between 41 and 50 years old (22.4%). Most of the respondents were

Table 1. Respondents' demographic background.

Variable	Sample (N = 450)	Percentage (%)	Variables	Sample (N = 450)	Percentage (%)
1.Gender			**6.Monthly Income**		
Male	187	41.6	(U.S. dollars per month)		
Female	263	58.4	Under $666	62	13.8
			$667 ~ 1,333	141	31.3
2.Age			$1,334 ~ 2,000	137	30.4
20 and below	6	1.3	$2,001 ~ 2,667	49	10.9
21 ~ 30	94	20.9	$2,668 ~ 3,333	32	7.1
31 ~ 40	154	34.2	$3,334 and above	29	6.4
41 ~ 50	101	22.4			
51 ~ 60	59	13.1	**7.Number of staying at a hotel per year**		
61 and above	36	8.0	1–3	239	53.1
3.Education			4 ~ 6	138	30.7
			7 ~ 9	39	8.7
Secondary	10	2.2	10 and above	34	7.6
High school degree	60	13.3			
College or university	274	60.9	**8. Average night per stay**		
Graduate degree	106	23.6	1 night	134	29.8
			2 ~ 3 nights	229	50.9
4.Marriage			4 ~ 6 nights	74	16.4
Single	190	42.2	7 ~ 9 nights	5	1.1
Married	247	54.9	10 and above	8	1.8
Others	13	2.9			
			9.Purpose of trips		
5.Occupation			Business	15	3.3
Student	37	8.2	Leisure	304	67.6
Service industry	128	28.4	Business & Leisure	111	24.7
Financial industry	83	18.4	Visiting relatives & friends	19	4.2
Technology industry	37	8.2	Others	1	0.2
Manufacturing industry	26	5.8			
Public official	39	8.7			
Free Lance	24	5.3			
Housewife	22	4.9			
Unemployed	3	0.7			
Retired	27	6.0			
Others	24	5.3			

university graduates (60.9%). More than half were married (54.9%). In terms of occupation, most were in the service industry (28.4%), followed by the finance industry (18.4%). The average monthly income was approximately US$667 to US$2,000 (61.4%). Slightly more than half of the respondents stayed at a hotel one to three times a year (53.1%), and about half of the respondents stayed two to three nights per stay (50.9%). Two-thirds of the respondents had stayed in hotels for leisure purposes (67.6%).

Kano analysis

According to the classification criteria proposed by Matzler and Hinterhuber (1998) (Table 2), the results of hotel attribute analysis using the Kano model are shown in Table 3. The analysis revealed 1 must-have attribute, 3 attractive attributes, 16 one-dimensional attributes, 31 indifferent attributes, and zero reverse or invalid attributes.

- The must-have attribute was access to Internet and Wi-Fi services, a hotel necessity that does not contribute to customer satisfaction; however, as hotel guests will be discontented with a lack of Internet access, a Wi-Fi connection has become a necessary condition for hotel selection.

- The three attractive attributes were control of lighting, temperature, curtains, television, and other amenities with a smartphone or an iPad in the hotel room; shuttle services to/from the airport or stations; and a wide variety of discount offers. The availability of these three attributes led to customer satisfaction, but their absence did not lead to dissatisfaction. As these attractive attributes can elevate customer satisfaction, hoteliers may want to refer to these qualities and consider introducing the corresponding services.

- The 16 one-dimensional attributes led to customer satisfaction when they were performed well but led to dissatisfaction when they were poorly executed. These attributes were front desk services; luggage services; supply of breakfast; cleanliness and size of guest rooms; comfortable beds/pillows; an option for (non-)smoking rooms; convenience of hotel location and transportation; overall service quality; service employees' enthusiasm, friendliness, and

Table 2. Kano two-dimensions attributes category.

Hotel Attribute		Does not have Attribute				
		I like it that way	It must be that way	It is indifferent	I can live with it	I dislike it that way
Does have Attribute	I like it that way	Q	A	A	A	O
	It must be that way	R	I	I	I	M
	It is indifferent	R	I	I	I	M
	I can live with it	R	I	I	I	M
	I dislike it that way	Q	R	R	R	Q

A: Attractive Quality; O: One-Dimensional Quality; M: Must-be Quality
I: Indifferent Quality; R: Reverse Quality; Q: Questionable

Table 3. Evaluation of KANO category for hotel attribute.

Item	Hotel Attribute	M	O	A	I	R	Q	Main Category	Second Category
1	Internet (Wi-Fi) connection	138	129	81	93	3	6	M	O
2	Hotel official website online reservation	97	79	89	175	5	5	I	
3	Third-party (OTA) website online reservation	28	54	104	247	12	5	I	A
4	Hotel APP (reservation, guiding, searching, etc.)	21	52	144	226	4	3	I	A
5	Robot service (Luggage delivery, etc.)	8	22	141	260	15	4	I	A
6	Self check-in & out	20	31	152	221	22	4	I	A
7	VR video room type choosing	11	36	180	207	13	3	I	A
8	Mobile APP check-in & out	9	27	168	215	26	5	I	A
9	Mobile APP instead of room card (key)	7	29	169	189	50	6	I	A
10	All room amenities (lights, temperature, curtain, TV, etc.) controlled by smart phone or iPad	11	38	192	183	23	3	A	I
11	VR and E-Entertainment	5	26	173	231	12	2	I	A
12	E-housekeeping service (E-system contact personal service)	7	24	148	256	13	2	I	A
13	Mobile APP/third-party payment system	9	36	149	234	19	3	I	A
14	Front Office service (Staff service personally)	97	152	94	103	3	1	O	I
15	Luggage service (Personally delivery & luggage for guests)	104	157	84	97	6	2	O	M
16	Provision of Food & Beverage	92	124	100	129	4	1	I	O
17	Free Breakfast	94	128	104	117	3	4	O	I
18	Cleanliness of room	159	230	23	30	5	3	O	M
19	Size of the room	89	136	87	131	2	5	O	I
20	Comfortable bedding	116	211	68	49	3	3	O	M
21	(Non) smoking room choice	120	186	62	72	6	4	O	M
22	Free toothbrush and toothpaste	94	96	56	194	6	4	I	
23	Free daily bottled water	102	129	82	130	2	5	I	O
24	Mini-bar	32	57	89	262	8	2	I	
25	Safety deposit boxes	55	58	58	274	4	1	I	
26	Location	56	164	139	81	5	5	O	A
27	Shuttle services	43	137	162	103	3	2	A	O
28	On-site Parking/ valet parking	76	106	78	182	2	6	I	O
29	Laundry service	23	39	74	309	3	2	I	I
30	Swimming pool	15	42	131	259	2	1	I	A
31	Exercise facilities/fitness center	15	48	128	255	1	3	I	A
32	Recreational facilities	28	55	130	232	2	3	I	A
33	Business meeting facilities	27	38	87	297	0	1	I	
34	Infant-related facilities and services	37	51	79	282	0	1	I	
35	Elderly or disability related facilities and services	45	55	92	254	1	3	I	
36	Friendly pet services	20	52	89	274	15	0	I	
37	Overall service quality	89	236	60	56	2	7	O	
38	High quality staff	91	238	67	45	2	7	O	
39	Respectful and friendly staff	104	249	50	38	1	8	O	M
40	Staff with foreign language skills	72	141	95	135	0	7	O	I
41	Hotel atmosphere is pleasant	89	223	75	55	1	7	O	
42	The ambience of the hotel is relaxing	92	239	60	48	2	9	O	
43	Hotel is themed	17	50	130	247	2	4	I	A
44	Hotel is well-known brand	24	30	121	270	2	3	I	A
45	Chain hotel	24	26	101	294	1	4	I	A
46	Star-rating hotel	31	45	145	225	1	3	I	A
47	Hotel adopt green/environmental activities	20	63	139	219	7	2	I A	A
48	Member reward program	20	56	122	242	7	3	I A	A
49	Reasonable hotel rates	80	228	81	49	4	8	O	
50	Value for money	45	185	148	60	2	10	O A	A
51	Offers a variety of discounts	38	133	173	95	1	10	A O	O

foreign language skills; creation of a pleasant mood and cozy atmosphere for guests; reasonable room prices; and great value for money. Most of these are general attributes considered by customers during hotel selection and are quality requirements that hotel managers should endeavor to fulfill.

Table 4. Factor analysis of hotel attributes.

Items	Factor Loading	Eigen value	% of Variance
Factor 1: Intangible service and ambience		4.320	18.512
37	Overall service quality	0.690	
38	High quality staff	0.825	
39	Respectful and friendly staff	0.851	
40	Staff with foreign language skills	0.583	
41	Hotel atmosphere is pleasant	0.758	
42	The ambience of the hotel is relaxing	0.760	
Factor 2: Hotel brand and chain star hotel		2.903	9.292
43	Hotel is themed	0.588	
44	Hotel is well-known brand	0.849	
45	Chain hotel	0.847	
46	Star-rating hotel	0.795	
Factor 3: Leisure facilities		2.805	5.837
30	Swimming pool	0.813	
31	Exercise facilities/fitness center	0.857	
32	Recreational facilities	0.773	
Factor 4: Room quality		2.603	4.229
18	Cleanliness of room	0.640	
19	Size of the room	0.726	
20	Comfortable bedding	0.743	
21	(Non) smoking room choice	0.484	
17	Free Breakfast	0.454	
16	Provision of Food & Beverage	0.461	
Factor 5: Extra specific facilities		2.484	3.736
33	Business meeting facilities	0.512	
34	Infant-related facilities and services	0.779	
35	Elderly or disability related facilities and services	0.725	
36	Friendly pet services	0.552	
Factor 6: E-housekeeping		2.381	3.233
10	All room amenities (lights, temperature, curtain, TV, etc.) controlled by smart phone or iPad	0.623	
11	VR and E-Entertainment	0.770	
12	E-housekeeping service (E-system contact personal service)	0.696	
Factor 7: Smart phone as room key and payment		2.200	2.892
8	Mobile APP check-in & out	0.723	
9	Mobile APP instead of room card (key)	0.803	
13	Mobile APP/third-party payment system	0.518	
Factor 8: Price and value		2.160	2.755
49	Reasonable hotel rates	0.734	
50	Value for money	0.789	
51	Offers a variety of discounts	0.757	
48	Member reward program	0.323	
Factor 9: Room spare parts		2.136	2.488
22	Free toothbrush and toothpaste	0.696	
23	Free daily bottled water	0.667	
24	Mini-bar	0.435	
25	Safety deposit boxes	0.560	
Factor 10: Online and APP usage		1.966	2.418
1	Internet (Wi-Fi) connection	0.738	
2	Hotel official website online reservation	0.718	
3	Third-party (OTA) website online reservation	0.658	
4	Hotel APP (reservation, guiding, searching, etc.)	0.667	
7	VR video room type choosing	0.483	
Factor 11: Location		1.865	2.326
26	Location	0.551	
27	Shuttle services	0.601	
28	On-site Parking/ valet parking	0.378	
Factor 12: Green hotel		1.725	2.171
47	Hotel adopt green/environmental activities	0.519	
Factor 13: Front office and luggage service		1.624	2.055
14	Front Office service (Staff service)	0.720	
15	Luggage service (Personally delivery & luggage for guests)	0.720	
Factor 14: Electronic Self-service		1.423	1.969
6	Robot service (Luggage delivery, etc.)	0.493	
7	Self check-in & out	0.686	

- The 31 indifferent attributes made no difference to guests' evaluation of the hotel whether they were present or not. These attributes included 11 services provided using innovative hotel technologies: the availability of restaurants; room supplies; leisure and entertainment; elderly, baby-, and pet-friendly amenities; the star ratings of chain hotels; eco-friendliness of the hotel; and membership reward programs. Most of the indifferent attributes above were deemed to be nonessential by general customers and were excluded from the basic factors for consideration during hotel selection. Despite being insignificant to most travelers, these attributes are appealing and important to specific groups. Hence, depending on the positioning and main target groups of the hotel, hoteliers may still want to allocate service items to this category.

Of the 13 items relating to hotel technological innovation, Internet service was considered a must-have attribute, whereas controlling the lighting, temperature, curtains, and television with a smartphone or an iPad was regarded as an attractive attribute. The remaining 11 items were indifferent attributes. However, after indifferent, the most frequently chosen category for these items was attractive attributes, implying that although most travelers are currently indifferent to hotel attributes pertaining to technological innovation, there are still a great deal of people who consider these attributes attractive. With the growing acceptance of and reliance on new technologies, these attributes are expected to become attractive qualities in the near future. Hence, hotels should consider gradually introducing technological services to attract more customers.

Factor analysis

A factor analysis was performed on 51 hotel attributes (Table 4). The KMO (Kaiser–Mayer–Olkin) value was 0.850, demonstrating that the distribution of values in the initial measurement of hotel attributes was adequate for factor analysis. The factor loadings of all relevant items in the rotated factor matrix were clearly related to only one factor each. Most of the factor loadings were greater than 0.5. "Laundry services" was removed because it carried a factor loading below 0.4 and could not be attributed to any factor. The other two factor loadings that were less than 0.4 (member reward program and on-site parking/valet parking) were not removed because the experts consulted for this study insisted they are important attributes for hotel selection. This produced a 14-factor solution with eigenvalues greater than one, accounting for 63.912% of the total variance.

(1) Overall service quality: service employees' enthusiasm, friendliness, and foreign language skills as well as the creation of a pleasant mood and cozy atmosphere for the guests of hotels. As this factor was mainly concerned with service quality and atmosphere, it was named "intangible service and ambience," which accounted for 18.512% of the total variance.

(2) Preferences for thematic hotels, well-known hotel brands, chain-brand hotels, and hotels with star ratings. As this factor mainly involved hotel brands and themes, it was named "hotel brand and chain star hotel," which accounted for 9.292% of the total variance.

(3) General leisure and entertainment amenities such as swimming pools, gyms, and other facilities. The factor was named "leisure facilities," which constituted 5.837% of the total variance.

(4) Quality of guest rooms and catering services, including the cleanliness and size of guest rooms, the option of a (non-)smoking room, the supply of breakfast, and the availability of restaurants. This factor was therefore called "room quality," which accounted for 4.229% of the total variance.

(5) "Extra specific facilities," which constituted 3.736% of the total variance and mainly involved hotel services and amenities targeted towards specific groups, such as those for business purposes; those related to infants, young children, and elderly people; and pet-friendly services.

(6) "E-housekeeping," which constituted 3.233% of the total variance and mainly involved the E-system services in guest rooms, including smartphone- or iPad-regulated lighting, temperature, curtains, television, and other amenities; VR and electronic audio-visual entertainment; and electronic housekeeping (E-system personal services).

(7) The "use of a smartphone as room key and for payment," which was responsible for 2.892% of the total variance. This was largely about mobile applications services, including using them to perform check in and check out, substitute room cards, as well as making payments via applications or third-party systems.

(8) "Price and value," which accounted for 2.755% of the total variance and mainly concerned the price and value of hotel services, such as reasonable room price, high value-for-money hotel experiences, a wide variety of discounts, and membership reward programs.

(9) "Room spare parts," which constituted 2.488% of the total variance and mainly concerned room supplies, including free toothbrushes and toothpaste, daily free bottled water, mini-bar, and safes.

(10) "Online and app usage," which constituted 2.418% of the total variance and was largely related to Internet services and online reservations, including access to the Internet/Wi-Fi, online reservation services on the official website, room booking services on third-party reservation websites, hotels' cellphone applications, and room selection through VR videos.

(11) "Location," which accounted for 2.326% of the total variance and mainly concerned hotel transportation, including convenience of hotel location and transportation, shuttle services to/from the airport or stations, and availability of car parks.

(12) "Green hotel," which accounted for 2.171% of the total variance and mainly concerned the implementation of eco-friendly measures and eco-friendly activities.

(13) "Front office and luggage service," which constituted 2.055% of the total variance and mainly pertained to the service quality at the front desk.

(14) "Electronic self-service," which accounted for 1.969% of the total variance and mainly concerned electronic self-services such as robot services and self-check in and check out.

The Kano analysis of hotel attributes and their corresponding factor analysis are illustrated in Table 5.

• Attractive attributes included items such as an electronic housekeeper, location, and price and value. As attractive attributes can be beyond customers' expectations, providing these three types of attributes can enhance customer satisfaction.

• Must-have attributes included online accessibility and app usage. Access to the Internet has become an essential service requirement that hotels must satisfy.

• One-dimensional attributes included front office and luggage service, room quality, location, intangible services and ambience, and price and value. Hoteliers must endeavor to improve attractive attributes such as front desk services, room qual-

Table 5. Evaluation of Hotel Attribute categorized to KANO model and factor analysis.

Kano Category	Number	Item	Factor
Attractive Quality	10	All room amenities (lights, temperature, curtain, TV, etc.) controlled by smart phone or iPad	Electronic Housekeeping
	27	Shuttle services	Location
	51	Offers a variety of discounts	Price and value
Must-be Quality	1	Internet (Wi-Fi) connection	Online and APP usage
One-dimensional Quality	14	Front Office service (Staff service personally)	Front office and luggage service
	15	Luggage service (Personally delivery & luggage for guests)	
	17	Free Breakfast	Room quality
	18	Cleanliness of room	
	19	Size of the room	
	20	Comfortable bedding	
	21	(Non) smoking room choice	
	26	Location	Location
	37	Overall service quality	Intangible service and ambience
	38	High quality staff	
	39	Respectful and friendly staff	
	40	Staff with foreign language skills	
	41	Hotel atmosphere is pleasant	
	42	The ambience of the hotel is relaxing	
	49	Reasonable hotel rates	Price and value
	50	Value for money	
Indifferent quality	2	Hotel official website online reservation	Online and APP usage
	3	Third-party (OTA) website online reservation	
	4	Hotel APP (reservation, guiding, searching, etc.)	
	7	VR video room type choosing	
	5	Robot service (Luggage delivery, etc.)	Electronic Self-service
	6	Self check-in & out	
	8	Mobile APP check-in & out	Smart phone as room key and payment
	9	Mobile APP instead of room card (key)	
	13	Mobile APP/third-party payment system	
	11	VR and E-Entertainment	E-housekeeping
	12	E-housekeeping service (E-system contact personal service)	
	16	Provision of Food & Beverage	Room quality
	22	Free toothbrush and toothpaste	Room spare parts
	23	Free daily bottled water	
	24	Mini-bar	
	25	Safety deposit boxes	
	28	On-site Parking/ valet parking	Location
	30	Swimming pool	Leisure facilities
	31	Exercise facilities/fitness center	
	32	Recreational facilities	
Indifferent quality	33	Business meeting facilities	Extra specific facilities
	34	Infant-related facilities and services	
	35	Elderly or disability related facilities and services	
	36	Friendly pet services	
	43	Hotel is themed	Hotel brand and chain star hotel
	44	Hotel is well-known brand	
	45	Chain hotel	
	46	Star-rating hotel	
	47	Hotel adopt green/environmental activities	Green hotel
	48	Member reward program	Price and value

ity, location, overall service quality and ambience, room price, and accommodation value because poor performance in these factors will trigger customer dissatisfaction.

- Indifferent attributes included online and app usage, electronic self-service, using a smartphone as room key and for payment, electronic housekeeper, room quality, room spare parts, location, leisure facilities, extra specific facilities, hotel brand and chain star hotel, green hotel, and price and value. At present, the first four factors have yet to exert any effects on customers' choice of hotel, whereas customer satisfaction is influenced by factors such as room

supplies, leisure and entertainment, services and amenities for specific groups, star ratings of hotel brands, and the implementation of eco-friendly measures. However, hoteliers should think about how they may convert these indifferent attributes into attractive ones.

Discussion

The Kano analysis indicated that access to the Internet and Wi-Fi was a must-have attribute; in other words, having Internet access is taken for granted by customers, who may be dissatisfied if they cannot gain access to the Internet. This finding was consistent with that of Shanka and Taylor (2003), who pointed out that Internet connection was an important hotel attribute. It is a must for hotels to set up an Internet or Wi-Fi connection and ensure that Internet services are available in every guest room, rather than just the hotel lobby.

One-dimensional attributes included front desk services, luggage services, supply of breakfast, cleanliness and comfort of guest rooms, overall service quality, staff's service, a cozy and pleasant atmosphere, reasonable room prices, and a great value-for-money hotel experience. Hotel operators should strive to improve these attributes continuously because they are required by customers.

Hotel technological innovation attributes were originally expected to be categorized as attractive attributes. However, the results showed that only the control of lighting, temperature, curtains, and television using by a smartphone or iPad in the hotel room was an attractive attribute (the remaining attributes were indifferent attributes). Further analysis revealed that the most chosen category after indifferent for these attributes was attractive. In other words, although most customers are indifferent to these technological attributes at present, a number of people still consider them attractive. The attributes of innovative technologies are very likely to become important requirements in the future.

Among the indifferent attributes were the availability of restaurants; room supplies; leisure and entertainment; elderly-, baby-, and pet-friendly amenities; star ratings and chain-brand hotels; eco-friendly hotels; and membership reward programs. However, these attributes could still be differentiating factors among hotels. In addition, age was shown to be a significant variable in respondents' demographic background. With low birth rates and changes in demographic composition in the future, senior travelers will become the main target group, which makes the provision of elderly- and baby-friendly amenities and services a potential marketing strategy for hotels, and this finding is consistent with that of the study of Chen et al. (2014).

Attractive attributes also included shuttle services to/from the airport and stations, as well as a wide variety of discounts. Despite convenience of transportation being a one-dimensional attribute, it can be transformed into an attractive attribute as long as hotels can provide shuttle services. Room price was yet another one-dimensional attribute in this study, but it can also be an attractive attribute with the help of marketing strategies and sales promotions, as well as a wide variety of discounts. With clear positioning and

strategies, both one-dimensional and indifferent attributes can turn into attractive attributes.

Factor analysis yielded 14 factors, with non-technological innovation attributes showing the similar results with those in previous studies on hotel attributes. The biggest contribution of this study was categorizing 13 attributes of innovative technologies into 4 factors – E-housekeeping, using a smartphone as a room key and for payment, online and app usage, and electronic self-service. This study found that the travelers identify innovative technologies that they might need during their hotel stays. Before check-in, travelers widely use the official OTA and hotel websites or cellphone applications of hotels for making room reservations. These findings also supported the studies of Rhee and Yang (2014) and Lee et al. (2013) that pointed out that customers' search information depends on online ratings and comments on online travel agency platforms. Upon arrival at the hotel, self-check-in is done using the cellphone application or at the hotel, and luggage is carried by automated robots. When customers arrive at the guest room, the guest room door is directly opened via the cellphone application. Inside the guest room, a smartphone or an iPad can be used to control and adjust lighting, temperature, curtains, and television, and e-housekeeper services are accessible in case room services are needed. VR or electronic audio-visual entertainment is also available in the guest room or in the leisure and entertainment area. When leaving the hotel, self-check-out is done via the mobile application or at the hotel, while bills are also paid on the mobile application. Yavas and Babakus (2005) suggested that hotel attributes should include the use of amenities related to computer networks. This study proved that future analysis of hotel attributes should definitely involve hotel attributes about technological innovation.

This study adopted the Kano model incorporating hotel technological innovation as new attributes and re-classifying hotel attributes. This study brings a better understanding of hotel attributes, categorizing them into attractive, one-dimensional, must-have and indifferent attributes perceived by guests, and it recommends hotel managers should not only improve the must-have attributes but also alter their one-dimensional and attractive attributes. The findings only partially supported some technological innovation attributes as attractive attributes and helps analyze the relative importance of hotel attributes in customers' current perceptions and better understand customers' needs in the future. Research findings supported the Kano model identifying the key attributes of customer value and providing criteria for decision-making. Therefore, the Kano model is a theoretical and empirical model that endorses classifying technological innovation attributes and hotel attributes.

Conclusion

Hotel attributes are important as customers give them consideration when choosing hotels. With consumers' growing reliance on the Internet and smartphones, hotel services should incorporate technological innovation continuously. Since past studies on hotel attributes pointed out only a few technological attributes (Lee et al., 2013; Rhee & Yang, 2014; Shanka & Taylor, 2003), this study filled the research gap by categorizing 13 attributes of innovative technologies into 4 factors to investigate travelers' perception of new technological innovation attributes and previous hotel attributes. This study adopted the Kano model as its theoretical basis and empirically showed that this model is especially advantageous for analysis and prioritization during product development. According to the results of this study, only the control of lighting, temperature, curtains, and television using a smartphone or iPad in the hotel room was an attractive attribute, and access to the Internet and Wi-Fi was categorized as a must-have attribute. All other technological attributes were indifferent attributes. Despite this finding, analysis of the second-most frequently selected categories implied that most innovative technologies considered were attractive attributes. In other words, although most customers are indifferent to them at present, with customers' increasing technological dependence, hotels should gradually introduce these innovative technologies because they are very likely to develop into attractive attributes. Hotel attributes in this study consisted of 50 items and 14 factors, where four factors were related to innovative technologies – E-housekeeping, use of a smartphone as room key and for payment, online and app usage, and electronic self-service. E-housekeeping was considered an attractive attribute. Both use of a smartphone as room key and for payment and electronic self-service were indifferent attributes, whereas online and app usage was a must-have attribute. This result implied that although hotels must provide access to the Internet and Wi-Fi, online room reservations via the official website, OTA, or cellphone applications are also a necessary conditions. Hotels may also consider adopting E-housekeeping to surprise hotel guests. Meanwhile, use of a smartphone as a room key and for payment and electronic self-service can serve as hotels' future directions for introducing technological innovation. Research findings can serve as references for hotel operators planning to introduce innovative technologies into their businesses, help hotel managers allocate their limited resources effectively, and provide a reference for hotel development strategies.

Future studies to focus on hotel technologies and investigate customers' perceptions and expectations in greater depth are suggested. More hotel technological innovation can provide more services, including using an iPad to order food in hotel restaurants and using cellphone applications to control the guest room air-conditioning remotely. Research on customer satisfaction or attitudes toward technological innovation attributes will also be feasible in the future when such technologies are employed by more hotels and experienced by more customers. Additional variables regarding the socioeconomic status or preferences of customers are required for future analysis. However, as the scope of this study was limited to guests' perception of innovative technologies implemented by four- or five-star hotels in Taipei, the results of this study cannot be generalized to the whole hotel industry. As this was a cross-sectional study, attractive attributes may turn into one-dimensional ones or must-have attributes with time. Therefore, hotel operators are advised to gather and introduce innovative technologies progressively based on longitudinal data, which can offer enhanced technological and marketing strategies.

Disclosure statement

No potential conflict of interest was reported by the authors.

ORCID

Chun-Fang Chiang http://orcid.org/0000-0003-1257-3191

References

Back, K.-J. (2012). Impact-range performance analysis and asymmetry analysis for improving quality of Korean food attributes. *International Journal of Hospitality Management*, *31*(2), 535–543.

Bitner, M. J., Ostrom, A. L., & Meuter, M. L. (2002). Implementing successful self-service technologies. *The Academy of Management Executive*, *16*(4), 96–108.

Bowen, J. T., & Shoemaker, S. (2003). Loyalty: A strategic commitment. *Cornell Hotel and Restaurant Administration Quarterly*, *44*(5), 31–46.

Chang, K. C., & Chen, M. C. (2011). Applying the Kano model and QFD to explore customers' brand contacts in the hotel business: A study of a hot spring hotel. *Total Quality Management*, *22*(1), 1–27.

Chen, H. T., & Chen, B. T. (2015). Integrating Kano model and SIPA grid to identify key service attributes of fast food restaurants. *Journal of Quality Assurance in Hospitality & Tourism*, *16*(2), 141–163.

Chen, L. F. (2012). A novel approach to regression analysis for the classification of quality attributes in the Kano model: An empirical test in the food and beverage industry. *Omega*, *40*(5), 651–659.

Chen, W. Y., Wang, K. C., Luoh, H. F., Shih, J. F., & You, Y. S. (2014). Does a friendly hotel room increase senior group package tourists' satisfaction? A field experiment. *Asia Pacific Journal of Tourism Research*, *19*(8), 950–970.

Choi, T. Y., & Chu, R. (2001). Determinants of hotel guests' satisfaction and repeat patronage in the Hong Kong hotel industry. *Hospitality Management*, *20*(3), 277–297.

Chu, R. (2002). Stated-importance versus derived-importance customer satisfaction measurement. *Journal of Services Marketing*, *16*(4), 285–301.

Chu, R. K. S., & Choi, T. (2000). An importance-performance analysis of hotel selection factors in the Hong Kong hotel industry: A comparison of business and leisure travelers. *Tourism Management*, *21*(4), 363–377.

Dolnicar, S. (2002). Business travellers' hotel expectations and disappointments: A different perspective to hotel attribute importance investigation. *Journal of Tourism Research*, *7*(1), 29–35.

Dominici, G., & Palumbo, F. (2013). The drivers of customer satisfaction in the hospitality industry: Applying the Kano model to Sicilian hotels. *International Journal of Leisure and Tourism Marketing*, *3*(3), 215–236.

Dube, L., & Renaghan, L. M. (1999). How hotel attributes deliver the promised benefits. *The Cornell Hotel and Restaurant Administration Quarterly*, *41*(5), 89–95.

Fawzy, A. (2010). Business travelers' accommodation selection: A comparative study of two international hotels in Cairo. *International Journal of Hospitality & Tourism Administration*, *11*(2), 138–156.

Gregory, A. M., & Parsa, H. G. (2013). Kano's model: An integrative review of theory and applications to the field of hospitality and tourism. *Journal of Hospitality Marketing & Management*, *22*(1), 25–46.

Kano, N., Seraku, N., Takahashi, F., & Tsuji, S. (1984). Attractive quality and must-be quality. *Journal of Japanese Society for Quality Control*, *14*(2), 39–48. in Japanese.

Kokkinou, A., & Cranage, D. A. (2013). Using self-service technology to reduce customer waiting times. *International Journal of Hospitality Management*, *33*, 435–445.

Kucukusta, D., Heung, V. C., & Hui, S. (2014). Deploying self-service technology in luxury hotel brands: Perceptions of business travelers. *Journal of Travel & Tourism Marketing*, *31*(1), 55–70.

Kuo, C. M., Chen, H. T., & Boger, E. (2016). Implementing city hotel service quality enhancements: Integration of Kano and QFD analytical models. *Journal of Hospitality Marketing & Management*, *25*(6), 748–770.

Kuo, C. M., Chen, L. C., & Tseng, C. Y. (2017). Investigating an innovative service with hospitality robots. *International Journal of Contemporary Hospitality Management*, *29*(5), 1305–1321.

Law, R., & Jogaratnam, G. (2005). A study of hotel information technology applications. *International Journal of Contemporary Hospitality Management*, *17*(2), 170–180.

Law, R., Leung, R., & Buhalis, D. (2009). Information technology applications in hospitality and tourism: A review of publications from 2005 to 2007. *Journal of Travel & Tourism Marketing*, *26*(5–6), 599–623.

Lee, J., Lee, J.-N., & Tan, B. C. Y. (2013). The contrasting attitudes of reviewer and seller in electronic word-of-mouth: A communicative action theory perspective. *Asia Pacific Journal of Information Systems*, *23*(3), 105–129.

Lema, J. D. (2009). Preparing hospitality organizations for self-service technology. *Journal of Human Resources in Hospitality & Tourism*, *8*(2), 153–169.

Lin, L. Z., Yeh, H. R., & Wang, M. C. (2015). Integration of Kano's model into FQFD for Taiwanese Ban-Doh banquet culture. *Tourism Management*, *46*, 245–262.

Matzler, K., & Hinterhuber, H. H. (1998). How to make product development projects more successful by integrating Kano's model of customer satisfaction into quality function deployment. *Technovation*, *18*(1), 25–38.

Orfila-Sintes, F., Crespí-Cladera, R., & Martínez-Ros, E. (2005). Innovation activity in the hotel industry: Evidence from Balearic Islands. *Tourism Management*, *26*(6), 851–865.

Qu, H., Ryan, B., & Chu, R. (2000). The importance of hotel attributes in contributing to travelers' satisfaction in the Hong Kong hotel industry. *Journal of Quality Assurance in Hospitality and Tourism*, *1*(3), 65–83.

Rhee, H. T., & Yang, S.-B. (2014). How does hotel attribute importance vary among different travelers? An exploratory case study based on a conjoint analysis. *Electronic Markets*, *25*(3), 211–226.

Shanka, T., & Taylor, R. (2003). An investigation into the perceived importance of service and facility attributes to hotel satisfaction. *Journal of Quality Assurance in Hospitality and Tourism*, *4*(3/4), 119–134.

Shen, X. X., Tan, K. C., & Xie, M. (2000). An integrated approach to innovative product development using Kano's model and QFD. *European Journal of Innovation Management*, *3*(2), 91–99.

Tan, K. C., & Pawitra, T. A. (2001). Integrating SERVQUAL and Kano's model into QFD for service excellence development. *Managing Service Quality*, *11*(6), 418–430.

Tanford, S., Raab, C., & Kim, Y.-S. (2012). Determinants of customer loyalty and purchasing behavior for full-service and limited-service hotels. *International Journal of Hospitality Management*, *31*(2), 319–328.

Victorino, L., Verma, R., Plaschka, G., & Dev, C. (2005). Service innovation and customer choices in the hospitality industry. *Managing Service Quality: An International Journal*, *15*(6), 555–576.

Vieregge, M., Phetkaew, P., Beldona, S., Lumsden, S. A., & DeMicco, F. J. (2007). Mature travelers to Thailand: A study of preferences and attributes. *Journal of Vacation Marketing*, *13*(2), 165–179.

Wei, W., Torres, E., & Hua, N. (2016). Improving consumer commitment through the integration of self-service technologies: A transcendent consumer experience perspective. *International Journal of Hospitality Management*, *59*, 105–115.

Wong, K. F., & Lam, C. Y. (2002). Predicting hotel choice decisions and segmenting hotel consumers: A comparative assessment of a recent consumer based approach. *Journal of Travel & Tourism Marketing*, *11*(1), 17–33.

Wuest, B. E. S., Tas, R. F., & Emenheiser, D. A. (1996). What do mature travelers perceive as important hotel/motel customer service?. *Hospitality Research Journal*, *20*(2), 77–93.

Yavas, U., & Babakus, E. (2005). Dimensions of hotel choice criteria: Congruence between business and leisure travelers. *International Journal of Hospitality Management*, *24*(3), 359–367.

The view from above: the relevance of shared aerial drone videos for destination marketing

Uglješa Stankov, James Kennell, Alastair M. Morrison and Miroslav D. Vujičić

ABSTRACT

The use of drones to produce videos has generated a large amount of visually appealing footage of various destinations. They attract much attention, but there are issues that affect their production, and their relevance to destination marketing. This research examines YouTube meta-data and spatial overlay analysis of shared aerial drone videos from the United Kingdom (UK). The results suggest that shared aerial drone videos have some unique user-generated content (UGC) characteristics and their spatial distribution tends to favor more populated areas. Theoretical and practical implications for destination marketing are further discussed.

Introduction

Despite the recent boom in the availability and use of drones (Goldman Sachs, 2016; Luppicini & So, 2016), and recent research into their application in other sectors (Almeida et al., 2017; Beadel et al., 2018; Braitenberg et al., 2016; Stark, Vaughan, Evans, Kler, & Goossens, 2018), their role in the tourism industry has received very little attention in the research literature (Hay, 2016; King, 2014; Mirk & Hlavacs, 2014, 2015). This research is the first to analyze shared aerial drone videos from the perspective of tourism destination marketing.

Drone is a broad term used to describe any kind of unmanned aerial vehicle (UAV) that is remotely controlled or pre-programmed to fly autonomously, which can look like either a small airplane with fixed-wings or a small helicopter with multirotor systems (Vergouw, Nagel, Bondt, & Custers, 2016). They can be controlled by mobile apps installed on smartphones or tablets, by wrist-worn devices, or by consoles as ground stations. Drones can be equipped with cameras, sensors and other electronics, providing live streaming or recording capabilities (King, 2014) Drones have uses with clear public benefits in the military, public safety, agricultural and industrial sectors (e.g., mapping and disaster management, surveillance, newsgathering, crime scene investigation) (Canis, 2015; Sandvik & Lohne, 2014), as well as being used an increasing range of ways related to entertainment and commerce. These have included,

for example, the use of drones to livestream and to monitor crowds at events (Sakiyama, Miethe, Leiberman, Heen, & Tuttle, 2017), to generate advertising footage for real estate developments (Babel, 2015) and to create dramatic footage for television and film (La Bella, 2016). Some uses of drones in sectors connected to, but not directly related to tourism, also provide benefits to the tourism industry, such as the use of drones in meteorology (PytlikZillig et al., 2018) or conservation (Bryan, 2017). An emerging area of drone use is delivery, with a number of retailers having investigated the possibilities of using drones for direct delivery of products to customers (Bamburry, 2015), although trials of these services have not progressed to viable mass-market offerings as yet.

The consumer drone market can be broken down into four distinct categories: aerial photography drones; toy drones; FPV (first person view) and racing drones; and hobbyist/hacker/developer drones (DroneDlyers, 2015). From these groups, the area of aerial filming was amongst the first commercial applications of drones (SESAR, 2016). The consumer and commercial drone market has seen significant growth in recent years (Global Market Insights, 2018; Luppicini & So, 2016). Most drones in 2014 were bought by the US (35%), Europe (30%) and China (15%) (Majumdar, 2016). By 2020 it is expected that drone shipments will reach 7.8 million, versus 450,000 shipments in 2014 (Goldman Sachs, 2016). However, differences in rates of adoption are largely dependent on differing national regulations, relating to drone applicability, technical requirements, operational limitations, administrative procedures, human resource requirements and the implementation of ethical and legal constraints (Stöcker, Bennett, Nex, Gerke, & Zevenbergen, 2017).

The tourism industry is a growth area for the use of drones (King, 2014; Mirk & Hlavacs, 2015), but this has not been mirrored in the growth of research in this field. Recently, Hay (2016) presented a study which investigated general current and potential uses of drones in hospitality and tourism, with a summary of the possible future uses. To this end, Dinhopl and Gretzel (2016b) explore the differences related to the technology and social practices of (re)presentation between the well-established practice of tourist photography and the new practice of using wearable cameras and drones to film from different perspectives, while Aaron (2016) analyzed the motivations and experiences of participants who employ drones for tourism.

In contrast to this lack of research, tourism practitioners are increasingly involved in innovative tourism industry-specific drone use. Based on the emerging research literature and various practical examples, two main scenarios of drone application in tourism can be distinguished. First is the physical use of drones to provide some transactions, services or just fun for tourists. Second is the application of drones as a means for carrying and controlling equipment for sensing or recording terrestrial objects or activities at a destination to use these products for management or marketing purposes. The first scenario includes, for example, drones intervening in case of emergency or even as "flying tour guides" that tourists can follow (King, 2014). Some applications, such as delivery of goods or fast-food, flying billboards or dropping flyers at festivals, although they seemed promising in earlier phases of drone adoption, did not reach their full potential mostly due to security limitations, technical issues or being labelled as a disruptive technology (Bamburry, 2015; Mancosu, 2016). For example, Rahman (2014) investigated the use of drones for assisting rescue services in a winter tourism context, and concluded that emerging technologies related to drones such as WiMAX and WiFi require further innovations before drones can be fully implemented within remote alpine settings.

The second scenario offers greater opportunities for the tourism industry. Mirk and Hlavacs (2014, 2015)) explored the use of real-time video images of different places of the world made by drone-flying webcams. This form of virtual tourism with the help of drone videos, can present new access to tourism destinations

and attractions for those unable to travel (Hay, 2016). Commercial drone producers market the necessary equipment for these virtual experiences from the same premise. For example, many new drones are now marketed as devices for filming traveler's adventures and are also offered with the addition of virtual reality (VR) goggles for the direct streaming of drone flights (Garrett, 2017). The rising popularity of adventure and extreme tours (Ingga, 2016) supports these trends, as travelers, athletes or artists more frequently showcase their experiences using affordable quality recording equipment (e.g., GoPro cameras) for the creation of professional-quality independent videos, distributed via websites and social media in common with other kinds of user-generated content in tourism (Munar & Jacobsen, 2014; Tussyadiah & Fesenmaier, 2009; Vannini & Stewart, 2017).

According to Hay (2016), drone videos are of interest to destination marketing organizations (DMOs), complementing static images and short videos in presenting and promoting a destination. For example, New Zealand's DMO acquired drones to create its own videos (Dinhopl & Gretzel, 2015) and subsequently created a successful social media campaign for sharing "ultimate holiday selfies" (Tourism New Zealand, 2015). The characteristics of destination videos shared on social media is a relatively unexplored academic topic, either as separate media type (Crowel, Gribben, & Loo, 2014; Huertas, 2018; Tussyadiah & Fesenmaier, 2009) or as a part of other social media content types (Ulrike Gretzel, Fesenmaier, Lee, & Tussyadiah, 2011; Kwok & Yu, 2013; Månsson, 2011; Mariani, Di Felice, & Mura, 2016). Lu, Chen, and Law (2018) reviewed the research literature on social media and tourism and hospitality management published between 2004–2014 and found that only 1.9% of the papers had engaged with the area of video within UGC, reflecting the relatively recent emergence of shared video content as an area of concern to tourism marketers.

When aerial drone videos are shared via social media sites they can be treated as other forms of user-generated content (UGC), such as text, pictures or audio. However, unlike other user-shared videos, the creation of drone videos encounters novel different technical and regulative limitations, as well as different users' motivations (Kreps, 2016), that mean that they can be considered as a specific type of UGC. Those specifics can be of relevance if aerial drone videos are considered as a means of destination marketing.

The overall aim of this research was to develop a greater understanding of this new form of UGC that will benefit researchers and practitioners, especially in terms of destination marketing. The three specific research objectives were to: 1. Determine the general characteristics of shared aerial drone videos based on UGC metadata analysis; 2. Map the spatial distribution of shared aerial drone videos within a country to reveal spatial patterns; and to, 3. Discuss the relevance of these videos for destination marketing.

Literature review

User-generated content in destination marketing

UGC is media content created or produced by consumers rather than by paid professionals, and primarily shared online (Daugherty, Eastin, & Bright, 2008). Johnson, Sieber, Magnien, and Ariwi (2012, p. 293) categorize the kinds of content posted in these websites as "data in the form of text, photos, tags, audio or video created by an individual and hosted online where it is accessible to others". User-generated content (UGC) has become an important source of information for tourists (Ayeh, Au, & Law, 2013; Carvão, 2010; Chung & Buhalis, 2008; Gretzel & Yoo, 2008) and can be situated on a variety of websites including social networks (e.g., Facebook), online travel communities (e.g., Lonely Planet), review sites (e.g., TripAdvisor), personal blogs, blog aggregators (e.g., Reddit), microblogging sites (e.g., Twitter, Weibo), wikis (e.g., WikiTravel) and video-hosting platforms (e.g., YouTube, Vimeo).

UGC can be shared both in "real time" during a tourism experience or after the experience has ended (Munar & Jacobsen, 2014), increasingly facilitated by the always-on nature of Internet-enabled smart devices carried by tourists. Content of this kind that relates to the experiences of tourists at destinations, attractions, or other sites has also been described as comprising part of "electronic word of mouth" (eWOM), an aspect of marketing that has become increasingly important for tourism and hospitality businesses (Carvão, 2010; Litvin, Goldsmith, & Pan, 2008; Rupert Hills & Cairncross, 2011 as well as for tourism destinations (Gretzel, 2006; Marchiori & Cantoni, 2015; Munar, 2011; Narangajavana, Callarisa Fiol, Moliner Tena, Rodríguez Artola, & Sánchez García, 2017; Shen, Liu, Yi, & Li, 2016).

UGC has proven to be an effective way for companies and organizations to capitalize on the new relations created with consumers in the digital economy (Dickey & Lewis, 2011). Before the emergence of Web 2.0, characterized by widespread social media usage, traditional "gatekeepers" such as newspaper editors, publishers and news shows had to digest information and report valuable content to the public in manageable ways. Nowadays, there are few or no "gatekeepers"

to filter online content, and audiences can participate in new forms of dialogue online, and interact directly with businesses, institutions, and opinion-formers (Chin-Fook & Simmonds, 2011).

Despite controversies over the reliability and credibility of UGC in tourism, especially concerning review sites such as TripAdvisor (Gao, Li, Liu, & Fang, 2018), some research has found that UGC in eWOM for tourism can be perceived as more reliable than other forms of information (Fotis, Buhalis, & Rossides, 2012) including that provided by businesses or destinations themselves, despite the fact that this does not appear to be true in other contexts such as retail (Ye, Law, Gu, & Chen, 2011). UGC is frequently viewed by tourists as more akin to standard "word of mouth" (WOM) recommendations from friends and family members (Wang, Yu, & Fesenmaier, 2002; Yoo, Lee, Gretzel, & Fesenmaier, 2009), despite more sophisticated consumers' ability to evaluate content in terms of its trustworthiness (Jin & Phua, 2016). Chen, Nguyen, Klaus, and Wu (2015, p. 964) found that eWOM "plays a primary role in the consumer decision-making process" and that consumers react more decisively to positive reviews than to negative ones. Mendes-Filho and colleagues (2018) linked this trend to the increasing empowerment of independent travel consumers, a broader trend affecting the industry (Marine-Roig & Anton Clavé, 2016). Despite this, Uşaklı, Koç, and Sönmez (2017) found in a study of 50 European destination management organizations (DMOs), that social media and UGC are not being harnessed effectively in destination marketing, which has also been found to be the case with a sample of international DMOs (Roque & Raposo, 2016). A study of 150 DMOs in France, Belgium and Switzerland found, for example, that only 20% of marketing budgets were spent on online content, with only 0.4% allocated to social media activities (Wozniak, Stangl, Schegg, & Liebrich, 2017). These findings have significant implications for increasing DMO engagement with tourists – especially the generation of "digital natives" (Gon, Pechlaner, & Marangon, 2016) who expect to interact with businesses and each other using these means. Kang and Schuett (2013) sound a cautionary note, however, when advocating the engagement in UGC by DMOs, noting the inherent difficulties in controlling the quality and quantity of UGC on their in-house or independent social media platforms.

Characteristics of drone videos as UGC

In addition to traditional tourist photography, an increasing number of visitors have experience of recording videos during their vacations and later sharing these on social media sites (Tussyadiah & Fesenmaier, 2009). Video content has rapidly grown as a proportion of UGC online, as video-making devices have become more mainstream and video content has been integrated into other social media platforms such as Facebook and Twitter (Dinhopl & Gretzel, 2016a). Because of its specificity in technological and social practices, tourism videography can even be considered as a separate media form, different from travel photography (Dinhopl & Gretzel, 2015, 2016b). From another perspective, using various social media sites, consumers now can easily search travel videos posted by other tourists and individuals, or by official DMOs, before making travel decisions (Lim, Chung, & Weaver, 2012). According to a USA-based study, two out of three consumers watch online travel videos when they are seeking information about their trips (Crowel et al., 2014).

Apart from the obvious perspective differences, the use of drones has brought several changes to travel video creation. To summarize these changes, Table 1 presents descriptions of the most common views on the issue.

The creation of drone videos, however, is characterized by specific technical (flight time, flight conditions, visual contact) and regulatory limitations (different restrictions on flights over densely populated areas, larger assembly of people, no-flight zones, privacy issues, ethics of the use, etc.), which can limit the spatial coverage of a destination (Kreps, 2016; Luppicini & So, 2016). This can be contrasted with the growing popularity with DMOs of the less visually interesting, but nearly universal coverage offered by Digital Earth systems (Craglia et al., 2012) such as online satellite and aerial imagery, or Bing Bird's Eye (Bartha & Kocsis, 2011), meaning that tourists can visually review almost any part of a destination. However, the method of the geo-localization of images and videos still remains a challenging task as many of Digital Earth systems are limited to highly visited urban regions while large, but less populated geo-spatial regions are left behind (Zamir, Hakeem, Van Gool, Shah, & Szeliski, 2016). In that sense, the spatial coverage capabilities of the shared image and video repositories are an important characteristic for destination marketing.

Many aerial drone videos are professionally produced and so are, in some respects, not genuine UGC. However, if they are made publicly available (shared), regardless of the main motivation of a user to showcase a company's or entrepreneur's business activities, they make a contribution to the existing body of UGC for a destination. Unlike other types of UGC, such as pictures or general videos, aerial drone videos by default require additional techniques and efforts from their creators and therefore it is sometimes hard to delineate professional content from UGC. However, from the perspective of destination marketing, this delineation is not essential as the drone video's value will depend on the individual video's characteristics and the specific features of the destination.

Methods

The analysis in this research is based on meta-data of United Kingdom (UK) aerial drone videos shared on YouTube and with added spatial references. This study focused on the UK for several reasons. The UK is, and will remain, one of the largest markets for drones in Europe, with a strong technology base, high levels of expertise, diverse industrial applications and an enthusiastic home market (EC, 2008; Goldman Sachs, 2016). The UK government is one of the first to set out a vision of a safe and proper use of drones in public and commercial services to contribute to the economy, create new jobs and encourage the development and learning of important new skills and rules of drone usage

Table 1. Major changes that drones brought to video creation.

Aerial filming perspectives	In drone videos people look at objects and landscapes from a view that they've never seen before, which is effective in gaining the attention of viewers. For example, rather than looking down at objects from an angle the "bird's-eye", or "God's eye" view is created when camera is pointing directly down, creating unique shots that have a lot of impact on the viewer (Smith, 2016).
Access to previously un-shootable scenarios	Previously, it was difficult or even impossible for amateurs to capture great footage of locations considered to be off limits, such as volcanoes, cliffs and waterfalls. Now, by using drones, getting to these difficult and harsh locations is much easier (Ingga, 2016).
Attractiveness of air mobility simulations	Flight imagery evokes the age-old dream of human flight (Johnson, 2016). Today the dream of personal vertical flight lives on in the public imagination of urban mobility. While this, in reality, is not a viable mobility option, technology allows viewers to indulge in the dream of flying in a realistic manner (Cwerner, 2006).
Democratization of aerial video production	Prior to the advent of inexpensive consumer drones, aerial video was a costly, heavily planned and mostly commercial activity that needed the use of helicopters, hot air balloons, etc. Now, drones with professional video capture devices are available to the public (Johnson, 2016)
A new media genre	The creation of drone videos has led to a new genre in aerial filming, both for professionals and amateurs (Johnson, 2016).
Multiple data forms	Apart from capturing videos, the same drone flight might be used for taking photos or video can be enchanted by acquiring other data using sensors (for example, 3D, Infra-Red, georeferencing) (Johnson, 2016; Kreps, 2016).

(Department for Transport, 2017). The sophistication and scale of the market for commercial and leisure drone use in the UK means that the research could draw on a large potential set of drone videos for analysis, and that recommendations could then be made for the use of destination drone videos in destinations in emerging drone markets.

Sampling

A purposive sample of drone videos of the UK was collected from YouTube. YouTube is the world's largest online video-sharing platform (Bärtl, 2018; Cheng, Liu, & Dale, 2013), meaning that it was the most appropriate source for these videos, but it does not georeference videos by their locations which were necessary for this sampling strategy. To address this, the website TravelbyDrone.com was used. This website allows consumers to share aerial drone videos uploaded on YouTube to a web-based map. TravelbyDrone.com is currently the world's largest collection of geo-located drone videos (TravelByDrone, 2017). Georeferenced drone videos clearly indicate the area in which the drone was used to film a destination and allowed for the identification of drone videos that were solely taken of the UK. Additionally, TravelbyDrone.com provides a quality check of drone videos. For example, videos that will not be included if they feature: poor editing, "roller-coaster"-like or low-quality footage, are too long, overly promotional in nature, with animated intros or endings beyond 5-10s, military-related footage, political, religious or other personal messages (TravelByDrone, 2017). In total, 614 drone videos that satisfy the above-mentioned criteria were gathered.

Youtube meta-data analysis

Given the absence of academic literature about the use of drone videos in tourism, this study was grounded on the existing common measurement variables for assessing social media videos and the measurement of user engagement. The first stage of the analysis was carried out to determine the characteristics of aerial drone videos based on measurement metrics of general YouTube videos (Cheng et al., 2013; Thelwall, Sud, & Vis, 2012). When uploading a video to YouTube, the user optimizes the metadata by choosing one of 15 self-explanatory categories where most people would expect to find the video, adds key words, key word phrases and tags (names, places, events, etc.) that accurately describe video and writes an accurate and thorough description (IMP, 2012). Thus, for every drone destination video, the following data were collected: category; title; description;

length; and age. *Webometric Analyst* (http://lexiurl.wlv.ac.uk/) software was used to retrieve drone video metadata from the *YouTube API*. The datasets were analyzed using SPSS statistical software.

Spatial analysis

The second part of the research, dedicated to spatial analysis, followed the approach of variable selection, which had been applied in the case of user contributions of drone pictures on a photo-sharing portal conducted by Hochmair and Zielstra (2015). *ESRI's ArcGIS for Desktop* software was used for data transformation and analysis. An overlay analysis and descriptive statistics were used for spatial analysis (Johnson & Arrowsmith, 2015; Stankov et al., 2014). Four primary sources of data were used for this part of research: drone video locations; population density, land use and nationally designated areas in the UK.

- Drone video locations were retrieved from TravebyDrone.com using manual extraction of geographical coordinates from web-map HTML. Geographical coordinates were transformed in point shapefile, a basic vector-based impute data format for ArcGIS software.
- The population layer was in the form of gridded population, with a spatial resolution of 1×1 km for the UK, based on Census 2011 and Land Cover Map 2007 input data (Reis et al., 2016).
- Land used data was based on vector datasets for the UK, Jersey and Guernsey containing the Corine Land Cover (CLC) for 2012. Data were published by the UK Centre for Ecology and Hydrology (Cole et al., 2015)
- For the protected areas, the nationally designated areas inventory (CDDA) polygon shapefile (version 14 for 2016) was obtained from the European Environment Agency (European Environment Agency, 2016).

Results

Drone video characteristics

Video category

Table 2 lists the number and percentage of all the categories in the sample used in this research. It is apparent that the distribution is highly skewed: the most popular category is "People & Blogs", and second and third are "Travel & Events" and "Film & Animation". Those three categories of videos constitute more than 2/3 of the entire selection of drone videos in the sample. The fact that the categories "People & Blogs", "Film & Animation" and

Table 2. The frequency of drone videos by YouTube video categories.

Category	Frequency	Percent
People and blogs	197	32.08%
Travel and events	117	19.06%
Film and animation	112	18.24%
Entertainment	67	10.91%
Science and technology	50	8.14%
Sports	31	5.05%
Autos and vehicles	11	1.79%
Education	9	1.47%
Comedy	4	0.65%
Gaming	4	0.65%
How to and style	4	0.65%
Music	4	0.65%
Non-profits and activism	2	0.33%
News and politics	1	0.16%
Pets and animals	1	0.16%
Total	614	100.0%

"Science & Technology" constitute more than half of the drone videos, suggest that drone videos are being categorized from the perspective of their creation, either as a hobby or professional activity. However, the presence of categories, such as "Travel & Events", "Entertainment", "Sports" and others, suggests the understanding of context-specific purpose of the drone videos, on behalf of their creators.

Video title and description
Table 3 shows the 50 most frequent nouns found in drone video titles and descriptions. Besides the annotation of geographical features shown, many drone video titles contain the brand of the equipment used for filming. As it can be seen from Table 3 more detailed explanations of drone video creation, procedures and post-production are shown in video descriptions (aircraft, camera, permission, gimbal, GHz etc.). These findings reconfirm the above-mentioned suggestion on the importance of drone video creation procedures for uploaders.

Video length and age
Figure 1 shows the histogram and normal curve of drone's video length. As can be seen, the drone Histogram exhibits a high positive skewness (1.92) calculated from the sample of drone's video length. The average drone video length is 3.45 min (σ 2.41, N = 614). Approximately every fourth drone video (25.73%) is shorter than 2 min, while 69.28% are up to 4 min long.

On average, the drone video age in the sample was about 3 years and 7 months. There were 8.8% videos older than 5 years. It suggests that, although a relatively new trend for the general market, filming with drones was practiced by early adopters.

Spatial analysis

Drone video locations and population density
Figure 2 depicts the spatial distribution of drone videos as point patterns, mapped on the top of the spatial density distribution of UK population as a raster

Table 3. Most frequent nouns in drone video titles and descriptions.

Video titles				Video descriptions			
Noun	Freq.	Noun	Freq.	Noun	Freq.	Noun	Freq.
Phantom	117	HD	13	*Phantom*	331	Scotland	57
DJI[a]	101	Hill	13	*DJI*[a]	257	film	54
drone	56	Ireland	12	UK	219	permission n	54
castle	45	River	12	video	191	area	53
Park	44	Bay	11	aircraft	145	gimbal	51
flight	34	Church	11	RPAS[2]	120	Wales	48
FPV	33	Dundee	11	*GoPro*	110	GHz (gigahertz)	46
view	31	Lake	11	camera	89	music	46
GoPro	30	(Phantom Vision) Plus	11	metres	88	(Phantom 2) Vision	46
North	27	Valley	11	CAA[b]	83	view	45
video	27	Forest	9	drone	80	location	44
footage	22	Northern (Ireland)	9	Facebook	79	time	43
beach	20	viaduct	9	castle	78	river	42
Wales	19	West	9	FPV	75	kg	41
Birds eye	18	Harbour	8	(GoPro) Hero	72	shot	41
Air	17	Head	8	footage	70	operator	40
Cornwall	17	South	8	park	69	RC4	40
Dropro	17	Country	7	quadcopter	67	regulations	40
(Phantom) Vision	17	Lancaster	7	*YouTube*	66	North	40
Scotland	16	Surrey	7	people	63	Twitter	40
UK	16	Devon	6	*Instagram*	62	channel	39
bridge	15	discovery	6	day	61	default	38
(GoPro) Hero	15	District	6	HD	61	views	37
coast	14	HeliMal	6	flight	58	bridge	35
Quadcopter	14	House	6	person	57	feet	35

[a] *Dà-Jiāng Innovations Science and Technology Company;* [2] Remotely Piloted Aircraft System;
[b] Civil Aviation Authority, UK; [4]Radio-controlled)

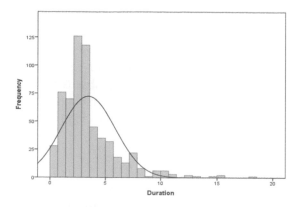

Figure 1. Distribution of aerial drone video length.

pattern. An overlay of locations and population density showed that 23.38% of drone videos were shot over areas that did not have registered inhabitants. Still, it does not imply that these areas with no recorded population are in remote areas. The original aim of the study was to use the smallest available spatial resolution size (1x1km), which can represent, for example, parks or recreation areas with no registered inhabitants, but within or near densely populated settlements. Figure 2 clearly shows that mostly unpopulated areas far from urbanized centres do not attract many videos.

The overlay of drone video location and land cover/use data showed that about two-thirds of all locations are classified as artificial surfaces (34.2%) or agricultural areas (34.0%) (Figure 3). Discontinuous urban fabric and pastures are the most popular places for drone filming. This is not a surprise, as current regulations in the UK restrict drone flights over densely populated areas or areas used by many people. Forested and semi-natural areas are present in the sample with 16.3%. However, mostly open areas are dominant, again because of regulations that require keeping the drone in the eyesight of a pilot. Wetlands (7.0%) and waterbodies (8.5%) are present in the list. However, if sub-categories are combined, for example, sea and oceans, estuaries, beaches, dunes, sands and bare rocks, seashores, as distinct geographical areas, are significantly present in the UK drone video sample.

Figure 4 shows areas mostly dedicated to recreation with fewer restrictions of drone usage. These were the video locations within nationally designated areas.

Figure 5 shows that 38.96% of all drone videos were filmed over protected areas. Areas of outstanding natural beauty (AONB) dominate with 32.9%, followed by national parks (21.3%), and sites of specific scientific interest (17.9%).

Discussion

The results section, above, has presented data gathered to answer the three research questions of this analysis, which have implications for both the academic understanding of the role of drone videos in destination marketing, as well as the use of drone videos by practitioners. The following section places these results into the context of the preceding literature review.

Videos filmed by drones, although depicting destinations, are not necessarily intended for tourism promotion purposes. Indeed, YouTube is not a tourism-specific social media site, and videos provided about a destination do not necessarily have a tourism focus (Munar, 2011). Similarly, the results of this analysis show that authors of drone videos, in many cases chose classifications other than "Travel and Events", which implicitly reveals that travellers are not the main expected audience of aerial drone videos and that the motivation for video-sharing is outside of the scope of tourism. This insight can be relevant for DMOs that could focus on engaging larger, non-tourist, audiences in drone video creation and sharing, although their motivation does not have to be related to destination promotion. Therefore, regardless of the category chosen, which originally helps in video search engine optimization, most aerial drone videos can be considered as partial visual presentations of a destination or a destination activity. The explicit mentioning of place names, landmarks and events at the destination in drone video metadata can be of more relevance. In fact, 80% of YouTube travel searches focus on destination names and local attractions (Crowel et al., 2014), indicating their importance for representing a destination as a form of UGC (Crowel et al., 2014; Mariani et al., 2016; Tussyadiah & Fesenmaier, 2009).

The research carried out discovered the frequent appearance of technical descriptions and specific drone systems in the video titles. These points towards the fact that there is a growing online community that has formed around drone videos, similar to GoPro videos (Dinhopl & Gretzel, 2016a), made of amateurs, professionals and expert authorities (Coleman, Georgiadou, & Labonte, 2009). It is not surprising to see greater engagement in this community, as they comment on each other's videos. This is also why it is important to them to provide technical descriptions of the drone videos, as our results suggest. There is often a professional element involved and so these additions are important for establishing expertise or influence in the community (Kozinets, 2002). However, as mentioned earlier, if those videos convey the representation of a destination (or just

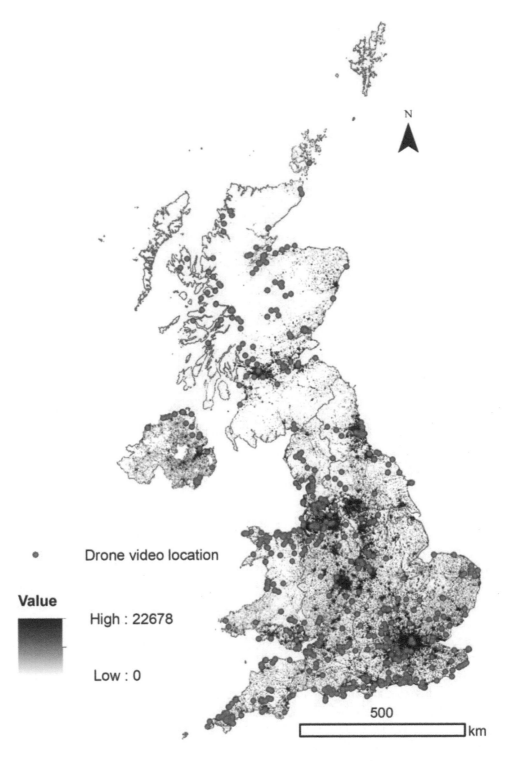

Figure 2. Drone video locations and population density.

a part of it) and if they are attractive to the public as well, that means that they potentially contribute to destination promotion through UGC.

This research revealed the dominance of shorter videos, which was expected, as YouTube is mostly comprised of short video clips. ComScore (2017) reported that in 2014 the duration of the average online content video was 4.4 min, but that there is a range in lengths. The presented data shows that the average aerial drone video is 1-min shorter if compared to the average online video. By default, users can upload videos to YouTube that are up to 15 min long, but with additional requirements, users can upload longer videos. In this sample, only three videos were longer than 15 min. The

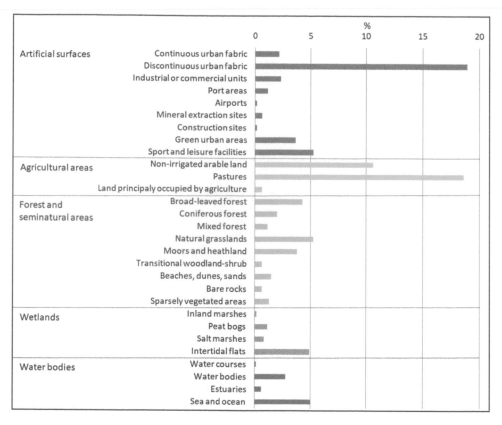

Figure 3. Distribution of drone video locations across CLC categories.

results could be biased by TravelByDrone recommendations to users to upload shorter videos. Looking from the specific point of drone video creation, if drone shooting is restricted to one flight the total video length will be limited by drone flying time, flight conditions and regulatory restrictions.

The results of this analysis suggested that aerial drone videos are not exclusively or dominantly related to certain geographical features. Therefore, the general aerial drone video properties make them suitable for visual presentation of a whole destination or its parts. Imposed restrictions on drone usage for certain areas or in certain situations could represent a challenge in achieving ubiquitous spatial continuity in Digital Earth presentations. Still, according to the geographic concept of a destination, the whole country's territory usually cannot be considered as travel destinations, as destinations are linked to geographical elements that act as nucleuses for development (Jovicic, 2016). In that sense, the initiative to setup and expand the use of "geofencing" in the UK that acts like an invisible shield around buildings or sensitive areas (e.g., prisons, military facilities or airports) and prevents drones from flying in will cover areas that are already away from general interest of tourists. On the other hand, some congested areas that are of tourist interest, as well as areas used for the organized open-air assembly of people at festivals

and events, which attract restrictions on drone flights, can still be covered with professional drone filming.

As a form of UGC in tourism, the role of shared aerial drone videos has not previously been examined, despite the growth of drone use (Luppicini & So, 2016). Aerial drone videos are a kind of UGC that is shared after the tourism experience itself (Munar & Jacobsen, 2014), and which are not part of the explosion of UGC related to the near ubiquitousness of smart-devices carried by tourists (Gretzel, 2006; Marchiori & Cantoni, 2015; Munar, 2011), due to their reliance on specialist equipment that has not yet completely crossed the hobbyist/leisure divide (Bamburry, 2015; Mancosu, 2016). The increasing amount of shared aerial drone videos should be considered part of the new body of information available to researchers to consider their role in destination marketing and to be evaluated along with other kind of online content that has previously been considered (Lim et al., 2012; Munar, 2011).

Practitioner implications

Increased consumer access to drones and consequentially, the increased production and sharing of aerial drone videos is not only theoretically interesting, but most importantly it is practically relevant for destination marketing.

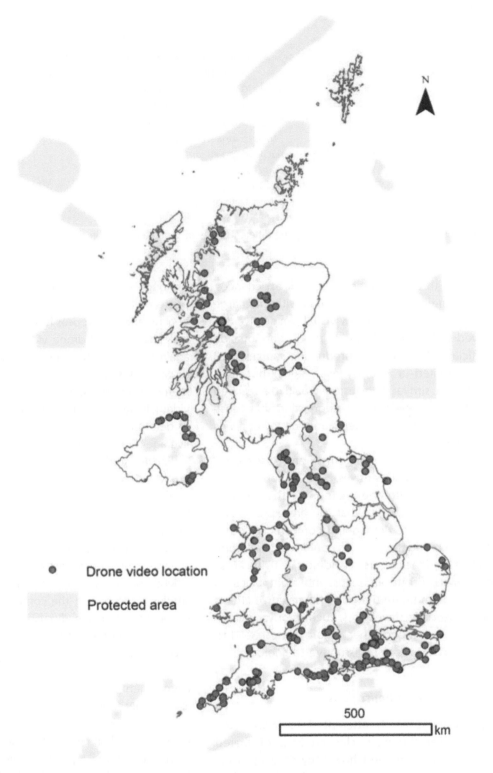

Figure 4. Drone video locations in protected areas (Nationally designated areas) in the UK.

Based on the characteristics of drone videos presented above, it is evident that DMOs can benefit from the trend of producing aerial drone videos by drone users. Videos captured from drones could help in differentiating a destination from its competitors (Hay, 2016). As in the case of other UGC, where some DMOs took the role of the content curator (Miralbell, Alzua-Sorzabal, & Gerrikagoitia, 2013), shared destination drone videos can be part of a DMO's content management strategies. The procuring, maintaining and using of drones in their own video production, as seen in the New Zealand DMO example, can be supplemented by leveraging the drone videos filmed by drone users, many of whom are not motivated by factors

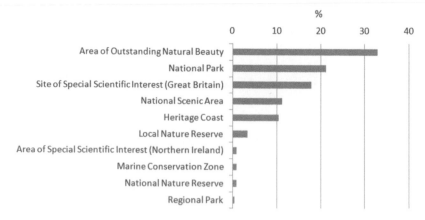

Figure 5. Frequency of aerial drone videos by the different types of protected areas in the UK.

connected to travel or sharing tourist experiences. These videos are often offered publicly without charge and the "Wow" effect of the new visual perspective can be achieved with various levels of production, outside of the official DMO's content production sources. This research presented a country-level study, but it is assumed that a similar conclusion would be reached in regional or city-level studies, suggesting that these practical implications can be replicated on lower levels of DMO structures.

By providing online platforms and assistance, together with other incentives, DMOs could more engage consumers into the creation of this form of UGC, as it was shown earlier that the process of drone video creation is more demanding compared to other forms of video production. DMOs could serve as "drone ambassadors" and facilitators providing safe flying areas for drone pilots, drone air maps and flight plans to reduce risks and mitigate the potential negative effects of drone presence at travel sites, such as privacy violations, noise pollution and other factors that can lead to a perception of drones as a disruptive technology.

Further research and limitations

This exploratory research attempted to answer the question of what the main characteristics of shared aerial drone videos are, and how they spatially cover a destination, along with their implications for destination marketing practices.

The study of Lim et al. (2012) showed that consumer-generated videos do not carry the same destination brand and have a little positive impact compared to destination marketing generated videos. Similarly, Google's study revealed that while there is an interest for community-generated travel content on YouTube, most travel-related views (67%) are branded or professionally related videos.

Although the number of views is not always the appropriate metric to measure online video performance, for benchmarking purposes it is reasonable to ascertain how well shared aerial drone videos perform in these terms against others in the same sector. Therefore, for further research it would be interesting to compare viewing metrics of aerial drone videos to other types of YouTube videos, including destination marketing generated videos, to determine whether they perform better or worse, on average (Crane & Sornette, 2008).

Further studies should be based on larger samples of drone videos from multiple destinations, with multiple methods, to go deeper in answering the question of why this trend is happening and what elements of aerial drone videos cause the biggest impression on viewers. For example, empirical research based on video content analysis is needed to test which element of aerial drone videos appeals the most to viewers. Further qualitative studies could dissect the comments to reveal the motivation for an online discussion on drone videos, as it would be useful to find out are they primarily related to production issues, destination or both, or the discussion is triggered by other topics. Moreover, in terms of effectiveness, an important additional question would be to ask whether there some other social media variables that influence the viewing of, and response to, aerial drone videos more than the content of the video itself?

The traditional spatial analysis tools used in the research included spatial distribution maps and descriptive statistics. While these methods can be of use for exploratory analysis, more advanced tools should be used to reveal statistically significant underlying patterns of georeferenced drone videos.

Additional explorations of organizational and human resource capabilities of DMOs to grasp the potential of drone destination videos and to tap into consumers' motivation to use drones are needed, as well as rethinking existing technical and legal issues related to drone usage in the context of destination marketing.

Disclosure statement

No potential conflict of interest was reported by the authors.

References

Aaron, T. (2016). Beam me up, Scottie! Drones and the production of a "Third Space" in Tourism. In A. C. C. Lu, Y. Rao, & D. Gursoy (Eds.), *6th advances in hospitality & tourism marketing & management conference* (pp. 6). Guangzhou: Sun Yat-Sen University, Washington State University. Retrieved from http://www.ahtmm.com/wp-content/uploads/2016/08/2016.pdf

Almeida, M., Azinheira, J. R., Barata, J., Bousson, K., Ervilha, R., Martins, M., … Viegas, D. X. (2017). Analysis of Fire Hazard in Campsite Areas. *Fire Technology, 53*(2), 553–575.

Ayeh, J. K., Au, N., & Law, R. (2013). "Do we believe in tripadvisor?" Examining credibility perceptions and online travelers' attitude toward using user-generated content. *Journal of Travel Research, 52*(4), 437–452.

Babel, J. (2015). Up in the air: The emerging issue of drones in the construction industry. *XL Catlin Construction Insider, 5*

Bamburry, D. (2015). Drones: Designed for product delivery. *Design Management Review, 26*(1), 40–48.

Bartha, G., & Kocsis, S. (2011). Standardization of geographic data: The European INSPIRE Directive. *European Journal of Geography, 2*(2), 79–89.

Bärtl, M. (2018). YouTube channels, uploads and views. *Convergence: the International Journal of Research into New Media Technologies, 24*(1), 16–32.

Beadel, S., Shaw, W., Bawden, R., Bycroft, C., Wilcox, F., McQueen, J., & Lloyd, K. (2018). Sustainable management of geothermal vegetation in the Waikato Region, New Zealand, including application of ecological indicators and new monitoring technology trials. *Geothermics, 73*, 91–99.

Braitenberg, C., Sampietro, D., Pivetta, T., Zuliani, D., Barbagallo, A., Fabris, P., … Mansi, A. H. (2016). Gravity for detecting caves: Airborne and terrestrial simulations based on a comprehensive Karstic Cave Benchmark. *Pure and Applied Geophysics, 173*(4), 1243–1264.

Bryan, P. (2017). 3D Recording, Documentation and Management of Cultural Heritage. *Conservation and Management of Archaeological Sites, 19*(2), 144–146.

Canis, B. (2015). Unmanned aircraft systems (UAS): Commercial outlook for a new industry. Retrieved from http://goodtimes web.org/industrial-policy/2015/R44192.pdf

Carvão, S. (2010). Embracing user generated content within destination management organizations to gain a competitive insight into visitors' profiles. *Worldwide Hospitality and Tourism Themes, 2*(4), 376–382.

Chen, C.-H., Nguyen, B., Klaus, P., Phil, & Wu, M.-S. (2015). Exploring electronic Word-of-Mouth (eWOM) in the consumer purchase decision-making process: The case of online holidays – evidence from United Kingdom (UK) consumers. *Journal of Travel & Tourism Marketing, 32*(8), 953–970.

Cheng, X., Liu, J., & Dale, C. (2013). Understanding the characteristics of internet short video sharing: A youtube-based measurement study. *IEEE Transactions on Multimedia, 15*(5), 1184–1194.

Chin-Fook, L., & Simmonds, H. (2011). Redefining gatekeeping theory for a digital generation. *The McMaster Journal of Communication, 8*(8), 7–34.

Chung, J. Y., & Buhalis, D. (2008). Information needs in online social networks. *Information Technology & Tourism, 10*(4), 267–281.

Cole, B., King, S., Ogutu, B., Palmer, D., Smith, G., & Balzter, H. (2015). Corine land cover 2012 for the UK, Jersey and Guernsey. Leicester, England: Centre for Ecology & Hydrology. doi:10.5285/32533DD6-7C1B-43E1-B892-E80D61A5EA1D

Coleman, D. J., Georgiadou, Y., & Labonte, J. (2009). Volunteered geographic information: The nature and motivation of producers. *International Journal of Spatial Data Infrastructures Research, 4*, 332–358.

ComScore. (2017, August 30). comScore Releases January 2014 U.S. Online Video Rankings - comScore, Inc. Retrieved from http://www.comscore.com/Insights/Press-Releases/2014/2/comScore-Releases-January-2014-US-Online-Video-Rankings

Craglia, M., de Bie, K., Jackson, D., Pesaresi, M., Remetey-Fülöpp, G., Wang, C., … Woodgate, P. (2012). Digital Earth 2020: Towards the vision for the next decade. *International Journal of Digital Earth*, (1), 4–21. doi:10.1080/17538947.2011.638500

Crane, R., & Sornette, D. (2008). Viral, quality, and junk videos on Youtube: Separating content from noise in an information-rich environment. In *AAAI Spring Symposium 2008 - Social Information Processing: Stanford University, CA, USA*, 18-20. Stanford: DBLP. Retrieved from https://vvvvw.aaai.org/Papers/Symposia/Spring/2008/SS-08-06/SS08-06-004.pdf

Crowel, H., Gribben, H., & Loo, J. (2014). Travel content takes off on YouTube. Retrieved from https://www.thinkwithgoo gle.com/consumer-insights/travel-content-takes-off-on-youtube/

Cwerner, S. B. (2006). Vertical flight and urban mobilities: The promise and reality of helicopter travel1. *Mobilities, 1*(2), 191–215.

Daugherty, T., Eastin, M. S., & Bright, L. (2008). Exploring consumer motivations for creating user-generated content. *Journal of Interactive Advertising, 8*(2), 16–25.

Department for Transport. (2017). Unlocking the UK's high tech economy: Consultation on the Safe Use of Drones in the UK Government Response Government Response. Retrieved from https://www.gov.uk/government/uploads/system/uploads/attachment_data/file/631638/unlocking-the-uks-high-tech-economy-consultation-on-the-safe-use-of-drones-in-the-uk-government-response.pdf

Dickey, I. J., & Lewis, W. F. (2011). An overview of digital media and advertising. In M. S. Eastin, T. Daugherty, & N. M. Burns (Eds.), *Handbook of research on digital media and advertising: User generated content consumption*, 1-31. Hershey: IGI Global.

Dinhopl, A., & Gretzel, U. (2015). Changing practices/new technologies: Photos and videos on vacation. In I. Tussyadiah & A. Inversini (Eds.), *Information and communication technologies in tourism 2015* (pp. 777–788). Cham: Springer International Publishing.

Dinhopl, A., & Gretzel, U. (2016a). Conceptualizing tourist videography. *Information Technology & Tourism, 15*(4), 395–410.

Dinhopl, A., & Gretzel, U. (2016b). GoPro panopticon: Performing in the surveyed leisure experience. In S. Carnicelli, D. McGillivray, & G. McPherson (Eds.), *Digital Leisure Cultures: Critical perspectives* (pp. 66–79). New York: Routledge.

DroneDlyers. (2015). The Drone Report 2016 - Droneflyers.com. Retrieved from http://www.droneflyers.com/the-drone-report-2016/

Ec, E., & I., D.-G. (2008). Study analysing the current activities in the field of UAV. Retrieved from https://ec.europa.eu/home-affairs/sites/homeaffairs/files/e-library/documents/policies/security/pdf/uav_study_element_2_en.pdf

European Environment Agency. (2016). CDDA v14 Shapefile. Retrieved from https://www.eea.europa.eu/data-and-maps/data/nationally-designated-areas-national-cdda-11/gis-data/cdda-v14-shape-file

Fotis, J., Buhalis, D., & Rossides, N. (2012). Social media use and impact during the holiday travel planning process. In M. Fuchs, F. Ricci, & L. Cantoni (Eds.), *Information and communication technologies in tourism 2012* (pp. 13–24). Vienna: Springer. doi:10.1007/978-3-7091-1142-0_2

Gao, B., Li, X., Liu, S., & Fang, D. (2018). How power distance affects online hotel ratings: The positive moderating roles of hotel chain and reviewers' travel experience. *Tourism Management, 65*, 176–186.

Garrett, J. (2017, July 28). Parrot Bebop and Disco Adventurer packs announced • GadgetyNews. Retrieved from http://gadgetynews.com/parrot-bebop-disco-adventurer-packs-announced/

Global Market Insights. (2018, August 5). Consumer Drone Market worth over $9bn by 2024. Retrieved from https://www.gminsights.com/pressrelease/consumer-drone-market

Goldman Sachs. (2016). Drones: Reporting for work. Retrieved from http://www.goldmansachs.com/our-thinking/technology-driving-innovation/drones/

Gon, M., Pechlaner, H., & Marangon, F. (2016). Destination management organizations (DMOs) and digital natives: The neglected "informal expertise" in web 2.0 implementation and social media presence. Insights from the Italian Friuli Venezia Giulia DMO. *Information Technology & Tourism, 16*(4), 435–455.

Gretzel, U. (2006). Consumer generated content - trends and implications for branding. *E-Review of Tourism Research, 4*(3), 9–11.

Gretzel, U., Fesenmaier, D., Lee, Y. J., & Tussyadiah, I. (2011). Narrating travel experiences: The role of new media. In S. Richard & R. S. Philip (Eds.), *Tourist Experience: Contemporary Perspectives* (pp. 171–182). New York: Routledge.

Gretzel, U., & Yoo, K. H. (2008). Use and impact of online travel reviews. In P. O'Connor, W. Höpken, & U. Gretzel (Eds.), *Information and communication technologies in tourism 2008* (pp. 35–46). Vienna: Springer - Verlang. doi:10.1007/978-3-211-77280-5_4

Hay, B. (2016). Drone tourism: A study of the current and potential use of drones in hospitality and tourism. In M. Scerri & L. K. Hui (Eds.), *CAUTHE 2016: The changing landscape of tourism and hospitality: The impact of emerging markets and emerging destinations* (pp. 49–68). Sydney: Blue Mountains International Hotel Management School.

Hochmair, H. H., & Zielstra, D. (2015). Analysing user contribution patterns of drone pictures to the dronestagram photo sharing portal. *Journal of Spatial Science, 60*(1), 79–98.

Huertas, A. (2018). How live videos and stories in social media influence tourist opinions and behaviour. *Information Technology & Tourism, 19*(1–4), 1–28.

IMP. (2012). Search engine optimization for Youtube videos. Retrieved from https://www.timlorang.com/SEO-for-YouTube-Updated

Ingga, Y. (2016). Drone Videos Lift up the Travel Industry's Charm - AVB Media Asia. Retrieved from http://avb.asia/drone-videos-lift-travel-industrys-charm/

Jin, S. V., & Phua, J. (2016). Making reservations online: The impact of consumer-written and system-aggregated user-generated content (UGC) in travel booking websites on consumers' behavioral intentions. *Journal of Travel & Tourism Marketing, 33*(1), 101–117.

Johnson, A., & Arrowsmith, C. (2015). Techniques for analyzing the relationship between population density and geographical features of interest. *Procedia Environmental Sciences, 27*, 89–93.

Johnson, J. (2016). How drones are changing the landscape of travel video. Retrieved from https://matadoru.com/drones-changing-landscape-travel-video/

Johnson, P. A., Sieber, R. E., Magnien, N., & Ariwi, J. (2012). Automated web harvesting to collect and analyse user-generated content for tourism. *Current Issues in Tourism, 15*(3), 293–299.

Jovicic, D. Z. (2016). Key issues in the conceptualization of tourism destinations. *Tourism Geographies, 18*(4), 445–457.

Kang, M., & Schuett, M. A. (2013). Determinants of sharing travel experiences in social media. *Journal of Travel & Tourism Marketing, 30*(1–2), 93–107.

King, L. M. (2014). Will drones revolutionise ecotourism? *Journal of Ecotourism, 13*(1), 85–92.

Kozinets, R. V. (2002). The field behind the screen: Using netnography for marketing research in online communities. *Journal of Marketing Research, 39*(1), 61–72.

Kreps, S. E. (2016). *Drones: What everyone needs to know.* New York, NY: Oxford University Press.

Kwok, L., & Yu, B. (2013). Spreading social media messages on facebook: an analysis of restaurant busine.ss-to-consumer communications. *Cornell Hospitality Quarterly, 54*(1), 84–94.

La Bella, L. (2016). *Drones and Entertainment.* New York, NY: Rosen Publishing Group.

Lim, Y., Chung, Y., & Weaver, P. A. (2012). The impact of social media on destination branding: Consumer-generated videos versus destination marketer-generated videos. *Journal of Vacation Marketing, 18*(3), 197–206.

Litvin, S. W., Goldsmith, R. E., & Pan, B. (2008). Electronic word-of-mouth in hospitality and tourism management. *Tourism Management, 29*(3), 458–468.

Lu, Y., (Tracy), Chen, Z., (Wade), & Law, R. (2018). Mapping the progress of social media research in hospitality and tourism management from 2004 to 2014. *Journal of Travel & Tourism Marketing, 35*(2), 102–118.

Luppicini, R., & So, A. (2016). A technoethical review of commercial drone use in the context of governance, ethics, and privacy. *Technology in Society, 46*, 109–119.

Majumdar, D. (2016). Russia vs. America: The race for underwater spy drones. The National Interest. Retrieved from https://nationalinterest.org/blog/the-buzz/america-vs-rus sia-the-race-underwater-spy-drones-14981

Mancosu, M. (2016). 4 ways drones are changing the market-ing industry. Retrieved from https://skytango.com/how-drones-are-changing-the-marketing-industry/

Månsson, M. (2011). Mediatized tourism. *Annals of Tourism Research, 38*(4), 1634–1652.

Marchiori, E., & Cantoni, L. (2015). The role of prior experience in the perception of a tourism destination in user-generated content. *Journal of Destination Marketing & Management, 4*(3), 194–201.

Mariani, M. M., Di Felice, M., & Mura, M. (2016). Facebook as a destination marketing tool: Evidence from Italian regional destination management organizations. *Tourism Management, 54*, 321–343.

Marine-Roig, E., & Anton Clavé, S. (2016). A detailed method for destination image analysis using user-generated content. *Information Technology & Tourism, 15*(4), 341–364.

Mendes-Filho, L., Mills, A. M., Tan, F. B., & Milne, S. (2018). Empowering the traveler: An examination of the impact of user-generated content on travel planning. *Journal of Travel & Tourism Marketing, 35*(4), 425–436.

Miralbell, O., Alzua-Sorzabal, A., & Gerrikagoitia, J. K. (2013). Content curation and narrative tourism marketing. In Z. Xiang & I. Tussyadiah (Eds.), *Information and communica-tion technologies in tourism 2014* (pp. 187–199). Cham: Springer International Publishing.

Mirk, D., & Hlavacs, H. (2014, July 9–11). Using Drones for virtual tourism. In D. Reidsma, I. Choi, & B. Robin (Eds.), *Intelligent technologies for interactive entertainment, 6th International Conference, INTETAIN 2014 Chicago, IL, USA* (pp. 144–147). Cham: Springer.

Mirk, D., & Hlavacs, H. (2015). Virtual tourism with drones: Experiments and lag compensation. In *Proceedings of the first workshop on micro aerial vehicle networks, systems, and applications for civilian use - DroNet '15* (pp. 45–50). New York, NY: ACM Press. doi:10.1145/2750675.2750681

Munar, A. M. (2011). Tourist-created content: Rethinking des-tination branding. *International Journal of Culture, Tourism and Hospitality Research, 5*(3), 291–305.

Munar, A. M., & Jacobsen, J. K. S. (2014). Motivations for sharing tourism experiences through social media. *Tourism Management, 43*, 46–54.

Narangajavana, Y., Callarisa Fiol, L. J., Moliner Tena, M. Á., Rodríguez Artola, R. M., & Sánchez García, J. (2017). The influence of social media in creating expectations. An empirical study for a tourist destination. *Annals of Tourism Research, 65*, 60–70.

PytlikZillig, L. M., Duncan, B., Elbaum, S., & Detweiler, C. (2018). A drone by any other name: purposes, end-user trust-worthiness, and framing, but not terminology, affect public support for drones. *IEEE Technology and Society Magazine, 37*(1),80-91.

Rahman, M. A. (2014). Enabling drone communications with WiMAX Technology. In *IISA 2014, The 5th International Conference on Information, Intelligence, Systems and Applications* (pp. 323–328). New York: IEEE Xplore doi:10.1109/IISA.2014.6878796

Reis, S., Steinle, S., Carnell, E., Leaver, D., Vieno, M., Beck, R., & Dragosits, U. (2016, January 1). UK gridded population based on Census 2011 and Land Cover Map 2007. *NERC Environmental Information Data Centre.* doi:10.5285/ 61F10C74-8C2C-4637-A274-5FA9B2E5CE44

Roque, V., & Raposo, R. (2016). Social media as a communication and marketing tool in tourism: An analy-sis of online activities from international key player DMO. *Anatolia, 27*(1), 58–70.

Rupert Hills, J., & Cairncross, G. (2011). Small accommodation providers and UGC web sites: Perceptions and practices. *International Journal of Contemporary Hospitality Management, 23*(1), 26–43.

Sakiyama, M., Miethe, T., Leiberman, J., Heen, M., & Tuttle, O. (2017). Big hover or big brother? Public attitudes about drone usage in domestic policing activities. *Security Journal, 30*(4), 1027–1044.

Sandvik, K. B., & Lohne, K. (2014). The rise of the humanitarian Drone: Giving content to an emerging concept. *Millennium: Journal of International Studies, 43*(1), 145–164.

SESAR. (2016). European Drones outlook study -unlocking the value for Europe. Retrieved from http://www.sesarju.eu/ sites/default/files/documents/reports/European_Drones_ Outlook_Study_2016.pdf

Shen, H., Liu, X., Yi, S., & Li, M. (2016, August 17-19). Understanding tourism image of cities through social semantic network analysis: A case study of Shanghai. In S. Chaperon & N. MacLeod (Eds.), *Tourism in contemporary cities: Proceedings of the international tourism studies asso-ciation conference*, 14-36. London: University of Greenwich.

Smith, C. (2016). *The photographer's guide to Drones - O'Reilly media*. San Rafael: Rocky Nook. Retrieved from http://shop. oreilly.com/product/9781681981147.do

Stankov, U., Marković, V., Savić, S., Dolinaj, D., Pašić, M., & Arsenović, D. (2014). Tourism resources in Urban Heat Island: A GIS analysis of Novi Sad, Serbia. In T. Bandrova & M. Konecny (Eds.), *5th International Conference on Cartography and GIS* (pp. 559–567). Sofia: Bulgarian Cartographic Association.

Stark, D. J., Vaughan, I. P., Evans, L. J., Kler, H., & Goossens, B. (2018). Combining drones and satellite tracking as an effec-tive tool for informing policy change in riparian habitats: A proboscis monkey case study. *Remote Sensing in Ecology and Conservation, 4*(1), 44–52.

Stöcker, C., Bennett, R., Nex, F., Gerke, M., & Zevenbergen, J. (2017). Review of the current State of UAV regulations. *Remote Sensing, 9*(5), 459.

Thelwall, M., Sud, P., & Vis, F. (2012). Commenting on YouTube videos: From guatemalan rock to El Big Bang. *Journal of the American Society for Information Science and Technology, 63* (3), 616–629.

Tourism New Zealand. (2015). Ultimate 'selfies' reach over 34 million - Tourism New Zealand. Retrieved from http:// www.tourismnewzealand.com/news/ultimate-selfies-reach-over-34-million/

TravelByDrone. (2017, May 9). About. Retrieved from http:// travelbydrone.com/

Tussyadiah, I. P., & Fesenmaier, D. R. (2009). Mediating tourist experiences: Access to places via shared videos. *Annals of Tourism Research, 36*(1), 24–40.

Uşaklı, A., Koç, B., & Sönmez, S. (2017). How "social" are destinations? Examining European DMO social media usage. *Journal of Destination Marketing & Management, 6* (2), 136–149.

Vannini, P., & Stewart, L. M. (2017). The GoPro gaze. *Cultural Geographies*, *24*(1), 149–155.

Vergouw, B., Nagel, H., Bondt, G., & Custers, B. (2016). Drone technology: Types, payloads, applications, frequency spectrum issues and future developments. In Custers and Bart (Eds.)., *The future of Drone use opportunities and threats from ethical and legal perspectives* (pp. 21–45). The Hague, NL: T.M.C. Asser Press.

Wang, Y., Yu, Q., & Fesenmaier, D. R. (2002). Defining the virtual tourist community: Implications for tourism marketing. *Tourism Management*, *23*(4), 407–417.

Wozniak, T., Stangl, B., Schegg, R., & Liebrich, A. (2017). The return on tourism organizations' social media investments: Preliminary evidence from Belgium, France, and Switzerland. *Information Technology & Tourism*, *17*(1), 75–100.

Ye, Q., Law, R., Gu, B., & Chen, W. (2011). The influence of user-generated content on traveler behavior: An empirical investigation on the effects of e-word-of-mouth to hotel online bookings. *Computers in Human Behavior*, *27*(2), 634–639.

Yoo, K.-H., Lee, Y., Gretzel, U., & Fesenmaier, D. R. (2009). Trust in travel-related consumer generated media. In W. Höpken, U. Gretzel, & R. Law (Eds.), *Information and communication technologies in tourism 2009* (pp. 49–59). Vienna: Springer. doi:10.1007/978-3-211-93971-0_5

Zamir, A. R., Hakeem, A., Van Gool, L., Shah, M., & Szeliski, R. (2016). Introduction to Large-Scale Visual Geo-localization. In A. R. Zamir, A. Hakeem, L. Van Gool, M. Shah, & R. Szeliski (Eds.), *Large-Scale Visual Geo-Localization* (pp. 1–18). Cham: Springer.

Using tracking technology to improve marketing: insights from a historic town in Tasmania, Australia

Bob Mckercher ⓘ, Anne Hardy ⓘ and Jagannath Aryal

ABSTRACT

This study examines the movement patterns of different market segments in an historic town. It combines traditional visitor surveys with a bespoke tourist tracking application. Two analytical stages were undertaken. The first involved analyzing the movements of tourist segments and revealed that "heritage" tourists tended to visit for the shortest lengths of time. The second phase revealed that a visit of between one and two hours seemed to provide the best opportunity to explore the village fully, while shorter and longer stays did not. The insights challenge traditional notions that heritage-oriented tourists should form the target market for historic communities.

Introduction

Understanding tourist movements in a destination have important implications for product development, destination planning, and the planning of new attractions, as well as management of the social, environmental, and cultural impacts of tourism (Lew & McKercher, 2006, p. 404). While it is relatively easy to track inter-destination movements, it has been much more challenging to track intra or within-destination movements, until recently, due primarily to technology limitations (McKercher & Zoltan, 2014). Moreover, tracking movements alone without understanding much about the tourist may produce impressive looking graphics, but offer few or no insights about how different segments whose motives and therefore behaviours may be quite different consume the destination.

The advent of GPS hand-held devices has resolved the first problem (Hardy, Hyslop, Booth, Robards, Aryal, Gretzel & Eccleston, 2016; Xia et al., 2010) by enabling a deeper understanding of tourist behaviour to be developed that may be used by marketers. It can be used by planners and marketers to assess the spatial travel patterns of tourists (Chancellor & Cole, 2008; Wu & Carson, 2008), it can be used by tourists to assist in decision-making (Feng & Morrison, 2002; Kramer, Modsching, Ten Hagen, & Gretzel, 2007) and ultimately, can be used to provide insights into the formation of emotional attachments to place. Detailed visitor surveys resolve the second problem. Combining both traditional surveys and GPS data capitalizes on the strengths of each technique (East, Osborne, Kemp, & Woodfine, 2017). In doing so, the method can provide guidance for the local destination marketing organizations (DMO) about how best to bundle their products to meet the observed needs of different types of tourists and how best to market these products to each segment (Snepenger, Snepenger, Dalbey, & Wessol, 2007; Weidenfeld, Butler, & Williams, 2010). Such an information is especially important for historic villages whose product mix often includes a range of dining, handicraft shops, small, trendy retail outlets, and other experiences that reflect the desired heritage ambience associated with the village (Frost, 2006; Huh & Uysal, 2004). Many of these places seem to rely solely on their historic character as their key selling point at the risk of ignoring other assets the community many have that appeal to different segments, with each looking for a somewhat different experience and each behaving in a somewhat different manner (Carson & Schmallegger, 2010; Donaire & Gali, 2008; Park & Yoon, 2009).

The failure to understand how different tourists consume places may result in a generic market positioning strategy that may appeal primarily to one segment while leaving others confused about what is on offer. This exploratory study seeks to address the question of how different tourist segments consume a small historic village through the combination of a paper-based survey to segment the markets and GIS analysis to track tourists. It further seeks to determine if such a mixed method approach can provide additional insights into tourist behaviour than the use of either alone. The study locale is the historic village of Richmond, Tasmania. It was founded in the 1820s and today is a popular day trip destination, attracting about one-fifth of all interstate and overseas tourists to the State (Balon, 2012). The three concepts of tourist space form the conceptual foundation for the paper.

Three types of "space" that influence tourist behaviour

Tourist behaviour involves movements through time and space. Time is arguably the most critical issue for it cannot be saved, only spent. But, conceptually time is an absolute concept. Space, on the other hand, has many dimensions. The United Nations World Tourism Organization (UNWTO 2004) defines local destinations as physical spaces offering tourism products, support services, attractions, and tourism resources that have physical and administrative boundaries defining their management, images, and perceptions. Building on this theme, Donaire and Gali (2008) suggest destinations involve three types of space: geographic space, mental space and social space. Tourist behaviour cannot be understood fully without considering the intersection of these three.

From a geographic perspective, geomorphology, the shape of the destination and the presence of hills, waterways and other landforms, along with the spatial distribution of attraction nodes and the road network linking them influence behaviour (Lew & McKercher, 2006). Wall (1996), for example, suggests that attractions can be grouped into three broad categories of points, lines, and areas. Points represent an individual, isolated attractions that have sufficient drawing power to pull tourists. Lines represent the linear routes that join sets of attractions, while areas represent concentrations of attractions that create nodes. Lines and areas usually have sufficient breadth of offerings to create tourism space, while some points may also have such appeal (Weidenfeld et al., 2010). However, isolated points will struggle to generate visitation unless the compulsion to visit is extremely high (Leiper, 1990; McKercher & Ho, 2006).

Mental space is signified by a series of markers that create an appealing destination image (Timothy & Boyd, 2006), motivate visitation (Leiper, 1990), signal it as a place worth seeing (MacCannell, 2001) and even signal how such places are to be consumed (Culler, 1988). McKercher, Wang, and Park (2015)

develop this idea further by suggesting that destinations consist of three types of semiotic space: tourist space that is signalled clearly for tourism use; shared space that both tourists and locals can use, and; non-tourism space that is signalled and signposted as places where tourists are not welcome. Tourism space in heritage communities may be signalled by the combination of an attractive streetscape along with shops, retail outlets and restaurants act as markers for historic villages that signify an authentic heritage place offering a variety of experiences (Frost, 2006). Here, the streetscape creates the ambience while a range of contemporary retail activities that evoke a sense of connection to its heritage atmosphere provide the tangible product to be consumed. Tourists may have to transit through non-tourism space to visit tourism and shared space.

Social space is signified by the behaviour of fellow tourists. Independent tourists like to believe their movements are guided by free will. In practice, though, they are guided consciously or unconsciously by a whole series of socially constructed itineraries, whereby behaviour patterns seem to be conditioned by fairly precise, yet unstated rules (Donaire & Gali, 2008). Indeed, Andreu, Kozak, Avci, and Cifter (2005) call this pattern the herding effect. This pattern may be a function of a number of inter-related factors. Time availability and the desire to spend time in the most efficient manner is one consideration, especially for those on limited time budgets (Shoval & Raveh, 2004). Becken and Wilson (2007) add further that the choice to deviate from known paths involves the necessary trade-off of time spent at other, perhaps less appealing objectives.

Together, the combination of geographic, mental and social space influences how tourists behave in a destination. While each may be assessed individually, in reality, they are closely linked, whereby one type of space influences or is influenced by the other types of space. For example, the perception of a site being geographically isolated may have as much to do with the lack of markers that signify it as appealing mental space and lack of other tourists that signify it as unappealing social space, even if it is quite proximate to other sites. Likewise, Wall's (1996) idea of lines that link attractions is similar to the need to transit through non-tourism mental space. Social space is influenced by both the geographic layout of a destination and the markers associated with it. It is for this reason that analyzing movements through time and space can identify discrete patterns and relationships (Miller, 2008) and can reveal the combined impact of these three dimensions.

Method

The purpose of the study is to see how different types of tourist behave in an historic village. A mixed methods approach was deemed most appropriate, through the use of a GPS tracking system to document movements, accompanied by a paper-based survey to segment the tourist population. Data were collected as part of a larger study investigating the movements of fully independent pleasure tourists (FITs) in the State of Tasmania, Australia. FITs are a highly significant market segment in Tasmania; the long-running Tasmanian Visitor Survey determined that between October 2017 and September 2018, only 10% of the 1.3 million visitors to the state were *not* free independent travellers and travelled through the state on an organized tour. Collection occurred in the first half of 2016 using a bespoke smartphone app with Global Navigation Satellite Systems (GNSS) networks that was loaded onto a Samsung Galaxy S3 smartphone and distributed to participating tourists (Hardy et al., 2016). The app contained an entry survey that sought information on the visitor's demographic profile, intended length of stay, main trip purpose and travel party composition. The entry survey included questions relating to participants' age, gender, income, groups size and structure, employment status, and previous visits to Tasmania. In addition, respondents were asked to identify a single, primary trip purpose. The trip purpose variables were the same as those used by Tourism Tasmania, in the Tasmanian Visitor Survey. Tourists' movements through their entire visit were tracked. Tracks were then synced with their demographic and travel characteristics, producing a large GNSS data set. This methodological approach and the decision behind the choice of technology, including its constraints and limitations, have been discussed in detail in Hardy et al. (2016).

A modified purposeful, convenience sampling technique was adopted. It was purposeful in that participants had to be independent tourists who were visiting Tasmania for between 4 and 14 days (3 and 13 nights). The lower bound was set to exclude short stay visitors, while the upper bound was selected to exclude the small number of extremely long stay visitors whose movements might be anomalous with those of the bulk of visitors. The sample was convenience based in that potential respondents were recruited at the State's three entry points: the Hobart and Launceston Airports and at the Devonport ferry terminal. Those who arrived by air subsequently rented a car, while those who arrived by ferry normally brought along their own transportation (car, bicycle, motorcycle, camper van, etc.). Few took public transport. A total of 472 people participated in the study. For the purpose of this study, only those tourists who visited Richmond were selected, reducing the valid sample to 136 participants who made a total of 164 trip-visits, as some tourists visited Richmond multiple times. The respondent profile is based on the sample of 136 participants, while movement patterns are analysed based on the 164 tracks.

Few differences were noted in the demographic profile, and general trip patterns of those who visited Richmond compared to those who did not. The key differences were in the travel party composition, with a clear majority of people who visited Richmond travelling as a couple, instead of travelling alone or as part of a larger group. As well, international tourists were over-represented among the Richmond sample (41% of the visitors, compared to less than 10% of the population of non-visitors). These differences translated into some significant differences in travel patterns. Those who visited Richmond were more likely to be on a multi-destination trip, where Tasmania was their main but not only Australian destination, while non-visitors to Richmond were more likely to state that Tasmania was either their only or a secondary destination.

The data points were cleaned to remove inaccurate points and points outside of the travel window. A region of 104.8 ha that covered Richmond was then created as a GIS polygon shape file. This polygon covered all tourist attractions in the town including the Richmond Bridge, churches, main streets and other significant built features. Further analysis was undertaken to determine features such as the speed between the subject point and the previous point based on Euclidean distance and the count of days since arrival date (day 1). Points were also joined in GIS software to the survey data collected at the beginning of the tracking project regarding tourist variables (i.e. reason for a visit to Tasmania). Finally, the raw data points for walking tourists were split into groups based on their reason for visiting Tasmania. These point groups were then used to create grid-based heat maps of tourist travel within Richmond. Each grid contained cells of 20 m x 20 m and within each grid, the percentage of points as a fraction of the total number of points in each group was calculated. Hot spot maps for the food, wine and art group, the history group, the wilderness and the visiting friends and relatives group were also developed.

Study locale–the historic site of Richmond, Tasmania, Australia

Richmond (see Figure 1) is one of Tasmania's most significant historic towns (Aussie Towns, 2017). The village

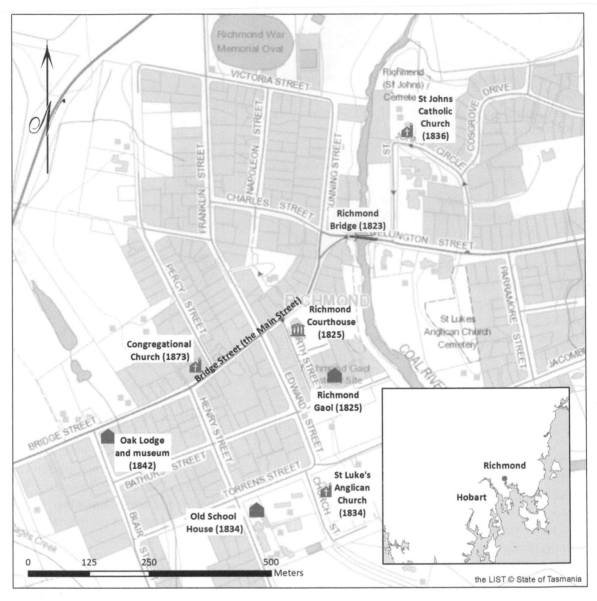

Figure 1. Richmond town located in Tasmania, Australia.

was founded in the 1820s, and is the site of Australia's oldest stone bridge (1823), oldest extant jail (1825) and the oldest still operating Catholic Church (1836) (Balon, 2012; Discover Tasmania, 2017). Its Victorian and Georgian streetscape is largely intact (Discover Tasmania, 2017). The village grew around a bridge crossing the Coal River constructed in 1823 to connect the capital, Hobart, to the eastern part of the Tasman Peninsula, home of the infamous Port Arthur prison (Shaw, n.d.). It grew quickly as an overnight waystation, police post, administrative centre, agricultural market community and convict station. By the 1860s Richmond had a population of over 1600 residents (anon, n.d.).

The future of the town changed dramatically in 1872, with the construction of the Sorell Causeway that bypassed the town and reduced the distance between Hobart and the Tasman Peninsula by some 15 km (Richmond, 2015), which in pre-automobile days meant a time saving of 3 h or more each way. The population stagnated for the next 100 years (CCC, 2003). More recently, additional road bypasses have been created to the west and east of the community, further exacerbating its isolation. Yet, its isolation, combined with strict planning regulations, has meant that rather than becoming a ghost town, Richmond has retained its feel as a quiet country town, locked in a time trap, enabling it to remain a classic example of a rural English Village, relatively untouched by modern development (Balon, 2012). Moreover, the preservation of its architecture, combined with rich agricultural land surrounding the town, has meant that there is an element of prestige associated with the village, reflected in its relatively high real estate prices.

According to its official history (CCC, 2003), the first tentative steps to attract tourists began only in the 1960s. Few services were available, until the first dedicated tourism business, a gallery selling Tasmanian arts and crafts, started in 1968. The Richmond Gaol was taken over by the National Parks and Wildlife Service in 1971, renovated and opened for visitation. At the same time, many historic buildings were renovated and converted into tourism-related retail and food businesses. By the 1980s, Richmond was firmly established as a premier tourist site. Its small size means that most people park their car and explore the town on foot (Balon, 2012). Like many other successful historic shopping communities (Frost, 2006), the village offers a wide array of shopping, eating, sightseeing and general socialising activities (Balon, 2012).

Today, Richmond is promoted primarily as an historic town. Tourism Tasmania, for example, indicates it is "a picture perfect town in the heart of the coal River valley wine region that tells the story of an early Australian colonial village. This is the perfect place to learn about Tasmania's past… (Tourism Tasmania, 2018)." Other travel websites also highlight is history (Ausemade 2018), with The Traveller (2018) website indicating "Richmond is best known for being old." The local government tourism promotion agency is the only one that attempts to position it more broadly by using the tag line "Richmond Village: history, fine wine and other temptations" (RCRVP, 2015). But even here, its home page highlights its history over other activities.

Findings

The analysis involved two stages. The first was to compare the profile and movement patterns of respondents by trip purpose. The original survey identified seven possible trip purposes. Subsequent analysis revealed these groups could be collapsed into four themed purpose categories of visiting friends and family (VFR); experiencing Tasmania's history and heritage; experiencing Tasmania's food, wine and arts; and to see natural scenery and wildlife. Using trip purpose allowed the study team to test the assumption that certain segments were interested principally in activities that satisfied their presumed specialist interests. The special interest tourists participated in only one activity related to their specialist interest (Read, 1980 as cited in Hall & Weiler, 1992) has led many destinations to create single-themed promotions that focus on specific interests while ignoring other activities or places tourists might engage in or visit. In reality, though most tourists are very active, for their travel decisions are influenced by a basket of needs (Herbert, 1996; Peters & Weiermair,

2000) that may comprise specialist and generalist needs (Dunn-Ross & Iso-Ahola's 1991; Heath & Wall, 1992) or simply generalist needs (Crompton, 1979). The result is that tourists participate in a wide array of activities when they visit a destination. The second involved analysing movements by the length of stay to enable further analysis of the depth of experience.

Profile of visitors to Richmond

No-one visits Richmond accidentally. Instead, a conscious decision must be made to deviate from the main highway, for a visit involves a 30 km detour if the person is heading south to the Tasman Peninsula and the world heritage listed Port Arthur Historic Site. A little extra distance is added if travelling between Hobart and the popular Freycinet National Park area to the north, but choosing this route entails driving along secondary and tertiary highways which adds to travel time.

Table 1 shows the profile of the sample. For the most part, few differences were noted in the trip profile of the four cohorts of visitors on such variables as average length of stay (mean 10.6 nights, with range 8.5 to 11.3 nights), however differences were not significant ($F = 1.202$, $p = .302$), and average travel party size (average 2.8 people) and no significant difference in size ($F = .734$, $p = .534$). The reader should note that the sample size for each cohort is relatively small. The small sample size is acceptable for the purposes of this study, given the vast amount of information generated by the GPS instrument and the small size of the study area. However, the results should be considered as indicative of the visitor and not necessarily as definitive.

Interestingly, the group who said they travelled to learn about history and heritage reported the lowest education levels with just over one-third holding a university degree. This figure compares to up to 70% for members of other groups. But, they were far more likely than any other group to state Tasmania was their only destination. A large majority of the heritage and food, wine and the arts cohorts indicated Tasmania was their only destination, while a majority of the people travelling to visit friends and relatives or for wilderness reasons indicated that they were visiting other areas in Australia as well. The wilderness and food, wine and arts groups comprised predominantly first-time visitors to Tasmania, while most members of the heritage and visiting friends and relatives were repeated visitors.

Movement patterns by trip purpose

Reflecting its status as a day trip destination, few tourists arrived before 10 am or after 4 pm. Instead, most

Table 1. Profile of visitors.

	VFR n = 16	History/Heritage n = 26	Food, Wine and Fine arts n = 19	Wilderness n = 75	Total n = 136
Origin					
Domestic Australia	10	19	16	54	80
International	6	7	3	21	56
Average Travel party size	2.8	2.4	2.7	2.7	2.7
Age group					
< 35	3	3	4	20	30
35 to 54	9	7	9	25	50
55 or older	4	16	5	29	54
Education					
High school or less	6	17	8	23	54
Post secondary	10	9	11	52	82
Entry point					
Hobart (air)	10	15	12	46	83
Launceston (air)	3	3	2	6	14
Devenport (ferry)	3	8	5	23	39
Mean length of stay (nights)	11.1	9.9	8.5	11.3	10.6
First or repeat visitor					
First time visitor	7	11	10	48	76
Repeat visitor	9	15	9	27	60

arrived at regular intervals between 10 am and 4 pm. Those travelling to visit friends and relatives arrived either earlier than others (before 10:30 am, 27%) or over the lunch period of 11:30 to 2 pm (46%). More than half of those whose trip purpose was food, wine or the arts arrived during the lunch hours (57%), while they were least likely to arrive early in the morning. Members of the wilderness group were more likely to arrive either before 11 am (30%) or after 3 pm (30%) than others, suggesting that Richmond represents an intermediate stop on either their outward or inward journeys of the day. Finally, more than half the history cohort arrived before noon (58.1%).

Figure 2(a–d) show the movement patterns of members of each trip purpose group, in the heat map form. All four groups follow a point and line model that is in accordance with Wall's (1996) proposition. In general, most visitors also showed evidence of Andreu et al.'s (2005) herding effect dictated by something similar to *Donaire and Galli's* (2008) unstated rules by walking from the southwest to the northeast or vice versa. This path brings them along the main street of the village (Bridge St) to a scenic photo spot where one can see Australia's oldest bridge and then continuing to St John's Cathedral. Also, popular is the downtown city block centred around the Richmond Courthouse, a bakery, art gallery and public toilet. The National trust listed Richmond Gaol is the only popular scenic spot not directly on this path. Visiting it required a deviation of only one block and takes tourists past a number of dining and retail outlets.

This pattern seems to reflect the combined impacts of geographic, mental and social space perceptions, regardless of purpose. The herding effect here may be influenced by the village's geographic spatial layout whereby most shops and restaurants are located along the main street. But evidence of herding being influenced by both markers and the behaviour of other tourists is supported by the fact that few people were interested in exploring the village more widely. In fact attractions such as St Luke's Anglican Church built in 1834, the Old School House (1834) and Oak Lodge (1831), and a heritage listed building that houses a local museum that were only 50 m to 100 m from where people concentrated their movements were seen to be too isolated to warrant a visit. Perhaps, they could "consume" these places at a distance and did not feel the need to enter. Likewise, no one followed the Richmond heritage walk and a few ventured for a pleasant walk along the river.

Those who are travelling to visit friends and relatives displayed the most concentrated movements largely staying in the core of the village, with a heavy emphasis on shopping and dining activities. The GIS hot spots correspond to a small number of local gift shops, antique stores and the bakery. Wilderness visitors are likely to walk the longest distances while in town, visiting antique shops, going for a stroll along the riverside and also visiting the built attraction of Old Hobart Town. Interestingly, while no members of the food, wine and the arts cohort stated an interest in visiting heritage places in their arrival survey, they were more likely to visit the largest number of historic sites and more out-of-the-way places than any other group. By contrast, the group of heritage tourists visited the fewest number of places and deviated rarely from the main road.

Movement patterns by the duration of the visit

Visitors who stopped in the village spent a median of about 1 h here, regardless of their trip purpose. However, as summarized in Table 2, substantial variations were noted

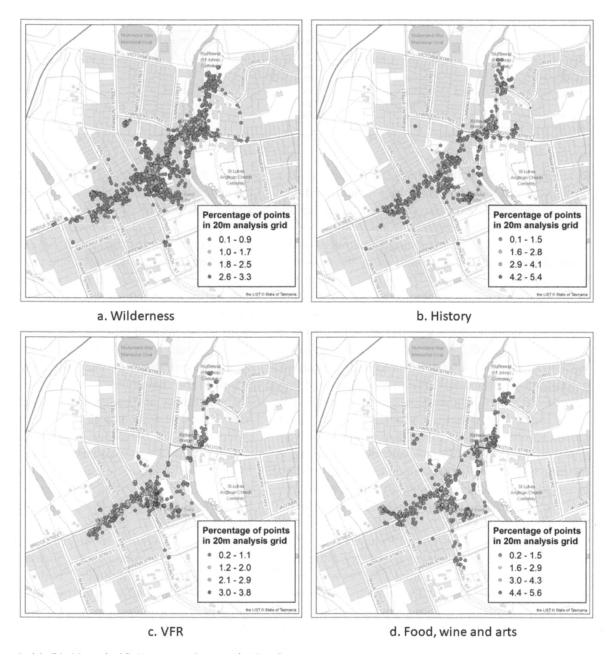

Figure 2. (a), (b), (c), and 2(d) Movement Patterns by Trip Purpose.
(Source: the LIST @ State of Tasmania for the original GIS data layers)

in the durations of stay by trip purpose. Somewhat unexpectedly, more than one-quarter of the members of the history cohort stayed for 10 min or less, with almost half staying 1 h or less. They were also the second least likely group to spend more than 2 h here. People travelling to visit friends and relatives either had a short visit of between 30 min and 1 h or had long stays of more than 2 h. The median stay of the food, wine and arts group was comparable to members of other groups. Indeed, almost two-thirds spent more than 1 h here, the largest share of any group although admittedly, their visits did correspond closely to the lunchtime period.

The GPS data were reanalysed to evaluate movement patterns by the duration of the visit. Five-time stay periods were produced depicting those who stayed 10 min or less, between 11 min and one half hour, between one half an hour and 1 h, between one and two hours and those who stayed more than 2 h (Figure 3(a–e)). While members of each time group displayed unique consumption patterns, the key delineator between what would appear to be a fairly quick experience and more prolonged experience seemed to be a visit of at least 30 min. Those who stayed less than 10 min tended to stop at one of three places: the

Table 2. Duration of Visit (among those who stopped).

	VFR (n = 16)	History/heritage (n = 26)	Food, wine and fine arts (n = 19)	Wilderness (n = 75)	All
≤ 10 minutes	12.5%	25.9%	5.0%	14.7%	15.3%
11 to 30 minutes	12.5%	11.1%	20.0%	16.2%	15.3%
31 minutes to 1 hour	31.3%	11.1%	10.0%	26.5%	21.4%
>1 hour to 2 hours	18.8%	33.3%	35.0%	32.4%	31.3%
> 2 hours	25.0%	18.5%	30.0%	10.3%	16.8%
Median stay (minutes)	99	62	59	57	59

Richmond Gaol, St John's Catholic Church or at a shop on the way into town that specializes in taking old time dress-up portraits. Secondary stops included historic buildings such as the Old Court House and the former Congregational Church. Interestingly, members of this group did not stop at the parking lot by the Richmond Bridge and instead drove by. Those who stayed for up to one half an hour again tended to do one of three things. Either they parked their cars at the parking lot near the Richmond Bridge and stayed there; parked in the centre of the village and went for a short walk or stopped at the shop that specialized in period photography. Unlike the shortest staying group, thought they did not visit either Richmond Gaol or St John's Church.

The movement patterns of members of the three groups who spent more than 30 min were somewhat similar, for in all cases they followed a linear route along the main street. Those who spent up to 1 h had the most restricted movements, not visiting attractions at the western end of the village and also rarely deviating from the main street, and therefore, missing the Richmond Gaol which is often considered one of Richmond's two icon attractions. They also stopped at the bakery, rather than stopping at a formal restaurant. Those who spent between one and two hours seemed to consume Richmond more deeply than any other group, including those who stayed longer than 2 h. Members of this group travelled widely throughout the village and made a number of stops at shops and restaurants. They also were most likely to take the scenic river walk and also visit St Luke's Anglican Church at the southern end of the village. The reason why most tourists spent more than 2 h here can be attributed to their tendency to devote a lot of time to visiting the Richmond Gaol and, most significantly, to visit the built attraction of Old Hobart Town, a model village depicting Hobart as it was in 1820, at the western entry to the village.

Discussion and conclusions

This paper makes a number of contributions to tourism methods and practice. It applied a mixed method approach of combining traditional visitor surveys with a bespoke tourist tracking application to analyze the movement patterns of different groups of tourists who visited a historic site. The unique integration of GPS and survey-based technology proved to be a highly efficient and accurate means by which to collect the fine-grained movement of tourists. Importantly, the purpose of the study was to gain insights into the behaviours of different types of tourist which could not be gathered by GPS or surveys alone. Survey data allowed respondents to be grouped into discrete segments, while GPS data permitted analysis of movements in two ways, by stated trip purpose and more generically by the length of visit in the community.

Operationally and conceptually, the study illustrates how Richmond embodies all three types of space that influence tourist behaviour. From a geographic perspective, it can be considered as a linear space defined by the main street, with specific highlight nodes that encourage people to stop. These nodes largely define the outer boundaries of the geographic tourist space (St Johns Catholic Church to the north and the Congregational Church to the southeast), as well as intermediate attraction nodes focused around the Richmond Gaol, the Richmond Bridge and the main shopping and dining node focused in the block dominated by the Richmond Courthouse. The unaltered historic streetscape marks the village as an aesthetically pleasing historic landscape that entices people to explore. Moreover, each of the geographic nodes is also signed and signalled semiotically as a tourism space where visitors are welcome. By the same token, tourists respect that residential areas are signalled as non-tourism space and rarely venture in them. However, this observation also meant that a number of places of interest located in non-tourism space were visited rarely. Better signage and semiotic signalling that these places are part of the product suite might encourage more visitation. Such places include St Luke's Church, the old school, Oak Lodge and built attractions on the edge of the village. Social space is signalled by the collective behaviour of other tourists, as shown in Figure 3, where regardless of the time spent in town, people generally follow the same route.

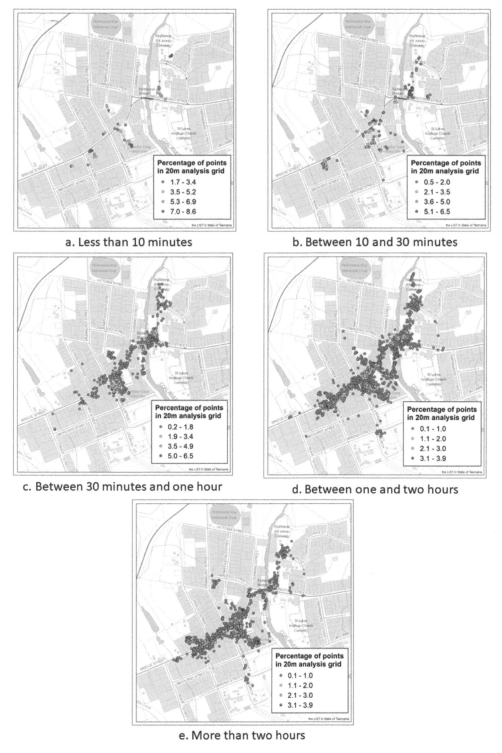

Figure 3. Movement patterns by the duration of the visit to Richmond.

Analysis by trip purpose indicated that each segment behaves somewhat differently in the community, and importantly demonstrated preferences for different bundles of attractions. Contrary to initial intuitive belief, one would have expected the heritage and VFR groups to have the strongest interaction with the village, by virtue of their stated interest in history or by benefiting from local knowledge of hosts, respectively. Yet, that was not the case. Instead, they displayed rather restricted movements. The heritage tourist, in particular, had the most fleeting experience, likely due to the fact that most visited Richmond on their way to Port Arthur. Additional time spent in this secondary attraction meant less time could be spent at the desired primary attraction for the day's trip, and so, most just captured a scenic streetscape experience and nothing deeper.

By contrast, the wilderness and food, wine, and arts groups seemed to engage the destination for longer periods of time level. In particular, the food, wine and arts group showed the greatest tendency to visit historic sites some distance from the main road. Counterintuitively, yet in hindsight logically, these individuals are more typical of classic "tourists" who are touring through the region seeking different experiences. They have more time to spend exploring interesting places and sites.

Analysis by the duration of stay also revealed some surprising results, for the findings suggest visitors who stayed between one and two hours tended to explore the community more widely than those who stayed either shorter or longer. Unsurprisingly, people on shorter stays tended to visit iconic sites conveniently located along the main road, but rarely deviated from it, while those on longer stays tended to concentrate their visits on single attractions.

These findings have a number of implications for other small historic villages. To begin, the study illustrates the potential application of GIS as a tourism marketing tool (Tussyadiah & Zach, 2012). Further, the results reveal that even though Richmond may be branded as a single product "heritage" destination, the diverse range of shopping, dining and sightseeing experiences have converted it into what Frost (2006) calls a multi-product historic shopping community that appeals to different market segments. The streetscape provides a scenic backdrop, while the shops and dining opportunities provide the primary attractions. Such focused branding may work against its best interests, for it, the historic streetscape only provides the ambience of the place while the specific shops, dining establishments and built attractions provide the product that is consumed. Promoting the place as a mixed product destination located in a heritage setting, as the local destination management organisation is attempting to do, is the way forward. The challenge is to convince other stakeholders involved in the provision of tourist information to follow suit.

The study also suggests different market segments prefer different bundles of attractions and sites in the community. While most people will visit or at least pass by the iconic sites, each segment also demonstrated some distinct preferences. The VFR segment, for example, preferred the bundle of shops and the bakery. The food, wine, and arts sector tended to eat at sit down restaurants and then explored the community widely, including more out of the way historic sites. The

wilderness group preferred a bundle of scenery, historic streetscapes and, somewhat surprisingly the built attraction of Old Hobart Town. This information suggests opportunities exist to create bundles of tours that can be delivered via different food and beverage outlets to cater for the needs of each group.

More than anything else, though, the study highlights the challenges of overcoming the three types of space in smaller destinations. Geographic space relates to the fact that many of the more appealing sites are located in a linear route, with a small node in the centre of town that encompasses the iconic attraction of the old Gaol. Mental space marks these places as being appealing, in part by the intact streetscape and also by the range of retail and food and beverage shops that complement the streetscape's ambience. But, it also marks the zone between the core and other historic other spaces as being unappealing, and therefore not warranting the short walk of even 100 m to transit through it. Social space exacerbates the issue, for the volume of tourists who follow dictates this path is the preferred route as most tourists follow it, with few deviating from it.

The study highlighted the benefits of using a mixed method approach. Traditional survey methods alone may have been able to segment the market by purpose, but could not demonstrate empirically different consumption patterns. GPS and GIS analysis could show movement patterns and perhaps differentiate use by time spent in the destination, but could not discriminate by purpose. Combined, the two formats enabled a deeper understanding of consumption of this historic village, which offered insights into both opportunities to bundle sites effectively, as well as the challenge of overcoming the combined impact of geographic, mental and social space.

Acknowledgments

The authors wish to acknowledge the support of Sense-T and the Institute for the Study of Social Change who provided funding and administrative support for this research project.

Disclosure statement

No potential conflict of interest was reported by the authors.

Funding

This work was supported by the Sense T [Sensing Tourist Tracking];

ORCID

Bob Mckercher http://orcid.org/0000-0001-7451-1266
Anne Hardy http://orcid.org/0000-0003-1461-2967

References

Andreu, L., Kozak, M., Avci, N., & Cifter, N. (2005). Market segmentation by motivations to travel. *Journal of Travel and Tourism Marketing, 19*(1), 1–14.

anon. (n.d.). *Richmond. Australian Heritage.* Retrieved from http://www.heritageaustralia.com.au/Tasmania/2649-richmond

Ausemade. (2018). *Richmond.* Retrieved from http://www.ausemade.com.au/tas/destination/r/richmond/richmond-information.htm

Aussie Towns. (2017). *Richmond, TAS. Aussie Towns.* Retrieved from http://www.aussietowns.com.au/town/richmond-tas

Balon, B. (2012). Clarence city council cultural heritage interpretation plan. Retrieved from http://www.ccc.tas.gov.au/webdata/resources/files/cultural_heritage_interpretation_plan.pdf

Becken, S., & Wilson, J. (2007). Trip planning and decision making of self drive tourists. *Journal of Travel and Tourism Marketing, 20*(3/4), 47–62.

Carson, D., & Schmallegger, D. (2010). Drive Tourism: A view from the road. In B. Prideaux & D. Carson (Eds.), *Drive tourism: Trends and emerging markets* (pp. 358–368). London: Routledge.

CCC (2003) *The Eastern shore: A history of clarence.* Retrieved from http://www.ccc.tas.gov.au/webdata/resources/files/FINALClarence_16_Richmond.pdf

Chancellor, C., & Cole, S. (2008). Using geographic information system to visualize travel patterns and market research data. *Journal of Travel & Tourism Marketing, 25*(3–4), 341–354.

Crompton, J. (1979). Motivations for Pleasure Vacation. *Annals of Tourism Research, 6*(4), 408–424.

Culler, J. (1988). The semiotics of tourism. In J. Culler (Ed.), *Framing the sign: Criticism and its institutions* (pp. 1–10). Norman: University of Oklahoma Press.

Discover Tasmania. (2017). *Richmond.* Retrieved from http://www.discovertasmania.com.au/about/regions-of-tasmania/hobart-and-south/richmond

Donaire, J., & Gali, N. (2008). Modeling tourist itineraries in heritage cities. Routes around the old district of Girona. *PASOS, 6*(3), 435–449.

Dunn-Ross, E., & Iso-Ahola, S. (1991). Sightseeing tourists' motivation and satisfaction. *Annals of Tourism Research, 18*(2), 226–237.

East, D., Osborne, P., Kemp, S., & Woodfine, T. (2017). Combining GPS & survey data improves understanding of visitor behaviour. *Tourism Management, 61*, 307–320.

Feng, R., & Morrison, A. (2002). GIS application in tourism and hospitality marketing: A case in brown country, Indiana. *Anatolia, 13*(2), 127–143.

Frost, W. (2006). From diggers to baristas: Tourist shopping villages in the victorian goldfields. *Journal of Hospitality and Tourism Management, 13*(2), 136–143.

Hall, C. M., & Weiler, B. (1992). Introduction: What's so special about special interest tourism? In B. Weiler & C. M. Hall (Eds.), *Special interest tourism* (pp. 1–14). London: Belhaven Press.

Hardy, A., Hyslop, S., Booth, K., Robards, B., Aryal, J., Gretzel, U., & Eccelston, R. (2016). Tracking tourists' travel with smartphone-based GPS technology: A methodological discussion. *Information Technology and Tourism, 17*(3), 255–274.

Heath, E., & Wall, G. (1992). *Marketing Tourism Destinations: A Strategic planning approach.* Brisbane: John Wiley.

Herbert, D. T. (1996). Artistic and literary places in france as tourist attractions. *Tourism Management, 17*(2), 77–85.

Huh, J., & Uysal, M. (2004). Satisfaction with cultural/heritage sites. *Journal of Quality Assurance in Hospitality & Tourism, 4*(3/4), 177–194.

Kramer, R., Modsching, M., Ten Hagen, K., & Gretzel, U. (2007). Behavioural impacts of mobile tour guides. In M. Sigala, L. Mich, & J. Murphy (Eds.), 53-64. *Information and communication technologies in tourism 2007.* Vienna: Springer.

Leiper, N. (1990). Tourist Attraction Systems. *Annals of Tourism Research, 17*(3), 367–384.

Lew, A., & McKercher, B. (2006). Modeling tourist movement: A local destination analysis. *Annals of Tourism Research, 33*(2), 403–423.

MacCannell, D. (2001). Tourist agency. *Tourist Studies, 1*(1), 22–37.

McKercher, B., & Ho, P. (2006). Assessing the tourism potential of smaller cultural attractions. *Journal of Sustainable Tourism, 14*(5), 473–488.

McKercher, B., Wang, D., & Park, E. (2015). Social impacts as a function of place change. *Annals of Tourism Research, 50*(52), 56.

McKercher, B., & Zoltan, J. (2014). Tourist flows and spatial behaviour. In A. A. Lew, C. M. Hall, & A. M. Willaims (Eds.), *The Wiley Blackwell Companion to Tourism* (2nd ed., pp. 34-44). West Sussex: Wiley Blackwell.

Miller, H. (2008). Time geography. In S. Shekhar & X. Hui (Eds.), *Encyclopedia of GIS* (pp. 1151–1156). Minneapolis: Springer.

Park, D., & Yoon, Y. (2009). Segmentation by Motivation in Rural Tourism: A Korean case study. *Tourism Management, 30*, 99–108.

Peters, M., & Weiermair, K. (2000). Tourist attractions and attracted tourists: How to satisfy today's 'fickle' tourist clientele? *Tourism Studies, 11*(1), 22–29.

RCRVP. (2015). *Richmond Village: History, fine wines and other temptations.* Richmond & Coal River Valley Promotions Inc. Retrieved from http://www.richmondvillage.com.au/

Richmond. (2015). *Richmond Village.* Retrieved from http://www.richmondvillage.com.au/

Shaw, R. (n.d.). *Richmond. Tasmanian Life.* Retrieved from http://www.tasmanianlife.com.au/historic-richmond/

Shoval, N., & Raveh, A. (2004). The categorization of tourist attractions: The modeling of tourist cities based on a new method of multivariate analysis. *Tourism Management, 25*(6), 741–750.

Snepenger, D., Snepenger, M., Dalbey, M., & Wessol, A. (2007). Meanings and consumption characteristics of places at a tourism destination. *Journal of Travel Research, 45*, 310–321.

Timothy, D., & Boyd, S. (2006). Heritage tourism in the 21st century: Valued traditions and new perspectives. *Journal of Heritage Tourism, 1*(1), 1–16.

Tourism Tasmania. (2018). *Richmond – Discover Tasmania.* Retrieved from https://www.discovertasmania.com.au/about/regions-of-tasmania/hobart-and-south/richmond

The Traveller. (2018). *Guide at a glance: Richmond.* Retrieved from http://www.traveller.com.au/guide-at-a-glance-richmond-254a3

Tussyadiah, L. P., & Zach, F. J. (2012). The role of geo-based technology in place experiences. *Annals of Tourism Research, 39*(2), 780–800.

United World Tourism Organization. (2004). *Indicators of sustainable development for tourism destinations: A guidebook.* Madrid:

UN World Tourism Organization. ISBN 92-844-0726-5. Retrieved from. www.world-tourism.org

Wall, G. (1996). Tourism Attractions: Points, lines and area. *Annals of Tourism Research, 24*(1), 240–243.

Weidenfeld, A., Butler, R., & Williams, A. (2010). Clustering and Comparability between Tourism Attractions. *International Journal of Tourism Research, 12*(1), 1–16.

Wu, C. L., & Carson, D. (2008). Spatial and temporal tourist dispersal analysis in multiple destination travel. *Journal of Travel Research, 46*(3), 311–317.

Xia, J. C., Evans, F. H., Spilsbury, K., Ciesielski, V., Arrowsmith, C., & Wright, G. (2010). Market segments based on the dominant movement patterns of tourists. *Tourism Management, 31*(4), 464–469.

Consequences of psychological benefits of using eco-friendly services in the context of drone food delivery services

Jinsoo Hwang, Sun-Bai Cho and Woohyoung Kim

ABSTRACT

This study examined the importance of psychological benefits of using eco-friendly services in the context of drone food delivery services. Based on the theoretical relationships between the conceptual constructs, a research model was developed and then assessed using data collected from 397 samples in Korea. The data analysis results showed that the three sub-dimensions of psychological benefits (i.e. warm glow, self-expressive benefits, and nature experiences) play an important role in the formation of positive and negative anticipated emotions. Furthermore, the positive and negative anticipated emotions had a significant influence on desire, which in turn positively affects intentions to use.

Introduction

As global warming accelerates and environmental pollution becomes increasingly severe, the need for environmental protection continues to rise (Singh & Sharma, 2018; Trenberth et al., 2014). In fact, many people around the world are committed to protecting the global environment and these efforts are reflected in their consumption culture (Han, Lee, & Kim, 2018; Yadav & Pathak, 2017). That is, consumers are willing to buy more environmentally friendly products/services and spend more money for such products/services (Liu, Yang, & Xu, 2017; Tang & Lam, 2017). In this situation, many companies naturally became interested in environmental management. They are trying to provide eco-friendly products/services to meet customers' environmental needs (Dubihlela & Ngxukumeshe, 2016; Kang & Hur, 2012).

Environmental management is also significant in the food service industry. In order to deliver food, many foodservice companies use cars or motorcycles that emit a lot of exhaust gas. Such delivery service methods are considered to be the main cause of environmental pollution (Cherry, Weinert, & Xinmiao, 2009). As a means of solving these problems, drone food delivery services are currently attracting attention in the food service industry. Drone food delivery services refer to the use of drones to deliver food to the customer's desired location. Currently, drones are being commercialized in some areas. For instance, in New Zealand,

Domino's Pizza has been approved by the New Zealand government to deliver food using drones after a successful test of drone food delivery services (CNBC, 2016). When compared with current methods of delivery services, such as cars or motorcycles, drone food delivery services are operated by electricity, so the services play a critical role in protecting the environment (Environmental Technology, 2018).

More importantly, eco-friendly services, such as drone food delivery services, play an important role in giving psychological benefits to their customers (Hartmann & Apaolaza-Ibáñez, 2008, 2012). Psychological benefits can be defined as "feelings of trust or confidence in the other party that result in greater peace of mind" (Sweeney & Webb, 2007, p. 476). That is, psychological benefits make people more comfortable and at ease (Gwinner, Gremler, & Bitner, 1998). Thus, if customers use drone food delivery services which help protect the environment, they are more likely to feel high levels of psychological benefits. In particular, the psychological benefits of eco-friendly services aid to increase an overall image of the brand (Hartmann & Apaolaza-Ibáñez, 2012), so it is necessary to identify the psychological benefits of using eco-friendly services in the context of drone food delivery services.

Despite the importance of the psychological benefits of using eco-friendly services, no research has investigated its role in the food service industry. Thus, to fill this gap, the purpose of this research was to examine the significance of the psychological benefits of using eco-friendly services in the context of drone food delivery services. To be more specific, this study investigated (1) the influence of the psychological benefits of using eco-friendly services on anticipated emotions when using drone food delivery services, (2) the effects of the anticipated emotions on desires to use drone food delivery services, and (3) the relationship between the desires and intentions to use drone food delivery services.

Literature review

In the literature review section, we tried to explain each concept in the proposed model and then showed how to develop the hypotheses after introducing the drones.

What are drone food delivery services?

Drones are a key industry in the fourth industrial revolution because they are useful in various fields. For instance, drones are used for spraying pesticides in agriculture. This improves crop productivity, because using drones saves time. Also, drones spray pesticides in places that are inaccessible for tractors (BBC, 2018). In addition, drones are also used for climate observation by collecting information about air quality and monitoring wildlife population (Green Matters, 2018). Due to the high utilization of these drones, the Korean government is working hard to foster the drone industry. The Korean government aims to raise the current market size of drones by about 60 times by 2026 (Dong-A Daily News, 2017). In addition the government plans to provide support by creating about 164,000 drones-related jobs by 2026 (NEWSIS, 2017).

Drones are expected to play an important role in the food service industry. For example, the use of drones has the advantage of delivering food to customers quickly, regardless of traffic jams. In fact, many food service companies are putting in a lot of effort to commercialize drone food delivery services. Yogiyo, one of the largest food delivery companies in Korea, has successfully completed a food delivery test using drones (Digital Daily, 2016). In addition, Flytrex, which is a drone delivery service company, provides drone food delivery services to golfers in North Dakota, USA (USA Today, 2018). Recently, the eco-friendly role of drone food delivery services has attracted attention. As previously described, food service companies currently use motorcycles or automobiles in order to deliver food. These types of delivery methods fume out exhaust gas, which leads to environmental pollution (Cherry et al., 2009). On the other hand, drones are significant from an environmental standpoint because they run on batteries that are charged with electricity. Empirical research also supported that drone food delivery services help protect the environment. For instance, Park, Kim, and Suh (2018) suggested that drone-based delivery services can reduce the global warming potential (GWP) rather than using motorcycle delivery. In addition, Stolaroff et al. (2018) also argued that drone delivery can reduce greenhouse gas emissions, which helps protect the environment.

Psychological benefits of using eco-friendly services

The concept of psychological benefits of using eco-friendly services originated from psychological benefits, which means spiritual comfort that consumers receive after using a certain product or service (Gwinner et al., 1998). Recently, the concept has been applied in green consumer behavior as people are voluntarily participating in environmental protection by using eco-friendly products or services (Han, Kim, & Lee, 2018; Trang, Lee, & Han, 2019). That is, consumers are comforted by the fact that they are protecting the natural environment by using eco-friendly products/services (Hartmann & Apaolaza-Ibáñez, 2008). For example, Hartmann and Apaolaza-Ibáñez (2012) suggested that consumers receive psychological benefits when using green energy brands (e.g. wind turbines and solar power plants) because they think that they take part in environmental protection by using such brands. Hwang and Choi (2018) also showed that passengers perceive high levels of psychological benefits when they take an environmentally friendly airline.

Empirical research has consistently proposed that psychological benefits of using eco-friendly services are composed of the following three sub-dimensions: (1) warm glow, (2) self-expressive benefits, and (3) nature experiences (e.g. Hartmann & Apaolaza-Ibáñez, 2008, 2012; Hwang & Choi, 2018; Lin, Lobo, & Leckie, 2017). First, warm glow refers to "satisfaction that goes beyond the benefits derived from aggregate provision of a public good through pro-environmental behavior" (Clark, Kotchen, & Moore, 2003, p. 239). Warm glow is his/her own moral satisfaction with actions contributing to environmental protection (Andreoni, 1990; Menges, Schroeder, & Traub, 2005). The theoretical basis for the concept of warm glow is neural evidence (Harbaugh, Mayr, & Burghart, 2007), suggesting that helping others in need stimulates the brain's reward center. Thus, it is also known as intrinsic satisfaction (De Young, 1996). That is, people think that they are rewarding themselves for their environmentally friendly behavior. In addition, the degree of warm glow depends on social responsibility (Brekke, Kverndokk, & Nyborg, 2003). For instance, if people think that social responsibility is important, they are more likely to have high levels of warm glow, while those who have no social responsibility are not interested in having warm glow.

The second component of psychological benefits of using eco-friendly services is self-expressive benefits. Self-expressive benefits can be defined as the benefits that consumers receive from themselves in an effort to signal concerns about environmental problems (Hartmann & Apaolaza-Ibáñez, 2009; Hwang & Choi, 2018). Signaling theory provides a theoretical background for the concept of self-expressive benefits. According to signaling theory, signaling is an important way to express personal tendency, such as likes and dislikes toward an object or phenomena (Aaker, 1999, 2012, Glazer & Konrad, 1996). This phenomenon can also be found in green consumer behavior. For example, people hope to express their environmental concern, so they are more likely to purchase eco-friendly products/services. More importantly such an effort makes them feel a high level of self-expressive benefits (Hartmann & Ibáñez, 2006). Hu (2012) also suggested when consumers try to buy eco-friendly products/services in order to convey information that they protect the environment, they are more likely to have a high level of self-expressive benefits.

Lastly, the concept of nature experiences is one of the most important psychological benefits of using eco-friendly services. It is widely known that nature experiences play a critical role in the enhancement of well-being perception, so people hope to spend time in a natural setting, such as in a forest, by a lake or next to a river stay where they can relax and recover from stress (Leather, Pyrgas, Beale, & Lawrence, 1998; Lee & Moscardo, 2005; Maller, Townsend, Pryor, Brown, & St Leger, 2006). In addition, nature experiences are deemed the basis for environmental awareness which helps form pro-environmental consumer behavior (Finger, 1994; Hartmann & Apaolaza-Ibáñez, 2008). That is, when people with high levels of nature experiences are more likely to have an awareness of protecting nature, they tend to purchase eco-friendly products/services. For this reason, many companies put beautiful natural landscapes in their advertisements, which encourage consumers to buy eco-friendly products/services (Bögeholz, 2006; Hartmann & Apaolaza-Ibáñez, 2012).

Effect of psychological benefits of using eco-friendly services on anticipated emotions

Next, this study proposed the effect of psychological benefits of using eco-friendly services on anticipated emotions. According to the model of goal-directed behavior (MGB), humans tend to have favorable or unfavorable emotions before taking any action in an uncertain situation and these prospect-based emotions are known as anticipated emotions (Perugini & Bagozzi, 2001, 2004). That is, anticipated emotions refer to a person's expected post-behavioral affective responses including positive or negative emotions (Perugini & Bagozzi, 2001). Thus, when consumers have positive anticipated emotions toward a certain service, they are more likely to use the service. On the other hand, if consumers have negative anticipated emotions toward a particular service, they will have low levels of intentions to use.

More importantly, environmental psychology has suggested that psychological benefits aid to form emotional responses, because consumers tend to have favorable emotions when they use products that can express their beliefs or values (Hu, 2012; Ulrich, 1981). Hartmann and Apaolaza-Ibáñez (2008) also suggested that when consumers get spiritual comfort through the consumption of environmentally friendly products, they have positive feelings toward the products. Empirical studies also supported the relationship between psychological benefits and anticipated emotions. Bögeholz (2006) argued that nature experiences aid to enhance evaluative aspects, such as attitudes. In addition, Hartmann and Apaolaza-Ibáñez (2009) developed a research model in order to identify the relationship between nature experiences and brand attitude using green advertisement. The results indicated that nature experiences play a critical role in the formation of brand attitude. Hartmann and Apaolaza-Ibáñez (2012) showed that when consumers have psychological benefits, such as nature experiences after using green-branded energy, they are more likely to have a favorable attitude toward the brand. Ahmad and Thyagaraj (2015) also suggested that self-expressive benefits positively affects attitude toward purchasing a green brand. More recently, Hwang and Choi (2018) found that if passengers have psychological benefits including warm glow, self-expressive benefits, and nature experiences when taking an environmentally friendly airline, they tend to have a good image of the airline. Thus, it can be inferred that if using environmentally friendly services, such as drone food delivery services, gives mental well-being to consumers, they are more likely to have positive anticipated emotions. Conversely, if consumers do not receive mental benefits because they think that drone food delivery services do not help the natural environment, they will have a bad feeling about the services. Based on the theoretical and empirical backgrounds, the following hypotheses were proposed.

Hypothesis 1a: Warm glow has a positive influence on positive anticipated emotion.

Hypothesis 1b: Warm glow has a negative influence on negative anticipated emotion.

Hypothesis 2a: Self-expressive benefits have a positive influence on positive anticipated emotion.

Hypothesis 2b: Self-expressive benefits have a negative influence on negative anticipated emotion.

Hypothesis 3a: Nature experiences have a positive influence on positive anticipated emotion.

Hypothesis 3b: Nature experiences have a negative influence on negative anticipated emotion.

Effect of anticipated emotions on desire and intentions to use

Desire has been widely used in order to understand consumer behavior in the hospitality and tourism industry since its introduction through the MGB. The concept of desire is defined as "a state of mind whereby an agent has a personal motivation to perform an action or to achieve a goal" (Perugini & Bagozzi, 2004, p. 71). Desire is a state in which humans are eager to take a certain action through internal stimulation (achievement, curiosity, shortage, etc.) (Han & Yoon, 2015; Perugini & Bagozzi, 2004). One of the important causes of the formation of desire is individuals' previous experiences (Leone, Perugini, & Ercolani, 2004). Thus, if consumers have a good feeling toward a certain product or service, they will have a high level of desire, and conversely when they have a bad feeling with the product or service, their desire will be low. Previous studies also have supported the relationship between anticipated emotions and desire. For instance, Han, Lee, and Hwang (2016) examined the role of anticipated emotions in the cruise industry using data from 350 passengers. The results of the structural equation modeling (SEM) analysis revealed that positive and negative anticipated emotions play an important role in the formation of desire. Piçarra and Giger (2018) tested the relationship between anticipated emotions and desire using 271 respondents and suggested that positive and negative anticipated emotions help form desire. Based on the above discussion, the following hypotheses are proposed:

Hypothesis 4: Positive anticipated emotion has a positive influence on desire.

Hypothesis 5: Negative anticipated emotion has a negative influence on desire.

In addition, intentions to use refer to "the degree to which a person has formulated conscious plans to perform or not perform some specified future behavior" (Warshaw & Davis, 1985, p. 214). It is widely accepted that consumers have intentions whether or not to use a certain product/ service after evaluating the product/service (Hwang & Lee, 2018; Hwang & Park, 2018). For instance, intentions to use a certain product/service are created after a favorable assessment of the product/service. Thus, intentions to use are directly related to actual consumption (Colgate & Lang, 2001; Han & Yoon, 2015). In addition, according to the MGB model, individuals' prospect-based emotions are key factors in forming behavioral intentions (Perugini & Bagozzi, 2001, 2004), suggesting that anticipated emotions can be a critical predictor of intentions to use. Prior studies also have confirmed the effect of anticipated emotions on intentions to use. For example, Han, Hwang, Kim, and Jung (2015) examined how anticipated emotions influence pro-environmental intention to revisit using 401 customers in the hotel industry. They suggested that positive and negative anticipated emotions significantly affect pro-environmental intention to revisit. Meng and Choi (2016) analyzed data collected from 387 tourists and found anticipated emotions including positive and negative anticipated emotions to be significant factors influencing intentions. Thus, it the following hypotheses can be proposed.

Hypothesis 6: Positive anticipated emotion has a positive influence on intentions to use.

Hypothesis 7: Negative anticipated emotion has a negative influence on intentions to use.

Effect of desire on intentions to use

According to the MGB, individuals take a certain action when they have a desire to engage in the action (Perugini & Bagozzi, 2001). In addition, the attention, interest, desire, and actions model (AIDA) suggested that desire is an important predictor of intentions to use. Empirical studies have also showed the positive relationship between desire and intentions to use. For example, Song, Lee, Reisinger, and Xu (2017) developed a research model to explain the effect of desire on behavioral intention in the tourism industry. They conducted the SEM analysis based on data collected from 648 tourists and suggested that desire plays a critical role in the formation of behavioral intention. Lee, Song, Lee, and Petrick (2018) examined how desire affects behavioral intentions using 529 tourists. They found that when tourists have high levels of desire to travel to Korea, they are more likely to have an intention to travel to Korea in the near future. In addition, Han, Meng, and Kim (2017) investigated the relationship between desire and loyalty using 394 respondents in the context of bicycle tourism. The results of the data analysis showed that when people's desire for bike-traveling is strong, they have high levels of intentions to travel by bike. Thus, it can be hypothesized that desire positively affects intentions to use.

Hypothesis 8: Desire has a positive influence on intentions to use.

Proposed model

Integrating the theoretical and empirical backgrounds, this study proposed a conceptual model with 11 theoretical concepts (see Figure 1).

Methodology

Measures

Validated measurement items were adapted from existing research and modified to fit the context of drone food deliver services. More specifically, psychological benefits of using eco-friendly services included three sub-dimensions, such as warm glow, self-expressive benefits, and nature experiences and were measured with nine items cited from Hartmann and Apaolaza-Ibáñez (2012) and Hwang and Choi (2018). Anticipated emotions consists of two sub-dimensions, positive and negative anticipated emotions, and were measured with six items adapted from

Perugini and Bagozzi (2001, 2004). Desire was measured with three items developed by Perugini and Bagozzi (2001, 2004). Intentions to use were measured with three items cited from Hwang and Lyu (2018) and Zeithaml, Berry, and Parasuraman (1996). All measurement items were measured using a seven-point Likert-type, ranging from 1 (strongly disagree) to 7 (strongly agree). The initial questionnaire was developed based on the measurement items in English. However, it was translated into Korean for data collection using the blind translation-back-translation method. And then the following two groups of experts carefully reviewed the questionnaire: (1) three faculty members with a primary research interest in the restaurant industry and (2) drone experts who hold a remote pilot certificate.

After confirming that the initial questionnaire was not problematic from the expert group, a pretest was conducted in order to check the reliability of the measurement items using 50 actual restaurant patrons through online surveys in Korea. A two-minute newspaper article was provided to respondents in order to make them clearly understand about the important role of drone food delivery services in protecting the environment before beginning the survey. The newspaper article was based on Stolaroff et al.'s paper (2018) that showed using drones instead of cars that depend on fossil fuels, such as gasoline, can reduce greenhouse gas emissions. Consequently, Cronbach's alpha values for the seven constructs used in this study were greater than 70, suggesting high levels of reliability (Nunnally, 1978).

Data collection

In Korea, the main survey was performed using an online survey from a market research firm, because the firm has

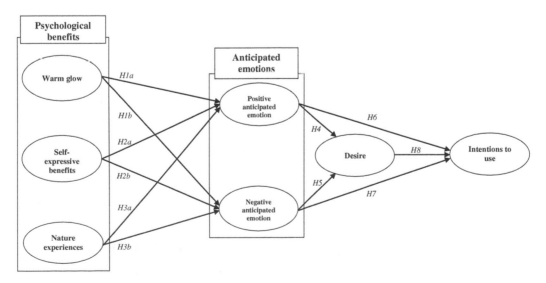

Figure 1. Proposed conceptual model.

the largest number of panels as a representative survey company in Korea. Before starting the survey, the following screening question was given to respondents:

"Have you used food delivery services within six months?"

If the respondents answered no, the survey ended. Using the same method as the pretest, a two-minute newspaper article involving the important role of drone food delivery services regarding protecting the environment was provided to respondents at the beginning of the survey. The company sent an invitation email to 4,524 people to participate in the survey. Although a total of 442 respondents answered the questionnaire, 45 of them were excluded because of multicollinearity problems and visual inspection. Consequently, 397 cases were used for statistical analysis.

Data analysis

Profile of survey respondents

Table 1 shows the profile of survey respondents. The 397 respondents included 195 males (49.1%) and 202 females (50.9%). The average age of respondents was 37.91 years. In terms of the respondents' monthly household income, most respondents answered that their income was between 1,001\$ US and 2,000\$ US and 2,001\$ US and 3,000\$ US (n = 109, 27.5%). In addition, 50.6% (n = 201) were single, while 48.4% (n = 192) were married. With regard to the respondents' education level, 63.5% (n = 252) held a bachelor's degree.

Confirmatory factor analysis

Table 2 provides the results of a confirmatory factor analysis (CFA). The CFA was employed in order to assess the appropriateness of construct measures. The results of the CFA revealed that the measurement structure of the proposed theoretical model had a satisfactory fit to the data (χ^2 = 470.014, df = 168, χ^2/df = 2.798, p < .001, NFI = .952, CFI = .968, TLI = .960, RMSEA = .067) (Byrne, 2001). The values of all the factor loadings were greater than .812 and were all significant at the .001 level.

As presented in Table 3, all values of composite reliability exceeded the minimum threshold of .70 (Hair, Black, Babin, Anderson, & Tatham, 2006), indicating that the measurement items used in this study had a high level of internal consistency. In addition, convergent validity was confirmed as average variance extracted (AVE) values were greater than .50 (Fornell & Larcker, 1981). Lastly, the values of AVE were higher than the squared correlations between constructs, which suggested high levels of discriminant validity.

Table 1. Profile of survey respondents (n = 397).

Variable	n	Percentage
Gender		
Male	195	49.1
Female	202	50.9
Monthly household income		
6,001\$ US and over	22	5.5
5,001\$ US –6,000\$ US	13	3.3
4,001\$ US –5,000\$ US	36	9.1
3,001\$ US –4,000\$ US	49	12.3
2,001\$ US –3,000\$ US	109	27.5
1,001\$ US –2,000\$ US	109	27.5
Under 1,000\$ US	59	14.9
Marital status		
Single	201	50.6
Married	192	48.4
Widowed/Divorced	4	1.0
Education level		
Less than High school diploma	48	12.1
Associate's degree	65	16.4
Bachelor's degree	252	63.5
Graduate degree	32	8.1
Mean age = 37.91 years old		

Structural equation modeling

The SEM analysis was performed in order to check the 11 hypotheses. The structural model had a satisfactory fit to the data (χ^2 = 538.712, df = 175, χ^2/df = 3.078, p < .001, NFI = .945, CFI = .962, TLI = .954, RMSEA = .072) (Byrne, 2001). The SEM analysis results showed all hypotheses were statistically supported at p < .05. More specifically, warm glow (β = .595, p < .05), self-expressive benefits (β = .150, p < .05), and nature experiences (β = .183, p < .05) had a positive influence on positive anticipated emotion. Hence, hypotheses 1a, 2a, and 3a were supported. In the case of the relationship between psychological benefits of using eco-friendly services and negative anticipated emotions, warm glow (β = −.182, p < .05), self-expressive benefits (β = −.153, p < .05), and nature experiences (β = −.276, p < .05) negatively affected negative anticipated emotion, which supports Hypotheses 1b, 2b, and 3b. Our results indicated that positive anticipated emotion (β = .735, p < .05) and negative anticipated emotion (β = −.111, p < .05) help form desire. Thus, hypotheses 4 and 5 were supported. In addition, positive anticipated emotion (β = .197, p < .05) and negative anticipated emotion (β = −.098, p < .05) played an important role in the formation of intentions to use. Hence, hypotheses 6 and 7 were supported. Lastly, desire had a positive influence on intentions to use (β = .590, p < .05), which supports Hypothesis 8. The results of SEM analysis are summarized in Table 4 and Figure 2.

Discussion and implications

The objective of this paper was to examine the significant role of psychological benefits of using eco-friendly services

Table 2. Confirmatory factor analysis: Items and loadings.

Construct and scale items	Standardized Loading[a]
Psychological benefits	
Warm glow	
With drone food delivery services, I can feel good because the services help to protect the environment.	.843
With drone food delivery services, I have the feeling of contributing to the well-being of humanity and nature.	.873
With drone food delivery services, I can feel better because the services don't harm the environment.	.937
Self-expressive benefits	
With drone food delivery services, I can express my environmental concern.	.879
With drone food delivery services, I can demonstrate to myself and my friends that I care about environmental conservation.	.952
With drone food delivery services, my friends would perceive me to be concerned about the environment.	.891
Nature experiences	
Drone food delivery services can make me feel close to nature.	.890
Drone food delivery services can make me think of nature, fields, forests and mountains.	.925
Drone food delivery services can evoke the sensation of being in nature.	.937
Anticipated emotions	
Positive anticipated emotion	
If I use environmentally friendly services, such as drone food delivery services, I will feel…	
Excited	.860
Delighted	.914
Happy	.904
Negative anticipated emotion	
If I use environmentally friendly services, such as drone food delivery services, I will feel…	
Disappointed	.812
Depressed	.935
Uncomfortable	.938
Desires	
I desire to use drone food delivery services when ordering food.	.938
My desire of using drone food delivery services when ordering food is strong.	.961
I want to use drone food delivery services when ordering food.	.971
Intentions to use	
I will use drone food delivery services when ordering food.	.941
I am willing to use drone food delivery services when ordering food.	.947
I am likely to use drone food delivery services when ordering food.	.949

Goodness-of-fit statistics: $\chi^2 = 470.014$, df = 168, χ^2/df = 2.798, $p < .001$, NFI = .952, CFI = .968, TLI = .960, RMSEA = .067

[a]All factors loadings are significant at $p < .001$
NFI = Normed Fit Index, CFI = Comparative Fit Index, TLI = Tucker-Lewis Index, RMSEA = Root Mean Square Error of Approximation

in the context of drone food delivery services. To be specific, based on the existing theoretical background, it was hypothesized that three sub-dimensions of psychological benefits of using eco-friendly services (i.e. warm glow, self-expressive benefits, and nature experiences) have a positive influence on anticipated emotions including positive and negative anticipated emotions. In addition, it was proposed that the anticipated emotions positively affect intentions to use. Based on the proposed theoretical relationships, a conceptual model was created and

assessed using empirical data collected from 397 respondents in Korea. The data analysis results have the following important theoretical and managerial implications.

Theoretical implications

First, the results of the data analysis showed that warm glow was found to have an important impact on both positive and negative anticipated emotions (hypotheses 1a and 1b). These findings are similar with previous studies (e.g. Hartmann & Apaolaza-Ibáñez, 2009; Hwang & Choi, 2018), suggesting the effect of warm glow on its outcome variables, such as attitude and image. The results of this study also indicated that warm glow significantly affects anticipated emotions. In this regard, this study confirmed and expanded the existing theoretical background by finding the significant effect of warm glow on positive and negative anticipated emotions in the context of drone food delivery services. These results can be interpreted to indicate that when consumers feel good because drone food delivery services don't harm the environment, they are more likely to have positive anticipated emotions. On the other hand, if consumers feel worse because drone food delivery services do not help to protect the environment, they would have negative anticipated emotions.

Second, the data analysis results revealed self-expressive benefits have a significant effect on positive and negative anticipated emotions (hypotheses 2a and 2b). That is, when consumers can/cannot express their environmental concern with drone food delivery services, they have a good/bad feeling about using the services. Prior studies have also confirmed the significance of self-expressive benefits in various industries, indicating that self-expressive benefits play an important role in explaining consumer behavior (e.g. Hartmann & Apaolaza-Ibáñez, 2012; Hwang & Choi, 2018). Unlike previous studies, this study found that self-expressive benefits are a critical factor affecting anticipated emotions in the context of drone food delivery services for the first time, which is an important theoretical implication of this study.

Third, nature experiences play an important role in the formation of positive and negative anticipated emotions (hypotheses 3a and 3b). These results highlight the significance of nature experiences, which has been consistently studied by prior research in diverse fields (e.g. Hartmann & Apaolaza-Ibáñez, 2009; Hwang & Choi, 2018; Kaplan, 1995). They argued that when eco-friendly products/services can make customers feel close to nature, they are more likely to have a favorable attitude or image on the products/services. In this respect, the results of this study verified the findings of existing research by empirically identifying

Table 3. Descriptive statistics and associated measures.

	No. of Items	Mean (SD)	AVE	(1)	(2)	(3)	(4)	(5)	(6)	(7)
(1) Warm glow	3	4.84 (1.19)	.784	**.916**[a]	.675[b]	.477	.764	−.425	.767	.678
(2) Self-expressive benefits	3	4.18 (1.25)	.824	.456[c]	**.934**	.532	.648	−.423	.596	.529
(3) Nature experiences	3	4.02 (1.31)	.842	.228	.283	**.941**	.517	−.444	.503	.464
(4) Positive anticipated emotion	3	4.45 (1.13)	.797	.584	.420	.267	**.922**	−.313	.745	.663
(5) Negative anticipated emotion	3	2.74 (1.26)	.804	.181	.179	.197	.098	**.925**	−.350	−.370
(6) Desire	3	4.42 (1.34)	.915	.588	.355	.253	.555	.123	**.970**	.780
(7) Willingness to pay more	3	4.49 (1.31)	.894	.460	.280	.215	.440	.137	.608	**.962**

SD = Standard Deviation, AVE = Average Variance Extracted
a. Composite reliabilities are along the diagonal, b. Correlations are above the diagonal, c. Squared correlations are below the diagonal

Table 4. Standardized parameter estimates for structural model.

			Standardized Estimate	t-value	Hypothesis
H1a Warm glow	→	Positive anticipated emotion	.595	11.078*	Supported
H2a Self-expressive benefits	→	Positive anticipated emotion	.150	3.500*	Supported
H3a Nature experiences	→	Positive anticipated emotion	.183	3.560*	Supported
H1b Warm glow	→	Negative anticipated emotion	−.182	−2.695*	Supported
H2b Self-expressive benefits	→	Negative anticipated emotion	−.153	−.2.184*	Supported
H3b Nature experiences	→	Negative anticipated emotion	−.276	−4.785*	Supported
H4 Positive anticipated emotion	→	Desire	.735	16.915*	Supported
H5 Negative anticipated emotion	→	Desire	−.111	−2.955*	Supported
H6 Positive anticipated emotion	→	Intentions to use	.197	3.419*	Supported
H7 Negative anticipated emotion	→	Intentions to use	.-.098	−2.704*	Supported
H8 Desire	→	Intentions to use	.590	10.161*	Supported

Goodness-of-fit statistics: χ^2 = 538.712, df = 175, χ^2/df = 3.078, p < .001, NFI = .945, CFI = .962, TLI = .954, RMSEA = .072

*p < .05
NFI = Normed Fit Index, CFI = Comparative Fit Index, TLI = Tucker-Lewis Index, RMSEA = Root Mean Square Error of Approximation

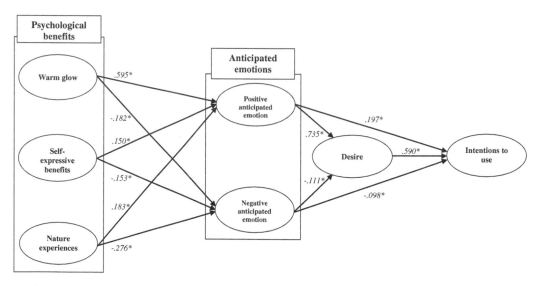

Figure 2. Standardized theoretical path coefficients.

the influence of nature experiences on anticipated emotions in the context of drone food delivery services.

Lastly, another significant finding of this study was the important role of anticipated emotions in the context of drone food delivery services. More specifically, the results of the data analysis indicated that positive and negative anticipated emotions were found to exert a significant impact on desire (hypotheses 4 and 5). That is, when consumers have a good/bad feeling

toward using drone food delivery services, their desire is strong/weak. In addition, this study found that positive and negative anticipated emotions are important predictors of intentions to use (hypotheses 6 and 7). And this can be interpreted that when consumers feel happy/unhappy with using drone food delivery services, they are more/less likely to use the services. These results are consistent with prior research (e.g. Han et al., 2015; Piçarra & Giger, 2018), suggesting that the importance of anticipated emotions in explaining consumer behavior. It is meaningful that this study empirically confirmed the argument using data collected from the context of drone food delivery services for the first time.

Managerial implications

First, this study found that warm glow significantly affects positive and negative anticipated emotions (hypotheses 1a and 1b). These findings include the following significant managerial implications. It is important to emphasize that using drone food delivery services contributes to the protection of the environment because satisfying environmental needs leads to purchase eco-friendly products/services (Dubihlela & Ngxukumeshe, 2016; SW Chan, 2013). Thus, it is necessary to make consumers fully understand that drone food delivery services are required for the environment. As previously explained, unlike current delivery services, such as cars or motorcycles, drone food delivery services play an important role in protecting the environment, because they are operated by electricity (Environmental Technology, 2018; Stolaroff et al., 2018), so food service companies should emphasize negative environmental impacts of the current delivery services through environmental campaigns. This type of effort keeps consumers alert and aware of environmental pollution, and they are more likely to acquire a good feeling about using drone food delivery services.

Second, the data analysis results revealed the effect of self-expressive benefits on positive and negative anticipated emotions (hypotheses 2a and 2b), so food service companies need to provide eco-friendly products/services like drone food delivery services because using the products/services helps consumers in expressing their environmental concern. In fact, many food service companies are making efforts to provide eco-friendly products/services. For instance, McDonald's plans to recycle customer trash at all 37,000 restaurants in 120 countries by 2025. The company also plans to make their packaging for products more eco-friendly (Fortune, 2018a). In addition, McDonald's and Starbucks are working together to create a fully recyclable, compostable cup by 2021 (Fortune, 2018b). Such efforts help consumers think that they participate in environmental protection. Therefore, food service companies that use drone food delivery services need to inform consumers that using environmentally friendly drones food delivery services has a major impact on the environment. For example, it is recommended to design an advertisement that compares drone food delivery services and traditional delivery methods, such as cars or motorcycles. By doing so, consumers would think that using drone food delivery services would contribute to environmental protection.

Third, the result of the data analysis indicated that nature experiences play an important role in the formation of positive and negative anticipated emotions (hypotheses 3a and 3b), which suggests the vital role of green advertising in the context of drone food delivery services because using an environmentally friendly way, such as drone food delivery services can make consumers feel close to nature (D'souza & Taghian, 2005; Hartmann & Apaolaza-Ibáñez, 2009). Prior research has also suggested the significance of green advertising in diverse industries (e.g. Hartmann & Apaolaza-Ibanez, 2010; Karna, Juslin, Ahonen, & Hansen, 2001; Muralidharan, La Ferle, & Sung, 2017). They found that advertising using the natural environment emphasizes the environmentally friendly image of products/services, which boosts consumption. Thus, it is necessary for food service companies to design green advertising that involve the natural environment. For instance, if the background of the advertisement for drone food delivery services is forests or mountains, consumers are more likely to have high levels of nature experiences. As a result, they would have positive feelings about using drone food delivery services.

Limitations and future research

Although this study provides important theoretical and practical implications, it has the following limitations. First, this study focuses only on food delivery services using drones in Korea, so it is rather difficult to apply the results of this study to other industries and areas. In future studies, it would be meaningful to apply the research model presented in this study to a new field and area. Second, it was impossible to receive questionnaires from customers who actually used the drone food delivery services, because these services have not been commercialized in Korea yet. In particular, the newspaper article we provided can cause biased results, because respondents rely heavily on the article. Therefore, it will be more meaningful to conduct a statistical analysis based on customers who actually have used the services in future research. Third, the online survey was used for data collection in this study. However, the convenience sampling technique using an online survey can lead to selection biases (Wright, 2005), so future research needs to use different data collection methods in order to reduce biases. Fourth, laws should be enacted regarding the operation of drone food delivery services, such as the weight of food and height restrictions, until the services are commercialized. It is also necessary to enact laws for accidents that occur during food delivery using drones. Lastly, consumers are reluctant to use new technology-based services because of unexpected risks, which are also known as perceived risks (Sun, 2014; Wu, Liao, Hung, & Ho, 2012). Thus, it is required to explore the perceive risks of drone food delivery services for future research.

Disclosure statement

No potential conflict of interest was reported by the authors.

References

Aaker, D. A. (2012). *Building strong brands*. Simon and Schuster. New York: The Free Press.

Aaker, J. L. (1999). The malleable self: The role of self-expression in persuasion. *Journal of Marketing Research, 36*, 45–57.

Ahmad, A. N. E. E. S., & Thyagaraj, K. S. (2015). Consumer's intention to purchase green brands: The roles of environmental concern, environmental knowledge and self expressive benefits. *Current World Environment, 10*, 879–889.

Andreoni, J. (1990). Impure altruism and donations to public goods: A theory of warm-glow giving. *The Economic Journal, 100*(401), 464–477.

BBC. (2018). *The crop-spraying drones that go where tractors can't*. Retrieved from https://www.bbc.com/news/business-45020853

Bögeholz, S. (2006). Nature experience and its importance for environmental knowledge, values and action: Recent German empirical contributions. *Environmental Education Research, 12*(1), 65–84.

Brekke, K. A., Kverndokk, S., & Nyborg, K. (2003). An economic model of moral motivation. *Journal of Public Economics, 87*(9–10), 1967–1983.

Byrne, B. M. (2001). *Structural equation modeling with AMOS: Basic concepts, applications, and programming*. Hillsdale, NJ: Erlbaum.

Cherry, C. R., Weinert, J. X., & Xinmiao, Y. (2009). Comparative environmental impacts of electric bikes in China. *Transportation Research Part D: Transport and Environment, 14*(5), 281–290.

Clark, C. F., Kotchen, M. J., & Moore, M. R. (2003). Internal and external influences on pro-environmental behavior: Participation in a green electricity program. *Journal of Environmental Psychology, 23*(3), 237–246.

CNBC. (2016). *Domino's delivers world's first ever pizza by drone*. Retrieved from https://www.cnbc.com/2016/11/16/dominos-has-delivered-the-worlds-first-ever-pizza-by-drone-to-a-new-zealand-couple.html

Colgate, M., & Lang, B. (2001). Switching barriers in consumer markets: An investigation of the financial services industry. *Journal of Consumer Marketing, 18*(4), 332–347.

D'souza, C., & Taghian, M. (2005). Green advertising effects on attitude and choice of advertising themes. *Asia Pacific Journal of Marketing and Logistics, 17*(3), 51–66.

De Young, R. (1996). Some psychological aspects of reduced consumption behavior: The role of intrinsic satisfaction and competence motivation. *Environment and Behavior, 28*(3), 358–409.

Digital Daily. (2016). *Yogiyo, drone food delivery test success*. Retrieved from http://news.naver.com/main/read.nhn?mode=LSD&mid=sec&sid1=105&oid=138&aid=0002045372

Dong-A Daily News. (2017). *The size of the drones industry is raised to 60 times by 2026*. Retrieved from http://news.donga.com/3/all/20171221/87862205/1

Dubihlela, J., & Ngxukumeshe, T. (2016). Eco-friendly retail product attributes, customer attributes and the repurchase intentions of South African consumers. *The International Business & Economics Research Journal (Online), 15*(4), 163.

Environmental Technology. (2018). *How does drone delivery impact the environment?* Retrieved from https://www.envirotech-online.com/news/environmental-laboratory/7/breaking-news/how-does-drone-delivery-impact-the-environment/46595

Finger, M. (1994). From knowledge to action? Exploring the relationships between environmental experiences, learning, and behavior. *Journal of Social Issues, 50*(3), 141–160.

Fornell, C., & Larcker, D. F. (1981). Evaluating structural equation models with unobservable variables and measurement error. *Journal of Marketing Research, 18*(1), 39–50.

Fortune. (2018a). *McDonald's plans environmental push to help boost its image*. Retrieved from http://fortune.com/2018/01/16/mcdonalds-recycling-environmentally-friendly-packaging/

Fortune. (2018b). *Starbucks and McDonald's team up to create a new sustainable cup*. Retrieved from http://fortune.com/2018/07/18/starbucks-mcdonalds-sustainable-cup/

Glazer, A., & Konrad, K. A. (1996). A signaling explanation for charity. *The American Economic Review, 86*(4), 1019–1028.

Green Matters. (2018). *The surprising way drones can help fight climate change*. Retrieved from https://www.greenmatters.com/technology/2018/05/15/1XUgFu/drones-climate-change

Gwinner, K. P., Gremler, D. D., & Bitner, M. J. (1998). Relational benefits in services industries: The customer's perspective. *Journal of the Academy of Marketing Science, 26*(2), 101–114.

Hair, J. F., Jr., Black, W. C., Babin, B. J., Anderson, R. E., & Tatham, R. L. (2006). *Multivariate data analysis* (6th ed.). Upper Saddle River, NJ: Prentice-Hall.

Han, H., Hwang, J., Kim, J., & Jung, H. (2015). Guests' pro-environmental decision-making process: Broadening the norm activation framework in a lodging context. *International Journal of Hospitality Management, 47*, 96–107.

Han, H., Kim, W., & Lee, S. (2018). Stimulating visitors' goal-directed behavior for environmentally responsible museums: Testing the role of moderator variables. *Journal of Destination Marketing & Management, 8*, 290–300.

Han, H., Lee, M. J., & Hwang, J. (2016). Erratum to "Cruise travelers' environmentally responsible decision-making: An integrative framework of goal-directed behavior and norm activation process"[Int. J. Hosp. Manag. 53 (2016) 94–105]. *International Journal of Hospitality Management, 56*, 138.

Han, H., Lee, M. J., & Kim, W. (2018). Antecedents of green loyalty in the cruise industry: Sustainable development and environmental management. *Business Strategy and the Environment, 27*(3), 323–335.

Han, H., Meng, B., & Kim, W. (2017). Bike-traveling as a growing phenomenon: Role of attributes, value, satisfaction, desire, and gender in developing loyalty. *Tourism Management, 59*, 91–103.

Han, H., & Yoon, H. J. (2015). Hotel customers' environmentally responsible behavioral intention: Impact of key constructs on decision in green consumerism. *International Journal of Hospitality Management, 45,* 22–33.

Harbaugh, W. T., Mayr, U., & Burghart, D. R. (2007). Neural responses to taxation and voluntary giving reveal motives for charitable donations. *Science, 316*(5831), 1622–1625.

Hartmann, P., & Ibáñez, V. A. (2006). Effects of green brand communication on brand associations and attitude. In *International Advertising and Communication: Current Insights and Empirical Findings,* ed. S Diehl, R Terlutter, pp. 217–36. Wiesbaden: Gabler DU.

Hartmann, P., & Apaolaza-Ibanez, V. (2010). Beyond savanna: An evolutionary and environmental psychology approach to behavioral effects of nature scenery in green advertising. *Journal of Environmental Psychology, 30*(1), 119–128.

Hartmann, P., & Apaolaza-Ibáñez, V. (2008). Virtual nature experiences as emotional benefits in green product consumption: The moderating role of environmental attitudes. *Environment and Behavior, 40*(6), 818–842.

Hartmann, P., & Apaolaza-Ibáñez, V. (2009). Green advertising revisited: Conditioning virtual nature experiences. *International Journal of Advertising, 28*(4), 715–739.

Hartmann, P., & Apaolaza-Ibáñez, V. (2012). Consumer attitude and purchase intention toward green energy brands: The roles of psychological benefits and environmental concern. *Journal of Business Research, 65*(9), 1254–1263.

Hu, H. H. S. (2012). The effectiveness of environmental advertising in the hotel industry. *Cornell Hospitality Quarterly, 53* (2), 154–164.

Hwang, J., & Choi, J. K. (2018). An investigation of passengers' psychological benefits from green brands in an environmentally friendly airline context: The moderating role of gender. *Sustainability, 10*(1), 80.

Hwang, J., & Lee, K. W. (2018). The antecedents and consequences of golf tournament spectators' memorable brand experiences. *Journal of Destination Marketing & Management, 9,* 1–11.

Hwang, J., & Lyu, S. O. (2018). Understanding first-class passengers' luxury value perceptions in the US airline industry. *Tourism Management Perspectives, 28,* 29–40.

Hwang, J., & Park, S. (2018). An exploratory study of how casino dealer communication styles lead to player satisfaction. *Journal of Travel & Tourism Marketing, 35*(9), 1246-1260.

Kang, S., & Hur, W. M. (2012). Investigating the antecedents of green brand equity: A sustainable development perspective. *Corporate Social Responsibility and Environmental Management, 19*(5), 306–316.

Kaplan, S. (1995). The restorative benefits of nature: Toward an integrative framework. *Journal of Environmental Psychology, 15*(3), 169–182.

Karna, J., Juslin, H., Ahonen, V., & Hansen, E. (2001). Green advertising, greenwash or a true reflection of marketing strategies: Greener management international, 59-71.

Leather, P., Pyrgas, M., Beale, D., & Lawrence, C. (1998). Windows in the workplace: Sunlight, view, and occupational stress. *Environment and Behavior, 30*(6), 739–762.

Lee, S., Song, H., Lee, C. K., & Petrick, J. F. (2018). An integrated model of pop culture fans' travel decision-making processes. *Journal of Travel Research, 57*(5), 687–701.

Lee, W. H., & Moscardo, G. (2005). Understanding the impact of ecotourism resort experiences on tourists' environmental attitudes and behavioural intentions. *Journal of Sustainable Tourism, 13*(6), 546–565.

Leone, L., Perugini, M., & Ercolani, A. P. (2004). Studying, practicing, and mastering: A test of the model of goal-directed behavior (MGB) in the software learning domain. *Journal of Applied Social Psychology, 34*(9), 1945-1973.

Lin, J., Lobo, A., & Leckie, C. (2017). Green brand benefits and their influence on brand loyalty. *Marketing Intelligence & Planning, 35*(3), 425–440.

Liu, Y., Yang, D., & Xu, H. (2017). Factors influencing consumer willingness to pay for low-carbon products: A simulation study in China. *Business Strategy and the Environment, 26*(7), 972–984.

Maller, C., Townsend, M., Pryor, A., Brown, P., & St Leger, L. (2006). Healthy nature healthy people:'Contact with nature'as an upstream health promotion intervention for populations. *Health Promotion International, 21*(1), 45–54.

Meng, B., & Choi, K. (2016). The role of authenticity in forming slow tourists' intentions: Developing an extended model of goal-directed behavior. *Tourism Management, 57,* 397–410.

Menges, R., Schroeder, C., & Traub, S. (2005). Altruism, warm glow and the willingness-to-donate for green electricity: An artefactual field experiment. *Environmental and Resource Economics, 31*(4), 431–458.

Muralidharan, S., La Ferle, C., & Sung, Y. (2017). Are we a product of our environment? Assessing culturally congruent Green advertising appeals, novelty, and environmental concern in India and the USA. *Asian Journal of Communication, 27*(4), 396–414.

NEWSIS. (2017). *Government, drone industry foundation… "Five major powers in the world".* Retrieved from http://www. newsis.com/view/?id=NISX20171228_0000188628&cID= 13001&pID=13000

Nunnally, J. C. (1978). *Psychometric theory.* New York, NY: McGraw-Hill.

Park, J., Kim, S., & Suh, K. (2018). A comparative analysis of the environmental benefits of drone-based delivery services in urban and rural areas. *Sustainability, 10*(3), 888.

Perugini, M., & Bagozzi, R. P. (2001). The role of desires and anticipated emotions in goal-directed behaviors: Broadening and deepening the theory of planned behavior. *British Journal of Social Psychology, 40,* 70–98.

Perugini, M., & Bagozzi, R. P. (2004). The distinction between desires and intentions. *European Journal of Social Psychology, 34,* 69–84.

Piçarra, N., & Giger, J. C. (2018). Predicting intention to work with social robots at anticipation stage: Assessing the role of behavioral desire and anticipated emotions. *Computers in Human Behavior, 86,* 129–146.

Singh, S. P., & Sharma, M. K. (2018). Impact of air pollution on global environment. *Research & Reviews: Journal of Ecology, 7*(1), 23–32.

Song, H., Lee, C. K., Reisinger, Y., & Xu, H. L. (2017). The role of visa exemption in Chinese tourists' decision-making: A model of goal-directed behavior. *Journal of Travel & Tourism Marketing, 34*(5), 666–679.

Stolaroff, J. K., Samaras, C., O'Neill, E. R., Lubers, A., Mitchell, A. S., & Ceperley, D. (2018). Energy use and life cycle greenhouse gas emissions of drones for commercial package delivery. *Nature Communications, 9*(1), 409.

Sun, J. (2014). How risky are services? An empirical investigation on the antecedents and consequences of perceived risk for hotel service. *International Journal of Hospitality Management, 37*, 171–179.

SW Chan, E. (2013). Gap analysis of green hotel marketing. *International Journal of Contemporary Hospitality Management, 25*(7), 1017–1048.

Sweeney, J. C., & Webb, D. A. (2007). How functional, psychological, and social relationship benefits influence individual and firm commitment to the relationship. *Journal of Business & Industrial Marketing, 22*(7), 474–488.

Tang, C. M. F., & Lam, D. (2017). The role of extraversion and agreeableness traits on Gen Y's attitudes and willingness to pay for green hotels. *International Journal of Contemporary Hospitality Management, 29*(1), 607–623.

Trang, H. L. T., Lee, J. S., & Han, H. (2019). How do green attributes elicit pro-environmental behaviors in guests? The case of green hotels in Vietnam. *Journal of Travel & Tourism Marketing*, 1–15.

Trenberth, K. E., Dai, A., Van Der Schrier, G., Jones, P. D., Barichivich, J., Briffa, K. R., & Sheffield, J. (2014). Global warming and changes in drought. *Nature Climate Change, 4*(1), 17.

Ulrich, R. S. (1981). Natural versus urban scenes: Some psychophysiological effects. *Environment and Behavior, 13*(5), 523–556.

USA Today. (2018). Drone delivers food and drinks at North Dakota golf course. Retrieved from https://www.usatoday.com/story/sports/golf/2018/09/07/kings-walk-golf-course-drone-food-grand-forks/1221146002/

Warshaw, P., & Davis, F. (1985). Disentangling behavioral intention and behavioral expectation. *Journal of Experimental Social Psychology, 21*, 213–228.

Wright, K. B. (2005). Researching Internet-based populations: Advantages and disadvantages of online survey research, online questionnaire authoring software packages, and web survey services. *Journal of Computer-Mediated Communication, 10*(3), JCMC1034.

Wu, C. H. J., Liao, H. C., Hung, K. P., & Ho, Y. H. (2012). Service guarantees in the hotel industry: Their effects on customer risk and service quality perceptions. *International Journal of Hospitality Management, 31*(3), 757–763.

Yadav, R., & Pathak, G. S. (2017). Determinants of consumers' green purchase behavior in a developing nation: Applying and extending the theory of planned behavior. *Ecological Economics, 134*, 114–122.

Zeithaml, V. A., Berry, L. L., & Parasuraman, A. (1996). The behavioral consequences of service quality. *The Journal of Marketing, 60*, 31–46.

Integrating virtual reality devices into the body: effects of technological embodiment on customer engagement and behavioral intentions toward the destination

Carlos Flavián ⓘ , Sergio Ibáñez-Sánchez ⓘ and Carlos Orús ⓘ

ABSTRACT

Virtual reality devices create a high integration of technologies with human senses. However, few studies analyze how embodied technologies affect customer pre-experiences with a destination. Results from a lab experiment show that compared to desktop PC and mobile phones, VR head-mounted displays generate more immersive experiences, higher sensory stimulation, more engagement, and higher behavioral intentions toward the destination. Immersion and sensory stimulation mediate the effects of technological embodiment on engagement and behavioral intentions. Furthermore, active (versus passive) tourism content strengthens these effects. Our results stress the role of technological embodiment to generate effective pre-experiences with potential tourists' destinations.

Introduction

The development of new technologies characterized by high degrees of portability and embodiment has brought virtual reality (VR) to a new level. Recent reports show that users are increasingly adopting this technology: in the third quarter of 2017, sales of VR HMD (Head-Mounted Displays) passed the 1 million for the first time (Canalys, 2017), and it seems that the growth of the VR HMD market is set to continue (Canalys, 2018). The launch of standalone VR devices (e.g. Oculus GO, HTC Vive Focus), together with the price decreases, may boost adoption of these technologies (Canalys, 2017). However, recent reports note a recent decline in the sales of VR devices (CCSInsight, 2018; IDC, 2018), showing that the growth in the adoption of VR is slower and more irregular than expected. Therefore, understanding how users interact with these technologies to support, empower, or create new experiences represents a challenge that must be addressed by researchers and practitioners (Flavián, Ibáñez-Sánchez, & Orús, 2018).

The particular features of tourism (e.g. service-intense industry, services that cannot be tested in advance; Guttentag, 2010; Neuhofer, Buhalis, & Ladkin, 2014; Yung & Khoo-Lattimore, 2017) make it an ideal industry in which to develop VR technologies and analyze their impact. In fact, users have shown high interest

in the use of VR devices in the travel and adventure field (Greenlight, 2016). Users perceive that VR adds value to their travel decision-making processes, so they are willing to use this technology at a travel agency as well as to book vacations based on in-store VR experiences (YouGov, 2016).

Marketers are striving to find innovative ways to attract potential customers to their destinations (Pike & Page, 2014). The use of VR devices can help tourism managers to design and deliver optimal customer experiences (Berg & Vance, 2017). More specifically, embodied VR devices have great potential to affect tourists' behaviors, especially in the pre-purchase stage of the customer journey (Guttentag, 2010; Lemon & Verhoef, 2016; Marasco, Buonincontri, van Niekerk, Orlowski, & Okumus, 2018; Tussyadiah, Wang, Jung, & Tom Dieck, 2018). Embodied VR devices can be said to be in direct contact with the human senses and can mediate the potential customers' experiences within a virtual environment, giving them the ability to explore virtually, and thereby assess, specific destinations (which cannot be pre-tested). Consequently, the consumer can make more confident decisions in relation to visiting that destination (Marasco et al., 2018).

Most studies about the implementation of VR technology in the tourism field focus on its antecedents (e.g. Disztinger, Schlögl, & Groth, 2017; Gibson & O'Rawe, 2017), its influence on decision-making process (e.g.

Marasco et al., 2018; Tussyadiah et al., 2018) or the benefits of its application (e.g. Barnes, 2016; Guttentag, 2010). However, the influence of technological embodiment, which is one of the main features of VR technologies (Tussyadiah, Jung, & Tom Dieck, 2017), has not been empirically analyzed. Technological embodiment occurs in situations in which the technological device mediates users' experiences, intertwining with their bodies and supporting them to perform sensorial and bodily functions (theory of technological mediation; Ihde, 1990). Technological embodiment allows users to extend their bodies to perceive, interpret and interact with the environment (Tussyadiah, Jung et al., 2017). Following the EPI Cube proposed by Flavián et al. (2018), technological embodiment ranges from the lowest level of integration (e.g. stationary desktop computers) to a full integration with the senses (e.g. smart contact lenses). In addition, few empirical studies investigate VR applications in tourism marketing, since most studies have been conducted with traditional virtual worlds (e.g. Second Life; Tussyadiah, Wang, & Jia, 2017).

This research analyzes how the degree of technological embodiment (high: VR HMD, medium: mobile phone, low: desktop PC) affects the customer pre-experience with a destination. Based on the Stimulus-Organism-Response (S-O-R) paradigm (Donovan & Rossiter, 1982; Mehrabian & Russell, 1974), we propose that level of embodiment (stimulus) affects users' perceptions of immersion and sensory stimulation (organism), which ultimately determine their experience in terms of engagement and behavioral intentions toward a destination (response). By better understanding the processes through which technological embodiment enhances customer experience, tourism managers will be able to create superior and more memorable experiences by offering their customers high-value propositions, especially in the pre-experience stage of their customer journey.

Theoretical background

The Stimulus-Organism-Response (S-O-R) paradigm is rooted in classic Stimulus-Response theory (classical conditioning; Pavlov, 1902), which posits that, after being shown a specific stimulus, subjects carry out a paired response. The classic conditioning model was extended by Mehrabian and Russell (1974) and Donovan and Rossiter (1982) to the S-O-R paradigm. Stimuli are the specific factors that arouse the organismic processes of the individual (Eroglu, Machleit, & Davis, 2001). Through the processing of these stimuli, internal processes are

generated (organism). Eventually, this finally leads to responses, such as approach or avoidance behaviors (Donovan & Rossiter, 1982). Thus, the S-O-R model proposes that stimuli cause organismic reactions, which lead to the performance (or not, as the case may be) of certain actions. The organism mediates the influence of a particular stimulus on the response. The S-O-R model has previously been used in online shopping environments (e.g. Eroglu et al., 2001; Ettis, 2017; Mummalaneni, 2005). In virtual environments, stimuli are the visual and auditory cues presented to the shopper, who processes these stimuli (organism) and, consequently, responds by buying (or not) a particular product (Eroglu et al., 2001).

Stimulus: technological embodiment

Recent technological developments have altered the processes of human-computer mediation. Theory of technological mediation (Ihde, 1990) describes embodiment as a situation in which a technological device mediates the users' experiences and, consequently, the technology becomes an extension of their bodies and helps them to interpret, perceive and interact with their immediate environment. Maximum levels of technological embodiment lead to human-technology symbiosis (Tussyadiah, 2014). As stated by Witmer and Singer (1998), technological devices are becoming more intertwined with human bodies, assisting and mediating the users' experiences (Tussyadiah, Jung et al., 2017).

The National Research Council (2012) proposes different levels of technological embodiment, ranging from minimum or no embodiment (e.g. desktop PCs) to devices that are fully integrated in the human body (e.g. microchips or smart contact lenses). Intermediate levels include portable external devices (e.g. mobile phones). Between portable external and fully integrated devices, we find advanced tools, commonly described as wearables (e.g. VR HMD) (Tussyadiah, Jung et al., 2017). In addition, the EPI cube (Flavián et al., 2018) notes that VR HMD are highly embodied technologies, while mobile phones and desktop PCs are in medium and low levels of embodiment, respectively. Recently developed wearable technologies have been compared to embodied technologies (Tussyadiah, 2014; Tussyadiah, Jung et al., 2017) since they reinforce the user´s sense of integration between the body and the technology. Therefore, devices with different levels of technological embodiment are the stimuli that are proposed to affect the organism components (immersion and sensory stimulation) and responses (engagement and behavioral intentions).

Organism: immersion and sensory stimulation

Immersion

Immersion is an individual experience, defined as the "psychological state characterized by perceiving oneself to be enveloped by, included in, and interacting with an environment that provides a continuous stream of stimuli and experiences" (Witmer & Singer, 1998, p. 227). This is related to the concept of "mental immersion", defined by Sherman and Craig (2003) as the state of being deeply involved in an experience with the suspension of disbelief. These authors state that physical immersion, in which the technological stimulus creates the sensation that the body has entered into the virtual environment, may have an important effect on mental immersion.

Cutting-edge technologies characterized by a high degree of immersion can generate experiences in which users feel as if they are actually part of the virtual environment (Tussyadiah et al., 2018). Furthermore, as the efficacy of traditional media is decreasing (Fransen, Verlegh, Kirmani, & Smit, 2015), marketers are continually on the lookout for more effective formats. Embodied VR technologies can enhance the communication of intangible experiences (i.e. tourism), resulting in an improvement of the destination image in the minds of potential visitors (Griffin et al., 2017). Embodied devices provide customers with a higher sense of closeness between the virtual environment and their senses, thus creating more immersive experiences than portable or external technologies (Biocca, 1997; Flavián et al., 2018). In addition, high embodied technologies create a greater sense of immersion in the virtual environment by matching their users' body movements with the information displayed (Witmer & Singer, 1998). Hence:

H$_1$: High vs. medium vs. low levels of technological embodiment have a positive effect on users' perceived immersion.

Sensory stimulation

According to Krishna (2012), sensory marketing aims to engage the customers' senses, resulting in changes in their perceptions, judgments, and subsequent behaviors. Consumers experience their surroundings through their senses, so sensory information and the related subjective experiences are crucial in human action and cognition (Krishna & Schwarz, 2014). Experiential products (such as tourism) need to provide vicarious experiences with sensory information to create an attractive destination (Hyun & O'Keefe, 2012).

VR technologies generate virtual environments where users obtain information directly through the stimulation of their senses, which provides them with a realistic representation of the simulated environment (Slater & Usoh, 1993). Sensorial richness is regarded as one of the variables that influences virtual experiences (Steuer, 1992), and VR offers elements that generate sensory stimulation (Cheong, 1995).

Sight is the sense most often stimulated by HMD devices. Audio is also important (Jung, Tom Dieck, Moorhouse, & Tom Dieck, 2017) and is widely used in realistic virtual environments (Gutierrez, Vexo, & Thalmann, 2008). For tourism, these two senses are regarded as paramount (Guttentag, 2010). In addition, haptic devices (e.g. gloves or haptic suits) can trigger tactile sensations. Finally, recent advances have been made regarding the olfactory and gustatory senses (Gutierrez et al., 2008). Thus, it has been demonstrated that more embodied technologies have the potential to create extensive multi-sensory experiences, which might result in better consumer responses.

Specifically, high embodied technologies use effectors (e.g. HMD, haptic devices), which stimulate the receptors of the perceptual human senses (Latta & Oberg, 1994). Therefore, devices with higher levels of technological embodiment generate stronger sensorial stimuli, resulting in more stimulating sensorial experiences (Biocca, 1997; Flavián et al., 2018; Tussyadiah, 2014), than non-embodied devices. Thus:

H$_2$: High vs. medium vs. low levels of technological embodiment have a positive effect on users' sensory stimulation.

Response: engagement and behavioral intentions

Engagement

User engagement is defined as the quality of the experience characterized by the depth of the users' cognitive, temporal, affective and behavioral investment when they are interacting in the digital environment (O'Brien, 2016). The underlying processes of user engagement in virtual environments are receiving great attention from both researchers and managers (O'Brien, 2016).

For tourism marketing, providing users with VR experiences (as they resemble direct experiences to a great extent) is expected to be more effective than giving them indirect experiences, favoring engagement with the real destination (Hyun & O'Keefe, 2012). High-embodied devices have great potential to engage tourists (Tussyadiah, Jung et al., 2017). Previous research has shown that advertising destinations using embodied VR devices is more engaging than with other, traditional formats (Griffin et al., 2017). In the same way, watching videos through highly embodied devices (e.g. VR HMD) generates more engagement than watching them on a flat screen (Nielsen, 2016). VR experiences generate customer engagement by creating emotional connections with the destination depicted (Barnes, 2016). Therefore, we propose that devices with high levels of technological embodiment will generate more engagement than devices with medium and low levels of embodiment:

H$_3$: High vs. medium vs. low levels of technological embodiment have a positive effect on users' engagement.

Behavioral intentions

Intentions are the main antecedents of actual customer behaviors (Ajzen, 1991). Intentions reflect the eagerness of users to carry out particular behaviors. Previous research has shown that there is a relationship between intentions and actual behaviors (Casaló, Flavián, & Ibáñez-Sánchez, 2017; Venkatesh & Davis, 2000).

Previous studies also show that VR technologies can provide "try-before-you-buy" experiences, which create a destination image in the mind of potential visitors, leading to positive behavioral intentions (Marasco et al., 2018; Tussyadiah et al., 2018). In fact, the study of the marketing opportunities that VR technologies offer, in terms of influence on potential visitors' decisions whether or not to visit a destination, is a growing research topic (Griffin et al., 2017; Marasco et al., 2018).

The impact of high embodied technologies on consumer behavior has been highlighted by previous literature. Kim, Lee, and Jung (2019) stress the potential of VR to enhance the behavioral intentions toward visiting a destination. Griffin et al. (2017) state that embodied devices, in comparison to less embodied technologies, generate greater willingness to seek out further information, and to share it, about a destination. Tussyadiah et al. (2018) also reveal the persuasive power of embodied devices (VR) in tourism marketing. Therefore, we propose that devices with high levels of technological embodiment will have a positive impact on behavioral intentions. Thus:

H$_4$: High vs. medium vs. low levels of technological embodiment have a positive effect on users' behavioral intentions toward the destination.

Mediation effects

Following the S-O-R framework (Donovan & Rossiter, 1982; Mehrabian & Russell, 1974), we propose that immersion and sensory stimulation are the organismic components that may mediate the relationship between the stimulus (devices different levels of technological embodiment) and the responses (engagement and behavioral intentions). On the one hand, high embodied technologies play a key role in providing immersive experiences that, as a result, generate a perception of engagement while users are in the virtual environment (Jennett et al., 2008; Sherman & Craig, 2003). On the other hand, one of the main advantages of embodied technologies for tourism marketing is that they provide potential tourists with sensory cues, which is crucial for the industry (Barnes, 2016; Guttentag, 2010). As a consequence, a sense of engagement in the virtual experience can be generated (Barnes, 2016). Therefore, both organismic components (immersion and sensory stimulation) may mediate the influence of devices with different levels of technological embodiment on users' engagement:

H$_5$: The levels of (a) immersion and (b) sensory stimulation mediate the effect of high vs. medium vs. low levels of technological embodiment on users' engagement.

Taking into account the particular features of the tourism industry (service domain and intangibility; Casaló, Flavián, & Guinalíu, 2010; Hyun & O'Keefe, 2012), providing potential visitors with a realistic "try-before-you-buy" experience can influence travel decision-making (Jang, 2005; Tussyadiah, Wang, & Jia, 2016). In this way, immersive technologies help potential visitors virtually to experience the actual destination before going there (Marasco et al., 2018; Tussyadiah et al., 2018). Previous research shows that the immersive capacity of VR devices can have a positive impact on subsequent behavior (Jung et al., 2017). Thus, high levels of immersion generated by embodied technologies may lead to favorable behavioral intentions toward a destination. In a similar vein, sensory cues can significantly influence the consumer's intention to visit a destination (Ghosh & Sarkar, 2016). Potential tourists can better evaluate and make better travel decisions if they are provided with useful and relevant information (Mendes-Filho, Mills, Tan, & Milne, 2017). Direct experiences can be simulated through the sensory power of high embodied technologies (VR), which will result in more positive behaviors (Huang, Backman, Backman, & Chang, 2016). Therefore:

H_6: The levels of (a) immersion and (b) sensory stimulation mediate the effect of high vs. medium vs. low levels of technological embodiment on users' behavioral intentions toward the destination.

Moderating effect: active/passive tourism

Previous studies reveal several motivations for tourism travel, such as leisure, escapism, novelty, and pleasure seeking (Guttentag, 2010; Kim, Chua, Lee, Boo, & Han, 2016; Kim & Prideaux, 2005). Tourists perform different activities during their stays to meet their own particular needs. In this sense, tourism activities can be classified according to the degree of physical energy that is expended (Pizam & Fleischer, 2005). Specifically, active (or dynamic) tourism encompasses activities in which tourists expend significant physical energy; these may include fast-moving, outdoor activities (vigorous sports, nature or adventure; Vohnout et al., 2014). Activities such as rafting or hiking can be considered as active tourism. On the other hand, passive (or static) tourism includes activities where the tourist does not expend significant amounts of physical energy. These activities are slow-paced, well planned and organized in advance, so they involve no risk. City-based activities, e.g. shopping, attending the opera, ballet, and theater, are often regarded as passive tourism.

According to the cognitive fit theory (Vessey, 1991), when users are presented with a particular task, the correspondence between the task and the format in which the relevant information is displayed results in superior task performance. Similarly, resource-matching theory (Peracchio & Meyers-Levy, 1997) suggests that the persuasiveness of a particular item of information is higher when the resources allocated to process it match that required to perform the related task. Therefore, the fit between the technology used to visualize a particular message and the features of the content displayed in the message is critical (task-technology fit; Goodhue & Thompson, 1995), especially taking into account that tourism services cannot be pre-tested by the consumers (Guttentag, 2010).

As technological embodiment is related to the extent that a device is integrated into the body, highly embodied devices (i.e. VR HMD; Flavián et al., 2018) will allow users to perceive more naturally the fast-paced movements, greater dynamism, and energy that featured active tourism activities. A greater correspondence between the active tourism video visualized and the technological device used strengthens users' perceptions (Goodhue & Thompson, 1995). However, for passive tourism activities videos (compared to active tourism), the role of embodiment is not substantial due to its main characteristics (e.g. slow-paced movements, less energetic activities). Additionally, embodied VR devices turn potential tourists into active participants since they can freely and naturally explore the virtual environment (Cho, Wang, & Fesenmaier, 2002), what reinforces their role in active tourism videos. Therefore, given the characteristics of active tourism, embodied devices (VR HMD) help to create a close match between users' actual movements and the ones in the virtual environment (Slater, 2009), what help potential travelers to better explore virtually the destination and strengthening their perceptions. Therefore:

H_7: The type of tourism (active/passive) moderates the effects of high vs. medium vs. low levels of technological embodiment on (a) immersion, (b) sensory stimulation, (c) engagement and (d) behavioral intentions; the effects of technological embodiment will be stronger for active tourism than for passive tourism.

Figure 1 shows the research model and related hypotheses.

Methodology

Participants, procedure, and measures

The data to test the hypotheses were collected from a lab experiment. The sample consisted of 202 participants, who took part in a 3 (technological embodiment: low vs medium vs high) x 2 (type of tourism: passive vs active) between-subjects factorial design. The respondents were 59.4% female and aged, on average, 22.10 years. We focused on this age range since members of the youngest generations are highly interested in VR technologies (Commscope, 2017; Greenlight, 2015).

The context of the experiment was a 360-degree tourism-related video as a pre-experience of a potential destination. First, the participants were gathered in one room and given a brief introduction about the study. Specifically, they were told that they were going to have a virtual pre-experience with a destination, and they had to answers related to it. At this point, the participants received a brochure with several pages containing the questionnaires. We used random procedures (different colored stickers) to hand out the brochures. In the first page, participants answered a series of control questions. Specifically, they indicated their previous touristic experience with different destinations (including the ones that were going to be displayed in the subsequent video) with four possible options: (1) "I have not visited the

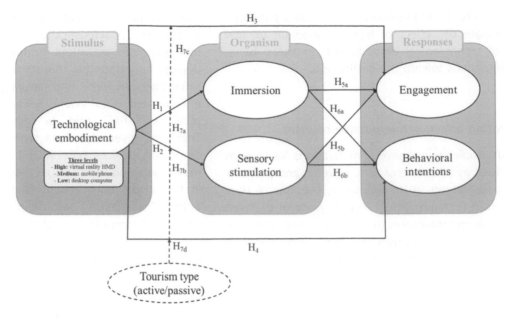

Figure 1. Research model.

destination, and I do not plan to"; (2) "I have not visited the destination, but I would like to"; (3) "I have visited the destination, and I would not visit it again"; (4) "I have visited the destination, and I would not mind to visit it again". After that, we asked the participants about their preferences (from 1 = "I do not like it at all", to 7 = "I like it very much") about different types of tourism (city, nature, adventure sports, sun, and beach). In addition, the participants indicated their degree of experience with 360-degree videos with different devices (desktop PC, laptop, tablet, mobile phone, VR HMD), on a 7-point scale (from 1 = "I have never used this device", to 7 = "I am very used to use this device"). Finally, we asked the participants about their degree of technological innovativeness (six 7-point Likert items adapted from Bruner & Kumar, 2007; Thakur, Angriawan, & Summey, 2016; Appendix).

Second, participants were directed to different experimental rooms, according to their assignment to the experimental condition (colored sticker). Each color corresponded to the visualization of a 360-degree video of a destination with a device with three levels of embodiment: low (desktop PCs), medium (mobile phones) and high (VR HMD). Participants entered individually into the room and, after some instructions they watched the video with the corresponding device. Regarding the type of tourism, participants in the passive tourism condition watched a video of a gondola ride in Venice. The video showed a quiet ride along the canals of the city on a sunny day; the viewer was placed on the gondola, plowed through the calm waters of the

canals in a slow-paced way. In the active tourism video, participants watched a video of a whitewater rafting in the Grand Canyon. In this video, the viewer was placed on a boat on a sunny day in the middle of nature; in this case, they sailed down through the rapids of a river, so that a great movement was generated in a fast-moving way. The original videos were modified to keep the duration and sound quality constant.

After visualizing the video, the participants completed the questionnaire (Appendix). We adapted scales previously validated in the literature for immersion (Fornerino, Helme-Guizon, & Gotteland, 2008), sensory stimulation (Witmer & Singer, 1998), engagement (O'Brien, Cairns, & Hall, 2018; O'Brien & Toms, 2010) and behavioral intentions toward the destination (Bigné, Sánchez, & Sánchez, 2001; Huang, Backman, Backman, & Moore, 2013). In relation to manipulation checks, we developed four items to measure the degree of technological embodiment, as we were not able to find any specific measure in previous studies (Appendix). All the items used 7-point Likert scales. In addition, the participants indicated their perceptions as to whether the depicted destination had passive (1) or active (7) tourism and whether they would categorize it as having "city" or "sports/nature" tourism.

Results

Before analyzing the data, the first control question allowed us to screen out those participants who had already visited the target destination (Venice or the

Grand Canyon) and would not visit it again. The resulting pre-experience and behavioral intentions of these participants might remain unaltered regardless of the experimental treatment, adding noise to the analysis. Thus, the final sample consisted of 196 participants (60.2% female; mean age = 22.10). Cell sizes ranged from 30 to 36 participants.

Scale validation

To validate the measurement model we performed a confirmatory factor analysis with SmartPLS 3 (Ringle, Wende, & Becker, 2015). Results confirmed that all the loadings from the items were higher than the recommended value of 0.7 (Henseler, Ringle, & Sinkovics, 2009). Additionally, the values of Cronbach Alphas were superior to 0.7 (Bagozzi & Yi, 1988) and composite reliabilities were higher than the recommended value of 0.65 (Steenkamp & Geyskens, 2006), proving their internal consistency. Convergent validity was confirmed since the values of the average variance extracted (AVE) were superior to the benchmark of 0.5 (Fornell & Larcker, 1981). Finally, the value of the square root of the AVE was higher than the correlations among the constructs (Fornell & Larcker, 1981) and the values of the HTMT ratio (Heterotrait–Monotrait ratio; Henseler, Ringle, & Sarstedt, 2015) were lower than 0.90 (Gold, Malhotra, & Segars, 2001), establishing the discriminant validity of the measures.

Manipulation checks

To check the manipulation of technological embodiment, we carried out a one-way ANOVA with device type as the independent variable with SPSS v22. As expected, technological embodiment was higher in the case of VR HMD ($M = 5.58$, $SD = 1.55$) than with mobile phones ($M = 4.30$, $SD = 1.12$) and desktop PCs ($M = 2.89$, $SD = 1.01$), and these differences were

significant ($F_{(2,195)} = 104.014$, $p < 0.001$). The post-hoc Tukey tests revealed significant differences between desktops and mobile phones ($p = 0.000$), desktops and VR HMD ($p = 0.000$) and mobile phones and VR HMD ($p = 0.000$). In addition, the Grand Canyon video was perceived as significantly more active ($M = 5.32$; $SD = 1.68$) than the Venice video ($M = 4.38$, $SD = 1.49$; $t_{(194)} = 4.126$, $p < 0.001$). Also, participants correctly classified the Venice video as city tourism and the Grand Canyon video as nature/sports tourism ($\chi^2_{(2)} = 196.000$, $p < 0.001$).[1]

Direct and moderation effects

The descriptive statistics per each experimental cell and treatment are shown in Table 1. We carried out a multivariate analysis of variance, which is appropriate since the correlations between the dependent variables were significant ($rs > 0.281$; Hair, Anderson, Tatham, & Black, 1998). We included the participants' previous experience in the destination (1 = yes, 0 = no), preference for the type of tourism displayed in their condition (city or adventure sports), their previous experience with 360-degree videos in the device they used in their condition (desktop PC, mobile phone, or VR HMD), and their degree of technological innovativeness as covariates. The MANCOVA revealed a significant multivariate effect of the type of device (Wilk's lambda= 0.469, $F_{(8, 374)} = 21.024$, $p < 0.001$; partial $\eta^2 = 0.315$; power= 1.000). Type of tourism did not have a significant multivariate effect ($p = 0.934$). However, the interaction term was significant at the multivariate level (Wilk's lambda= 0.895, $F_{(8, 374)} = 2.597$, $p < 0.05$; partial $\eta^2 = 0.054$; power= 0.921). Regarding the control variables, the MANCOVA showed a significant multivariate effect of the participants' previous experience in the destination (Wilk's lambda= 0.945, $F_{(4, 183)} = 2.679$, $p < 0.05$; partial $\eta^2 = 0.055$; power= 0.737). Their preference for the type of tourism ($p = 0.741$), their previous experience with the

Table 1. Descriptive statistics per experimental cell.

Device	Type of tourism	Immersion M (SD)	Sensory stimulation M (SD)	Engagement M (SD)	Behavioral intentions M (SD)
Desktop PC	Passive	3.35 (1.405)	3.96 (1.197)	4.16 (1.280)	4.44 (1.616)
	Active	2.62 (1.277)	3.50 (1.427)	3.82 (1.385)	4.18 (1.729)
	Total	**3.02 (1.387)**	**3.75 (1.316)**	**4.00 (1.329)**	**4.33 (1.661)**
Mobile phone	Passive	4.11 (1.420)	4.57 (1.260)	5.08 (1.203)	5.03 (1.438)
	Active	4.01 (1.168)	4.58 (1.151)	4.85 (1.033)	4.95 (1.340)
	Total	**4.06 (1.287)**	**4.58 (1.195)**	**4.95 (1.116)**	**4.99 (1.377)**
VR HMD	Passive	5.47 (1.123)	5.30 (0.695)	5.78 (0.947)	4.89 (1.348)
	Active	6.46 (0.649)	6.18 (0.723)	6 46 (0.677)	5.31 (1.426)
	Total	**5.99 (1.026)**	**5.76 (0.831)**	**6.14 (0.879)**	**5.11 (1.395)**
Total	Passive	4.28 (1.585)	4.59 (1.208)	4.97 (1.332)	4.77 (1.486)
	Active	4.49 (1.917)	4.84 (1.569)	5.12 (1.514)	4.85 (1.555)
	Total	**4.38 (1758)**	**4.71 (1.402)**	**5.04 (1.424)**	**4.81 (1.518)**

technology (p= 0.074) and their degree of technological innovativeness (p= 0.524) had no significant effects.

Overall, we observed gradual increases in all the dependent variables as the degree of technological embodiment increases (Table 1). The results for the univariate effects are shown in Table 2. Specifically, the type of device was found to positively affect the levels of immersion and sensory stimulation. The effects were significant and strong. The post-hoc Tukey test indicated that both variables were higher for participants in the VR condition than those in the mobile phone condition (Table 1; ps < 0.001) and those in the desktop PC condition (Table 1; ps < 0.001). The differences between mobile phone and desktop PC were also significant (Table 1; ps < 0.001). Thus, hypotheses H1 and H2 were supported. None of the covariates had a significant influence on immersion or sensory stimulation (Table 2).

Regarding the influence of embodiment on engagement, we found a significant strong effect (Table 2). The high level of technological embodiment (VR HMD) was found to positively affect the participants' engagement (Table 1). The post-hoc Tukey test indicated that all differences between conditions were significant (all ps < 0.001), thus supporting H3. The effect of the type of device on behavioral intentions was also significant, although the effect size was medium (Table 2); however, the difference between mobile phones and VR HMD was not significant (Table 1; p= 0.751). Therefore, H4 was partly supported. The control variables did not affect engagement and behavioral intentions, except for a small, significant impact of the previous experience in the destination on behavioral intentions (Table 2). Specifically, behavioral intentions were higher for participants who had not been in the destination previously (n=154; M= 4.91, sd = 1.449) than for those who had already been in the destination (n=42; M= 4.44, sd = 1.715).

Type of tourism had no direct effects on the dependent variables (Tables 1 and 2). However,

significant interaction effects were found for immersion, sensory stimulation, and engagement (Table 2). The effect sizes were medium for immersion and sensory stimulation, and small for engagement. Figure 2 shows these interaction effects. Specifically, we observed that the effects of high embodied technologies on immersion (Figure 2(a)), sensory stimulation (Figure 2(b)) and engagement (Figure 2(c)) were stronger for the active tourism video than for the passive tourism video. The interaction between technological embodiment and tourism type on behavioral intentions was not significant (p = 0.400). Altogether, the results support H7a, H7b, and H7c, yet H7d must be rejected.

Mediation effects

We used the PROCESS macro v3.1 for SPSS (Hayes, 2018; http://www.processmacro.org) to test the mediating role of the organismic components (immersion and sensory stimulation) in the relationship between the stimulus (technological device) and the participants' responses (engagement and behavioral intentions). The PROCESS macro is a simple, user-friendly modeling system that uses OLS regression procedures (Hayes, 2018). Similar to other techniques which rely on ML procedures, such as Structural Equation Modeling (SEM), the PROCESS macro estimates indirect effects and does not require separate tests to assess the significance of the mediation effect. However, unlike SEM, PROCESS can be used with smaller samples with irregular sampling distributions, given that it uses bootstrapping methods to estimate indirect effects (Hayes, 2018; Hayes, Montoya, & Rockwood, 2017). By using bootstrap confidence intervals, the inferences are likely to be more accurate, and the test has higher power than when using ordinary methods (Bernardo, Tan-Mansukhani, & Daganzo, 2018; Hayes, 2018). Hayes et al. (2017) argue that both methods are equally valid for mediation models, and produce similar results for observed variables (as is our case, given that the scales

Table 2. Results of the univariate effects.

Variable	Immersion			Sensory stimulation			Engagement			Behavioral intentions		
	F	Partial η^2	Power	F	Partial η^2	Power	F	Partial η^2	Power	F	Partial η^2	Power
Experience in the destination	1.461	0.008	0.225	2.853	0.015	0.390	0.001	0.000	0.050	4.001*	0.021	0.512
Pref. for the type of tourism	0.083	0.000	0.059	0.125	0.001	0.064	0.034	0.000	0.054	1.646	0.009	0.248
Experience with the technology	0.026	0.000	0.053	1.309	0.007	0.207	0.313	0.002	0.086	2.802	0.015	0.384
Technological innovativeness	1.810	0.010	0.268	1.014	0.005	0.171	2.136	0.011	0.307	1.456	0.008	0.225
Device	98.827**	0.515	1.000	56.428**	0.378	1.000	57.436**	0.382	1.000	6.411**	0.064	0.899
Type of tourism	0.671	0.001	0.071	0.905	0.000	0.052	0.823	0.000	0.056	0.805	0.000	0.057
Device x type of tourism	9.211**	0.090	0.975	6.408**	0.064	0.899	4.572*	0.047	0.771	0.955	0.010	0.214

are formed by the average of the items). In addition, PROCESS can be particularly useful given the particularities of our model: two parallel mediators and one multicategorical independent variable with three levels. PROCESS allows researchers to analyze direct, indirect, and total effects simultaneously with the total sample and does not require subgroup analysis (Hayes, 2018).

We ran two separate models for each response variable (model 4 with parallel mediators). As the independent variable was an ordinal multicategorical variable with three levels, sequential coding was used (Hayes, 2018). Thus, two dummy variables (X1: 0 = Desktop PC, 1 = mobile phone and VR HMD; X2: 1 = VR HMD, 0 = otherwise) were included in each model. The participants' previous experience in the destination and with the technology, their preference for the type of tourism displayed in the video, and their degree of technological innovativeness were also included as covariates.

The results of the mediation model on engagement are displayed in Table 3. The results of the effects of the device on immersion and sensory stimulation replicated those found in the MANCOVA. When the organismic variables were included in the model, the direct effects of technological embodiment became non-significant. Both immersion and sensory stimulation had significant effects on engagement. The bootstrap results for the indirect effects revealed mediation for both organismic variables, given that the zero value was not included in the 95% confidence intervals (Table 3). Therefore, H5a and H5b were supported. Regarding the control variables, we found that participants who had already been in the destination reported higher levels of engagement. However, the total effect of this variable was not significant, and no other effects were found (Table 3).

The same analysis was carried out for behavioral intentions. Taking into account that the effects of the independent variable (type of device) on the mediators (immersion and sensory stimulation) are similar to those calculated in the previous model (Table 3), Table 4 displays the results of the regression on behavioral intentions. In this case, the mediation model followed a similar pattern, yet with some remarkable differences. The direct effect of the device on behavioral intentions disappeared when the mediators were included in the regression. However, immersion had no significant effect on behavioral intentions; only sensory stimulation had a significant influence (Table 4). The significance of the indirect effects revealed that sensory stimulation mediated the effect of technological embodiment (low versus medium + high) on behavioral intentions. Support for H6b is found; H6a must be rejected. The participants' previous experience with the destination and the

technology, their preference for the type of tourism and their degree of technological innovativeness did not have a direct impact on behavioral intentions when the mediators were included in the model (Table 4). In the total effects model, the results replicated those found in the MANCOVA (negative of previous experience in the destination on behavioral intentions). Nevertheless, the explanatory power of the model was low, suggesting that the mediator (sensory stimulation) has a more powerful effect on behavioral intentions than the type of device used in the pre-experience with the destination.

Discussion and implications

VR technologies can allow potential tourists to have realistic "try-before-you-buy" experiences that help them make better travel decisions (Jang, 2005; Tussyadiah et al., 2016). Specifically, embodied VR devices are in close contact with the human senses, mediate users' experiences, create immersive and sensory-stimulating experiences that improve tourists' information search processes and, thus, help them make final decisions (Huang et al., 2016). This research uses the S-O-R model to provide a better understanding of the impact of this particular feature of VR devices on tourists' responses.

First, in line with previous notions, the results of the analysis show that technologies with high levels of embodiment (VR HMD) produced higher levels of immersion and sensory stimulation than technologies with medium and low levels of embodiment (Biocca, 1997; Shin, 2017; Tussyadiah, 2014). Furthermore, embodied technologies improve user engagement with the pre-experience of the destination. This finding highlights the role of embodied VR technologies for the tourism industry in terms of engaging tourists (Griffin et al., 2017). Finally, we found partial support for the effect of technological embodiment on behavioral intentions. Although there are clear differences between VR HMD, mobile phones, and desktop PCs, it appears that medium levels of technological embodiment may be enough to increase the potential tourist's behavioral intentions toward the destination. This could be due to the fact that tourists are accustomed to using their mobile phones during all the stages of their touristic experiences (Wang, Park, & Fesenmaier, 2012). In the pre-experience stage, tourists are determined to fulfill their informational needs (Lu, Gursoy, & Lu, 2016) and, therefore, they may be more concerned about the usefulness of the information for decision-making than about the integration of the technology with their senses.

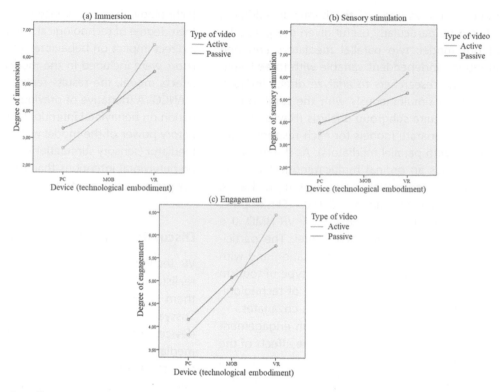

Figure 2. Interaction effects.

Furthermore, the results reveal that the particular features of the type of tourism moderate the effects of technological embodiment. Active tourism content is better perceived with embodied VR devices (high technological embodiment) in comparison to less embodied devices. We found that active tourism videos viewed through VR HMD stimulate more immersive and sensorial experiences, and higher perceptions of engagement, than passive tourism videos viewed through VR HMD. Watching passive tourism videos through low-embodied devices may be, at the very least, equally as effective as using high-embodied devices. This may be explained by the matching of the users' real movements and their actions in the virtual environment, facilitated by embodied VR technologies (Slater, 2009). This leads the potential tourist to have active involvement in the virtual environment which provides him or her with a better pre-experience of the destination (Cho et al., 2002). Our results are in line with the cognitive fit theory (Vessey, 1991). However, this moderating effect was not significant for behavioral intentions. These antecedents of actual behaviors (Ajzen, 1991) can be influenced by the type of tourism, while the rest of the variables are more related to the experience itself.

Finally, the results confirm mediation in the relationship between technological embodiment and engagement through the two organismic variables, immersion and sensory stimulation. The immersive and sensory power provided by highly embodied technologies drive perceptions of engagement with the virtual destination (Barnes, 2016; Jennett et al., 2008). In addition, sensory stimulation mediates the effect of high technological embodiment on behavioral intentions. As previously stated, sensory cues can impact on the users' senses and influence their behaviors through emotions, memories, perceptions, and preferences (Krishna, 2010). In tourism, this effect can be even stronger due to the particular features of the industry (Guttentag, 2010). Our findings confirm that embodied VR devices provide extensive sensory information, so their use in the tourism industry can lead to positive behavioral intentions. On the other hand, the mediating effect of immersion is not significant. This might be because immersion appeals to experiential processes and not their outcomes (Chen & Chen, 2010). Thus, sensory cues may be more important than perceptions of immersion for inducing certain behaviors.

Implications for research and practice

At the theoretical level, this research contributes to the body of knowledge about the application of VR technologies in the pre-experience stage of travelers' decision-making processes. VR devices can differ from mobile phones and stationary PCs in several

Table 3. Results of the analysis of the mediation model on engagement.

Predictor	Coeff.	SE	t	p	LLCI	ULCI
Immersion						
Constant	3.398	0.40	8.587	0.000	2.617	4.179
X1 (desktop PC vs. otherwise)	1.011	0.22	4.515	0.000	0.569	1.452
X2 (VR HMD vs. otherwise)	1.951	0.23	8.364	0.000	1.491	2.411
Experience in the destination	−0.245	0.23	−1.082	0.281	−0.692	0.202
Pref. for the type of tourism	−0.015	0.055	−0.278	0.781	−0.123	0.092
Experience with the technology	0.003	0.045	0.074	0.941	−0.086	0.093
Technological innovativeness	−0.076	0.067	−1.125	0.262	−0.208	0.057
Model summary			$R^2 = 0.512$; $F_{(6, 189)} = 33.513$, $p < 0.001$			
Sensory stimulation						
Constant	3.783	0.36	10.600	0.000	3.077	4.489
X1 (desktop PC vs. otherwise)	0.753	0.20	3.721	0.000	0.354	1.153
X2 (VR HMD vs. otherwise)	1.306	0.21	6.192	0.000	0.890	1.723
Experience in the destination	−0.387	0.20	−1.886	0.061	−0.791	0.018
Pref. for the type of tourism	0.010	0.05	0.196	0.845	−0.088	0.107
Experience with the technology	0.055	0.04	1.336	0.183	−0.026	0.135
Technological innovativeness	−0.049	0.06	−0.801	0.424	−0.169	0.071
Model summary			$F_{(6, 189)} = 19.090$, $p < 0.001$			
Engagement						
Constant	1.277	0.28	4.531	0.000	0.721	1.833
X1 (desktop PC vs. otherwise)	0.267	0.13	2.015	0.045	0.005	0.528
X2 (VR HMD vs. otherwise)	−0.065	0.15	−0.425	0.671	−0.368	0.237
Immersion	0.237	0.06	4.266	0.000	0.127	0.347
Sensory stimulation	0.589	0.06	9.582	0.000	0.468	0.710
Experience in the destination	0.263	0.13	2.047	0.042	0.009	0.516
Pref. for the type of tourism	−0.002	0.03	−0.069	0.945	−0.063	0.058
Experience with the technology	−0.049	0.02	−1.915	0.057	−0.099	0.002
Technological innovativeness	−0.032	0.04	−0.847	0.398	−0.107	0.043
Model summary			$R^2 = 0.770$; $F_{(8, 187)} = 78.299$, $p < 0.001$			
Total effect model: Engagement						
Constant	4.310	0.36	12.008	0.000	3.602	5.018
X1 (desktop PC vs. otherwise)	0.950	0.20	4.480	0.000	0.550	1.351
X2 (VR HMD vs. otherwise)	1.167	0.21	5.513	0.000	0.749	1.584
Experience in the destination	−0.023	0.21	−0.111	0.912	−0.428	0.383
Pref. for the type of tourism	0.000	0.05	−0.001	0.999	−0.098	0.098
Experience with the technology	−0.016	0.04	−0.391	0.696	−0.097	0.065
Technological innovativeness	−0.080	0.06	−1.290	0.198	−0.199	0.042
Model summary			$R^2 = 0.393$; $F_{(6, 189)} = 20.399$, $p < 0.001$			

Relative total effects of X on Y	Effect	SE	t	p	LLCI	ULCI
X1 (desktop PC vs. otherwise)	0.950	0.20	4.679	0.000	0.550	1.351
X2 (VR HMD vs. otherwise)	1.167	0.21	5.513	0.000	0.749	1.584
Omnibus test of total effect of X on Y			R^2 change = 0.359 $F_{(2, 189)} = 55.922$, $p < 0.001$			

Relative indirect effects of X on Y	Effect	BootSE	BootLLCI	BootULCI
Embodiment → Immersion → Engagement				
X1 (desktop PC vs. otherwise)	0.240	0.09	0.091	0.450
X2 (VR HMD vs. otherwise)	0.463	0.12	0.232	0.706

Bootstrap results for indirect effects	Effect	BootSE	BootLLCI	BootULCI
Embodiment → Sensory stimulation → Engagement				
X1 (desktop PC vs. otherwise)	0.311	0.09	0.130	0.486
X2 (VR HMD vs. otherwise)	0.540	0.11	0.336	0.764

dimensions. This research examines the role embodiment as one of the main differentiating features of these technologies and proposes a measurement instrument of perceived technological embodiment. Our findings stress that technological embodiment must be taken into consideration in the study of customer experiences with VR technologies. In addition, we contribute to the call for empirical research regarding the application of VR devices in tourism marketing (Griffin et al., 2017), since most of the previous literature is mainly focused on virtual worlds (e.g. Second Life; Tussyadiah et al., 2017).

At the managerial level, destination marketers can give tourists more effective promotional messages using embodied VR devices, integrating immersive and sensory experiences into their communication strategies to provide positive potential outcomes (Huang et al., 2016). This research sheds light on the psychological-technological processes that managers must take into account when presenting visual information to

Table 4. Results of the analysis of the mediation model on behavioral intentions.

Predictor	Coeff.	SE	t	p	LLCI	ULCI
Behavioral intentions						
Constant	2.154	0.55	3.932	0.000	1.073	3.235
X1 (desktop PC vs. otherwise)	0.248	0.26	0.962	0.338	−0.261	0.756
X2 (VR HMD vs. otherwise)	−0.165	0.30	−0.552	0.581	−0.753	0.424
Immersion	−0.132	0.11	−1.219	0.224	−0.345	0.081
Sensory stimulation	0.594	0.12	4.971	0.000	0.358	0.830
Experience in the destination	−0.368	0.25	−1.472	0.143	−0.860	0.125
Pref. for the type of tourism	0.086	0.06	1.440	0.151	−0.032	0.203
Experience with the technology	0.061	0.05	1.232	0.219	−0.037	0.159
Technological innovativeness	−0.074	0.07	−0.999	0.319	−0.219	0.072
Model summary			$R^2 = 0.234$; $F_{(8, 187)} = 7.158$, $p < 0.001$			
Total effects model: Behavioral intentions						
Constant	3.953	0.47	8.481	0.000	3.034	4.873
X1 (desktop PC vs. otherwise)	0.562	0.26	2.131	0.034	0.042	1.082
X2 (VR HMD vs. otherwise)	0.354	0.27	1.288	0.199	−0.188	0.896
Experience in the destination	−0.565	0.27	−2.115	0.036	−1.091	−0.038
Pref. for the type of tourism	0.094	0.06	1.456	0.147	−0.033	0.220
Experience with the technology	0.093	0.05	1.751	0.082	−0.019	0.198
Technological innovativeness	−0.093	0.08	−1.168	0.244	−0.249	0.064
Model summary			$R^2 = 0.098$; $F_{(6, 189)} = 3.424$, $p < 0.05$			
Relative total effects of X on Y	*Effect*	SE	t	p	LLCI	ULCI
X1 (desktop PC vs. otherwise)	0.562	0.26	2.131	0.034	0.042	1.082
X2 (VR HMD vs. otherwise)	0.354	0.27	1.288	0.199	−0.188	0.896
Omnibus test of total effect of X on Y			R^2 change = 0.061 $F_{(2, 189)} = 6.396$, $p < 0.01$			
Relative indirect effects of X on Y	*Effect*	BootSE	BootLLCI		BootULCI	
Embodiment → Immersion → Behavioral intentions						
X1 (desktop PC vs. otherwise)	−0.133	0.12	−0.382		0.074	
X2 (VR HMD vs. otherwise)	−0.257	0.21	−0.691		0.145	
Bootstrap results for indirect effects	*Effect*	BootSE	BootLLCI		BootULCI	
Embodiment → Sensory stimulation → Behavioral intentions						
X1 (desktop PC vs. otherwise)	0.447	0.16	0.171		0.771	
X2 (VR HMD vs. otherwise)	0.776	0.19	0.452		1.185	

potential tourists that may affect their virtual travel experiences (Choi, Hickerson, & Lee, 2018) and increase the likelihood of them actually visiting the destination. Travel agencies can use embodied VR technologies to offer vicarious experiences that help potential visitors to make better travel decisions, especially in the case of active tourism offers. These embodied technologies can generate superior, memorable experiences that will be perceived as high-value propositions by potential customers, particularly in the pre-experience stage of their customer journey. Therefore, investing in this emerging technology and the creation of attractive and suitable content may help companies to overcome the decreasing efficacy of traditional media (Fransen et al., 2015).

Limitations and future research lines

This research has several limitations that may serve as bases for future research. First, the empirical study was undertaken in artificial laboratory settings. Although this approach serves to achieve internal validity for testing purposes, it would be interesting to carry out field studies to ensure external validity and generalize

the results. Second, although several features may serve to characterize these technologies, we focused on one of the main differentiating factors of VR devices (i.e., technological embodiment) to compare their effectiveness with less embodied devices. However, future research should consider additional physical variables in which these devices differ (e.g., weight, screen size). Third, the research examines the pre-experience stage of the customer journey; it would be interesting to study the effects of embodied VR devices in later stages (experience stage, post-experience stage) to obtain a global picture of the customer journey. Fourth, we focused on active/passive tourism as a moderator of the proposed relationships. However, other types of tourism (e.g. cultural, relaxing) may moderate these effects. Fifth, while our millennial sample is an interesting target group (Commscope, 2017; Greenlight, 2015), it would be convenient to analyze market segments to enrich and generalize the results of the analysis.

Furthermore, we have taken into account several control variables (previous experience with the destination, preference for the type of tourism, previous experience with the technology, degree of technological innovativeness). However, as the newness effect of VR HMD dissipates over time (Diffusion of Innovations Theory; Rogers, 2010), users can become bored or even abandon these technologies once the initial excitement is overcome. Therefore, future studies should consider variables to reflect on the potential downsides of VR technologies (e.g. skepticism toward new technologies, novelty-seeking tendency). In addition, future studies could analyze the role that personality traits (e.g. capacity to imagine, personal involvement) play in these relationships, since previous research has shown that individual characteristics can alter the impact of VR technologies (Disztinger et al., 2017). Additionally, in the empirical study, we kept the level of interactivity constant, allowing the participants to control the navigation but not manipulate it (low interactivity; Flavián et al., 2018). However, future studies should consider this variable to analyze if these devices by themselves can generate different levels of perceived interactivity in this context of the study. Finally, this research offers a first step in the validation of a scale that measures effectively the level of technological embodiment perceived by users. Future studies are needed to develop and confirm scales for the more precise measurement of technological embodiment.

Note

1. The same analyses were carried out including the control variables (previous experience with the destination, preference for the type of tourism, previous experience with the technology, degree of technological innovativeness) as covariates. The results of the ANCOVAs replicated those of the ANOVAs. None of the control variables had a significant impact on the perceptions of technological embodiment ($ps > 0.182$) and on the perceptions of active/passive tourism ($ps > 0.406$).

Disclosure statement

No potential conflict of interest was reported by the authors.

Funding

This work was supported by the Spanish Ministry of Economy and Competitiveness (ECO2016-76768-R); the European Social Fund and the Government of Aragon (group "METODO" S20_17R and pre-doctoral grant 2016–2020 BOA IIU/1/2017).

ORCID

Carlos Flavián http://orcid.org/0000-0001-7118-9013
Sergio Ibáñez-Sánchez http://orcid.org/0000-0003-3088-4102
Carlos Orús http://orcid.org/0000-0002-8253-4713

References

Ajzen, I. (1991). The theory of planned behavior. *Organizational Behavior and Human Decision Processes*, *50*(2), 179–211.

Bagozzi, R. P., & Yi, Y. (1988). On the evaluation of structural equation models. *Journal of the Academy of Marketing Science*, *16*(1), 74–94.

Barnes, S. (2016). Understanding virtual reality in marketing: Nature, implications and potential. Retrieved from SSRN http://dx.doi.org/10.2139/ssrn.2909100.

Berg, L. P., & Vance, J. M. (2017). Industry use of virtual reality in product design and manufacturing: A survey. *Virtual Reality*, *21*(1), 1–17.

Bernardo, A. B., Tan-Mansukhani, R., & Daganzo, M. A. A. (2018). Associations between materialism, gratitude, and well-being in children of overseas Filipino workers. *Europe's Journal of Psychology*, *14*(3), 581.

Bigné, J. E., Sánchez, M. I., & Sánchez, J. (2001). Tourism image, evaluation variables and after purchase behaviour: Inter-relationship. *Tourism Management*, *22*(6), 607–616.

Biocca, F. (1997). The cyborg's dilemma: Progressive embodiment in virtual environments. *Journal of Computer-Mediated Communication*, *3*(2), 1–29.

Bruner, G. C., & Kumar, A. (2007). Gadget lovers. *Journal of the Academy of Marketing Science*, *35*(3), 329–339.

Canalys (2017). Media alert: Virtual reality headset shipments top 1 million for the first time. Retrieved from http://www.bit.ly/2ohSplJ.

Canalys (2018). VR headset market grows 200% in China in Q1 2018, driven by standalone models. Retrieved from http://www.bit.ly/2NcVFtT.

Casaló, L. V., Flavián, C., & Guinalíu, M. (2010). Determinants of the intention to participate in firm-hosted online travel communities and effects on consumer behavioral intentions. *Tourism Management*, *31*(6), 898–911.

Casaló, L. V., Flavián, C., & Ibáñez-Sánchez, S. (2017). Understanding consumer interaction on Instagram: The role of satisfaction, hedonism, and content characteristics. *Cyberpsychology, Behavior, and Social Networking*, *20*(6), 369–375.

CCSInsight (2018). Virtual reality device market declines in 2018 but outlook remains positive. Retrieved from http://www.bit.ly/2Rrnqh7.

Chen, C. F., & Chen, F. S. (2010). Experience quality, perceived value, satisfaction and behavioral intentions for heritage tourists. *Tourism Management*, *31*(1), 29–35.

Cheong, R. (1995). The virtual threat to travel and tourism. *Tourism Management*, *16*(6), 417–422.

Cho, Y. H., Wang, Y., & Fesenmaier, D. R. (2002). Searching for experiences: The web-based virtual tour in tourism marketing. *Journal of Travel & Tourism Marketing*, *12*(4), 1–17.

Choi, Y., Hickerson, B., & Lee, J. (2018). Investigation of the technology effects of online travel media on virtual travel experience and behavioral intention. *Journal of Travel & Tourism Marketing*, *35*(3), 320–335.

Commscope (2017). The generation Z. Study of tech intimates. Retrieved from http://www.bit.ly/2LYgSmZ.

Disztinger, P., Schlögl, S., & Groth, A. (2017). Technology acceptance of virtual reality for travel planning. In R. Schegg & B. Stangl (Eds.), *Information and communication technologies in tourism 2017* (pp. 255–268). Cham: Springer.

Donovan, R., & Rossiter, J. (1982). Store atmosphere: An environmental psychology approach. *Journal of Retailing, 58*(1), 34–57.

Eroglu, S. A., Machleit, K. A., & Davis, L. M. (2001). Atmospheric qualities of online retailing: A conceptual model and implications. *Journal of Business Research, 54*(2), 177–184.

Ettis, S. A. (2017). Examining the relationships between online store atmospheric color, flow experience and consumer behavior. *Journal of Retailing and Consumer Services, 37*, 43–55.

Flavián, C., Ibáñez-Sánchez, S., & Orús, C. (2018). The impact of virtual, augmented and mixed reality technologies on the customer experience. *Journal of Business Research, 100*, 547-560.

Fornell, C., & Larcker, D. (1981). Evaluating structural equation models with unobservable variables and measurement error. *Journal of Marketing Research, 18*(3), 39–50.

Fornerino, M., Helme-Guizon, A., & Gotteland, D. (2008). Movie consumption experience and immersion: Impact on satisfaction. *Recherche Et Applications En Marketing (English Edition), 23*(3), 93–110.

Fransen, M. L., Verlegh, P. W., Kirmani, A., & Smit, E. G. (2015). A typology of consumer strategies for resisting advertising, and a review of mechanisms for countering them. *International Journal of Advertising, 34*(1), 6–16.

Ghosh, T., & Sarkar, A. (2016). "To feel a place of heaven": Examining the role of sensory reference cues and capacity for imagination in destination marketing. *Journal of Travel & Tourism Marketing, 33*(1), 25–37.

Gibson, A., & O'Rawe, M. (2017). Virtual reality as a promotional tool: Insights from a consumer travel fair. In T. Jung & M. C. Tom Dieck (Eds.), *Augmented reality and virtual reality - Empowering human, place and business* (pp. 93–107). London: Springer.

Gold, A. H., Malhotra, A., & Segars, A. H. (2001). Knowledge management: An organizational capabilities perspective. *Journal of Management Information Systems, 18*(1), 185–214.

Goodhue, D. L., & Thompson, R. L. (1995). Task-technology fit and individual performance. *MIS Quarterly, 19*(2), 213–236.

Greenlight (2015). 2015 Virtual reality consumer report. Retrieved from http://www.bit.ly/2znYAs7.

Greenlight (2016). Virtual reality consumer report. Retrieved from http://www.bit.ly/2LZQvN9.

Griffin, T., Giberson, J., Lee, S. H. M., Guttentag, D., Kandaurova, M., Sergueeva, K., & Dimanche, F. (2017). Virtual reality and implications for destination marketing. *Proceedings of the Tourism Travel and Research Association: Advancing Tourism Research Globally*, Québec, Canada.

Gutierrez, M., Vexo, F., & Thalmann, D. (2008). *Stepping into virtual reality*. London: Springer Science & Business Media.

Guttentag, D. A. (2010). Virtual reality: Applications and implications for tourism. *Tourism Management, 31*(5), 637–651.

Hair, J. F., Anderson, R. E., Tatham, R. L., & Black, W. C. (1998). *Multivariate data analysis*. Englewood Cliffs, NJ: Prentice-Hall.

Hayes, A. F. (2018). *Introduction to mediation, moderation, and conditional process analysis: A regression-based approach* (2nd edn). New York, NY: The Guilford Press.

Hayes, A. F., Montoya, A. K., & Rockwood, N. J. (2017). The analysis of mechanisms and their contingencies: PROCESS versus structural equation modeling. *Australasian Marketing Journal (AMJ), 25*(1), 76–81.

Henseler, J., Ringle, C., & Sarstedt, M. (2015). A new criterion for assessing discriminant validity in variance-based structural equation modeling. *Journal of the Academy of Marketing Science, 43*(1), 115–135.

Henseler, J., Ringle, C. M., & Sinkovics, R. R. (2009). The use of partial least squares path modeling in international marketing. *Advances in International Marketing, 20*(1), 277–319.

Huang, Y. C., Backman, K. F., Backman, S. J., & Chang, L. L. (2016). Exploring the implications of virtual reality technology in tourism marketing: An integrated research framework. *International Journal of Tourism Research, 18* (2), 116–128.

Huang, Y. C., Backman, S. J., Backman, K. F., & Moore, D. (2013). Exploring user acceptance of 3D virtual worlds in travel and tourism marketing. *Tourism Management, 36*, 490–501.

Hyun, M. Y., & O'Keefe, R. M. (2012). Virtual destination image: Testing a telepresence model. *Journal of Business Research, 65*(1), 29–35.

IDC (2018). Despite a sharp decline in VR headset shipments in Q2 2018, the market outlook remains positive, says IDC. Retrieved from http://www.bit.ly/2CK6RtV.

Ihde, D. (1990). *Technology and the lifeworld: From garden to earth*. Indiana, IN: Indiana University Press.

Jang, S. (2005). The past, present, and future research of online information search. *Journal of Travel & Tourism Marketing, 17*(2–3), 41–47.

Jennett, C., Cox, A. L., Cairns, P., Dhoparee, S., Epps, A., Tijs, T., & Walton, A. (2008). Measuring and defining the experience of immersion in games. *International Journal of Human-Computer Studies, 66*(9), 641–661.

Jung, T., Tom Dieck, M. C., Moorhouse, N., & Tom Dieck, D. (2017). Tourists' experience of virtual reality applications. Proceedings of the *2017 IEEE International Conference on Consumer Electronics (ICCE)* (pp. 208–210). Las Vegas, LV: IEEE.

Kim, H. C., Chua, B. L., Lee, S., Boo, H. C., & Han, H. (2016). Understanding airline travelers' perceptions of well-being: The role of cognition, emotion, and sensory experiences in airline lounges. *Journal of Travel & Tourism Marketing, 33*(9), 1213–1234.

Kim, M. J., Lee, C. K., & Jung, T. (2019). Exploring consumer behavior in virtual reality tourism using an extended stimulus-organism-response model. *Journal of Travel Research*. Article in press. Retrieved from https://doi.org/10.1177/0047287518818915.

Kim, S. S., & Prideaux, B. (2005). Marketing implications arising from a comparative study of international pleasure tourist motivations and other travel-related characteristics of visitors to Korea. *Tourism Management, 26*(3), 347–357.

Krishna, A. (2010). An introduction to sensory marketing. In A. Krishna (Ed.), *Sensory marketing: Research on the sensuality of products* (pp. 1–13). New York, NY: Routledge.

Krishna, A. (2012). An integrative review of sensory marketing: Engaging the senses to affect perception, judgment and behavior. *Journal of Consumer Psychology, 22*(3), 332–351.

Krishna, A., & Schwarz, N. (2014). Sensory marketing, embodiment, and grounded cognition: A review and introduction. *Journal of Consumer Psychology, 24*(2), 159–168.

Latta, J. N., & Oberg, D. J. (1994). A conceptual virtual reality model. *IEEE Computer Graphics and Applications, 14*(1), 23–29.

Lemon, K. N., & Verhoef, P. C. (2016). Understanding customer experience throughout the customer journey. *Journal of Marketing, 80*(6), 69–96.

Lu, A. C. C., Gursoy, D., & Lu, C. Y. R. (2016). Antecedents and outcomes of consumers' confusion in the online tourism domain. *Annals of Tourism Research, 57*, 76–93.

Marasco, A., Buonincontri, P., van Niekerk, M., Orlowski, M., & Okumus, F. (2018). Exploring the role of next-generation virtual technologies in destination marketing. *Journal of Destination Marketing & Management, 9*, 138–148.

Mehrabian, A., & Russell, J. A. (1974). *An approach to environmental psychology*. Cambridge, MA: The MIT Press.

Mendes-Filho, L., Mills, A. M., Tan, F. B., & Milne, S. (2017). Empowering the traveler: An examination of the impact of user-generated content on travel planning. *Journal of Travel & Tourism Marketing, 35*(4), 425–436.

Mummalaneni, V. (2005). An empirical investigation of web site characteristics, consumer emotional states and on-line shopping behaviors. *Journal of Business Research, 58*(4), 526–532.

National Research Council. (2012). *Human performance modification: Review of worldwide research with a view to the future*. Washington, WA: National Academies Press.

Neuhofer, B., Buhalis, D., & Ladkin, A. (2014). A typology of technology-enhanced tourism experiences. *International Journal of Tourism Research, 16*(4), 340–350.

Nielsen (2016). Case study: Exploring immersive technologies. Retrieved from http://www.bit.ly/2LtV9mm.

O'Brien, H. L. (2016). Theoretical perspectives on user engagement. In H. O'Brien & P. Cairns (Eds.), *Why engagement matters: Cross-disciplinary perspectives and innovations on user engagement in digital media* (pp. 1–26). Cham: Springer.

O'Brien, H. L., Cairns, P., & Hall, M. (2018). A practical approach to measuring user engagement with the refined user engagement scale (UES) and new UES short form. *International Journal of Human-Computer Studies, 112*, 28–39.

O'Brien, H. L., & Toms, E. G. (2010). The development and evaluation of a survey to measure user engagement. *Journal of the American Society for Information Science and Technology, 61*(1), 50–69.

Pavlov, I. P. (1902). *The work of the digestive glands*. London: Griffin.

Peracchio, L. A., & Meyers-Levy, J. (1997). Evaluating persuasion-enhancing techniques from a resource-matching perspective. *Journal of Consumer Research, 24*(2), 178–191.

Pike, S., & Page, S. J. (2014). Destination marketing organizations and destination marketing: A narrative analysis of the literature. *Tourism Management, 41*, 202–227.

Pizam, A., & Fleischer, A. (2005). The relationship between cultural characteristics and preference for active vs. passive tourist activities. *Journal of Hospitality & Leisure Marketing, 12*(4), 5–25.

Ringle, C. M., Wende, S., & Becker, J. M. (2015). SmartPLS 3. Boenningstedt: SmartPLS GmbH. Retrieved from https://www.smartpls.com.

Rogers, E. M. (2010). *Diffusion of innovations* (4th edn). New York: Free Press.

Sherman, W. R., & Craig, A. B. (2003). *Understanding virtual reality*. San Francisco, CA: Morgan Kauffman.

Shin, D. H. (2017). The role of affordance in the experience of virtual reality learning: Technological and affective affordances in virtual reality. *Telematics and Informatics, 34*(8), 1826–1836.

Slater, M. (2009). Place illusion and plausibility can lead to realistic behaviour in immersive virtual environments. *Philosophical Transactions of the Royal Society of London B: Biological Sciences, 364*(1535), 3549–3557.

Slater, M., & Usoh, M. (1993). Representations systems, perceptual position, and presence in immersive virtual environments. *Presence: Teleoperators & Virtual Environments, 2*(3), 221–233.

Steenkamp, J. B. E., & Geyskens, I. (2006). How country characteristics affect the perceived value of web sites. *Journal of Marketing, 70*(3), 136–150.

Steuer, J. (1992). Defining virtual reality: Dimensions determining telepresence. *Journal of Communication, 42*(4), 73–93.

Thakur, R., Angriawan, A., & Summey, J. H. (2016). Technological opinion leadership: The role of personal innovativeness, gadget love, and technological innovativeness. *Journal of Business Research, 69*(8), 2764–2773.

Tussyadiah, I. P. (2014). Expectation of travel experiences with wearable computing devices. In Z. Xiang & I. Tussyadiah (Eds.), *Information and communication technologies in tourism 2014* (pp. 539–552). Switzerland: Springer International Publishing.

Tussyadiah, I. P., Jung, T. H., & Tom Dieck, M. C. (2017). Embodiment of wearable augmented reality technology in tourism experiences. *Journal of Travel Research, 57*(5), 597–611.

Tussyadiah, I. P., Wang, D., & Jia, C. H. (2016). Exploring the persuasive power of virtual reality imagery for destination marketing. *Proceedings of the 2016 International Conference Leading Tourism Research Innovation for Today and Tomorrow, Travel and Tourism Research Association*. Vail, U.S.

Tussyadiah, I. P., Wang, D., & Jia, C. H. (2017). Virtual reality and attitudes toward tourism destinations. In R. Schegg & B. Stangl (Eds.), *Information and communication technologies in tourism 2017* (pp. 229–239). Cham: Springer.

Tussyadiah, I. P., Wang, D., Jung, T. H., & Tom Dieck, M. C. (2018). Virtual reality, presence, and attitude change: Empirical evidence from tourism. *Tourism Management, 66*, 140–154.

Venkatesh, V., & Davis, F. D. (2000). A theoretical extension of the technology acceptance model: Four longitudinal field studies. *Management Science, 46*(2), 186–204.

Vessey, I. (1991). Cognitive fit: A theory-based analysis of the graphs versus tables literature. *Decision Sciences, 22*(2), 219–240.

Vohnout, P., Cerba, O., Kafka, S., Fryml, J., Krivanek, Z., & Holy, S. (2014). SmartTouristData approach for connecting local and global tourist information systems. *Proceedings of the 2014 IST-Africa Conference* (pp. 1–6). Mauritius: IEEE.

Wang, D., Park, S., & Fesenmaier, D. R. (2012). The role of smartphones in mediating the touristic experience. *Journal of Travel Research, 51*(4), 371–387.

Witmer, B. G., & Singer, M. J. (1998). Measuring presence in virtual environments: A presence questionnaire. *Presence, 7*(3), 225–240.

YouGov (2016). Travel booking trends in the Middle East, North Africa and South Asia. Retrieved from http://www.bit.ly/2bZDxBq.

Yung, R., & Khoo-Lattimore, C. (2017). New realities: A systematic literature review on virtual reality and augmented reality in tourism research. *Current Issues in Tourism*, 1–26. Article in press. Retrieved from https://doi.org/10.1080/13683500.2017.1417359.

Appendix

Please rate from 1 (strongly disagree) to 7 (strongly agree) the extent to which you agree with the following sentences.

Technological innovativeness *(adapted from* Thakur et al., 2016; Bruner & Kumar, 2007)
I get a kick out of buying new high tech items before most other people know they exist.
It is cool to be the first to own high tech products.
I get a thrill out of being the first to purchase a high technology item.
Being the first to buy new technology devices is very important to me.
I want to own the newest technological products.
When I see a new technology in the store (web), I often buy it because it is new.

Please rate from 1 (strongly disagree) to 7 (strongly agree) the extent to which you agree with the following sentences in relation to your (destination) experience with (technology).

Technological embodiment

The (technology) technology is nearly integrated into my body.

The (technology) technology is in direct contact with my senses.

The (technology) technology becomes part of my actions.

The (technology) technology is an extension of my body.

Immersion *(adapted from* Fornerino et al., 2008)

The technology created a new world that suddenly disappeared at the end of the experience.

During the experience with the technology, I was unaware of my real surroundings.

The technology made me forget about the realities of the world outside.

Sensory stimulation *(adapted from* Witmer & Singer, 1998)

During the (technology) experience, the visual aspects of the virtual environment involve me.

During the (technology) experience, the auditory aspects of the virtual environment involve me.

During the (technology) experience, I was able to actively survey or search the environment using vision.

During the (technology) experience, my sense of moving around inside the virtual environment was compelling.

Engagement *(adapted from* O'Brien et al., 2018; O'Brien & Toms, 2010)

I was absorbed in the (technology) experience.

Using (technology) in the experience was worthwhile.

My (technology) experience was rewarding.

The time I spent using (technology) just slipped away.

I felt interested in this (technology) experience.

Behavioral intentions *(adapted from* Huang et al., 2013; Bigné et al., 2001)

After the (place + technology) experience, I want to find out more information about the destination.

After the (place + technology) experience, I will try to visit the destination in person in the future.

Type of tourism

I consider that this video is related to…	City tourism	Nature tourism	Sports tourism

The approach of this video is…

Passive (lower leading role, more static) Active (higher leading role, more motion)

TOURISTS AS MOBILE GAMERS: GAMIFICATION FOR TOURISM MARKETING

Feifei Xu
Feng Tian
Dimitrios Buhalis
Jessica Weber
Hongmei Zhang

ABSTRACT. Gaming as a cutting-edge concept has recently been used by some innovative tourism sectors as a marketing tool and as a method of deeper engagement with visitors. This research aims to explore the gamification trend and its potential for experience development and tourism marketing. Using a focus group, this paper discusses gaming and tourism, and explores what drives tourists to play games. The results suggest tourists' game playing motivation is multidimensional. Players tend to start with purposive information seeking, then move on to an intrinsic stimulation. Socialization is also an important dimension. The research demonstrates several implications for tourism marketing.

INTRODUCTION

Gaming or electronic games (often simply called "games") provide players with an immersive and interactive entertainment experience often through dynamic and real-time interaction with their context, local organizations, and fellow players. With the rapid development of mobile devices, such as smartphones and tablets, gaming becomes mobile (Gentes, Guyot-Mbodji, & Demeure, 2010) and allows dynamic interaction at the location of the user. Smartphones enable players to interact with their real-world environment in real time (Hinske, Lampe, Magerkurth, & Röcker, 2007). Researchers suggest that mobile games have changed the game players' experiences in many ways (Blum, Wetzel, Mccall, Oppermann, & Broll, 2012). One of the fundamental changes is that gaming experiences have been extended into the real world, and are potentially available at any place and at any time (Benford,

Magerkurth, & Ljungstrand, 2005; Grüter, 2008).

Recently, persuasive technologies such as gaming and the application of game elements have been used in a non-gaming context (so-called gamification), such as business, health, and education (Xu, Webber, & Buhalis, 2014). Persuasive technology is broadly defined as technology that is designed to change attitudes or behavior of users through persuasion and social influence (Bogost, 2007). Persuasive applications are often computerized software or information systems designed to reinforce, change, or shape attitudes or behaviors or both, without using coercion or deception (Oinas-Kukkonen & Harjumaa, 2008).

Gaming, as a cutting-edge concept, is emerging as a useful tool and has been used by some tourism organizations for marketing and for dynamic engagement with users. As a new approach to promote tourism destinations, gaming provides tourism organizations and destination marketers with an opportunity to create informative and entertaining settings for successful brand awareness, interaction, and communication. Indeed, Middleton (1994) mentions that tourist decision-making is affected by both formal (e.g. advertising, internet, and sale promotion) and informal channels of communication, which form stimulus inputs. As the tourism industry is primarily an experience industry (Pine & Gilmore, 2011), several researchers have argued about the importance of using experiential information in promotional stimuli for tourism marketing (Goossens, 2000; Gretzel, Yuan, & Fesenmaier, 2000; Stamboulis & Skayannis, 2003). Gaming as a technological tool therefore has the potential to help develop such experiences and support dynamic interactions. For example, location-based games can be a way of experiencing points of interests for tourists through a treasure hunt. "Tourists can follow a list of recommendations given by a mobile game and can learn something about their environment by solving mini games related to their experiences" (Linaza, Gutierrez, & Garcia, 2014, p. 498).

Serious games are designed for purposes other than mere entertainment for players. They primarily perform tasks and achieve objectives that address key user requirements, including education, on-the-job training, cultural heritage, and medical applications. Serious games often collect information about brand consumers, determine behavior patterns, thought processes, priorities, and interests, and use gaming technologies and methodologies to engage users/learners/tourists at a deeper level in order to help them conceptualize and improve their experience. An example is the Dublin Augmented Reality Project, in Dublin, Ireland. It is developed to support Dublin's brand development to become the "innovative city" in Europe (Han, Jung, & Gibson, 2014, p. 512). The project is funded by Dublin City Council to develop a mobile augmented reality (AR) application for the tourism industry in Dublin,

> which will be applied via tourist trails in various parts of the destination by considering various tourism stakeholders. This application will provide a platform to superimpose tourism relevant information, reconstruct and revive stories of the past, assisting the tourists in creating an emotional experience of the intangible product (Han et al., 2014, p. 512)

With this innovative project Dublin aimed to be the first European city to implement an AR infrastructure, not only benefiting tourists but also its citizens and other stakeholders.

Gaming is in its infancy in many industries and also in tourism, as very few successful examples have so far been established, mainly specialized treasure hunts and cultural heritage applications. Gaming in tourism is a new and emerging area. Technically, it is very challenging in two aspects. One is that the game designers need to understand both the tourists' needs and the gamers' desires, and then blend them seamlessly to deliver memorable, fun, and engaging gaming experiences, for this particular segment; the other is that, from a game programmer's point of view, developing location-based tourism games such as those based on AR is more complex because AR still faces some technical issues itself, for example real-time calibration. Non-technically, the business model of these games needs to be explored and investigated further. Compared with generic or traditional games, tourism-specific games require very specific information of a particular destination, which sometimes is difficult to incorporate into the games. A game company must also take a tourist game's commercial viability into account as the target group of customers/players is relatively small.

Gradually some serious games are being designed for the purpose of introducing tourism information, specifically targeting tourist players. However, they are not always successful due to a lack of understanding of tourist players (Fernandes, Almeida, & Rosseti, 2013). Compared with traditional game players at home, tourist players often play in an unfamiliar environment with a limited time at their disposal (Fernandes et al., 2013), and they are also interested in their surrounding environment. Although tourists are important users of mobile games, hitherto little is known about their gaming motivation and experiences.

Previous studies on gaming motivations have mainly studied traditional games and games as pure entertainment (see for example Ryan, Rigby, & Przybylski, 2006). These studies have demonstrated the importance of researching players' motivations. Indeed, a deep understanding of motivations will help game designers create convincing and worthwhile games for users to enhance their experiences.

However, the research on traditional games (de Souza e Silva, 2013) is not sufficient as mobile games are different, they can be played at any time and any place, and the player's interaction with the surrounding environment via smartphone could result in motivations that differ from those associated with other traditional games (Goh, Ang, Lee, & Chua, 2011), particularly in the case of tourist players. There is very limited research on mobile games (Schønau-Fog, 2011) and whether traditional game play motivation would be suitable for mobile games is unsure.

Using a focus group, this research discusses gaming and tourism, and introduces the cutting-edge concept of game-based marketing for tourism. It explores what drives tourists to play mobile games on holiday, what their requirements are, and discusses whether traditional game play motivation would be suitable for mobile tourist players.

LITERATURE REVIEW

The Concept of Gaming

Gaming in this study concentrates on electronic games, often played on mobile devices and smartphones. Gaming is the running of software artefacts known as electronic games (often simply called "games"). It is regarded as a closed system in which the guidelines have to be clearly stated beforehand (Salen & Zimmerman, 2004). McGonigal (2011) suggests that goals, rules, feedback systems, and voluntary participation are important characteristics of gaming. Juul (2003) adds emotional attachment of a player assigned to the game itself and its specific outcome.

The proliferation of smartphones and tablets has empowered mobile gaming and is changing the gaming experience. With the popularity of smart phones, tablets, and personal digital assistants (PDAs), gaming experiences become much more mobile and context plays a critical role in the gaming experience. Particularly those location-based, Geographical Positioning System (GPS) supported mobile games, such as *Geocaching* and *Shadow Cities*, provide players with a more exciting and real experience (Benford, 2012). Location-based mobile games have taken the players from the virtual world to a real/mixed world environment (Gentes et al., 2010; Hinske et al., 2007). Grüter (2008) states that mobile games emphasize mobility and positioning, often using the context of their location as the background for the game. The physical location and the movement of the players are important in location-based mobile games (Jacob, 2011). Klopfer and Squire (2008) observe that mobile gaming is expanding to more context-sensitive, supporting game applications (apps) that relate the player to his physical location and encourage users to complete local tasks, as well as connect with and compete against other players. The latest generation of smart devices have introduced gaming experiences into entirely new experiences. From smartphone game apps to online social interaction, technology and social media have made gaming rapidly acceptable for both males and females, young and old, as well as people who have never played games before.

Motivation of Game Players

Motivation plays an important part in game playing. Ryan et al. (2006) suggest that understanding the motivation of game players is an under-researched area. Boyle, Connolly, Hainey, and Boyle (2012) state that studies of motives for playing digital games are mainly grounded in rigorous theoretical models, and they are mostly based on satisfaction of needs. The main motivations identified by researchers are summarized in Table 1. Although different methodological approaches are used, researchers tend to agree that games are used for enjoyment and to satisfy the needs for competence and relatedness.

Bartle's (1996) work on player type is one of the early works exploring player motivation. Based on Massively Multiplayer Online Game (MMOG) players, Bartle (1996) divides players into four types, namely achievers, socializers, explorers, and killers. The majority of players (80%) are socializers: they look for social engagement with other people. Achievers are always looking for challenge. Explorers are eager to know the breadth of the game by discovering every angle, while killers, interested in competing with and defeating others, only account for less than 1% of the total population of game players; they are most active and most engaging. Bartle's (1996) work has provided an important foundation for many researchers, although the use of his work applies to

TABLE 1. Game Players' Motivations Divided Into Intrinsic and Extrinsic Motivations

Motivation	Literature
Challenge, achievement, and competition	Deci & Ryan (1985); Lucas & Sherry (2004); Ryan et al. (2006); Yee (2006); Li & Counts (2007); Tychsen, Hitchens, & Brolund (2008); Frostling-Henningsson (2009); De Carvalho & Ishitani (2012); Engl & Nacke (2012)
Freedom in a virtual world	Ryan et al. (2006)
Sense of belonging	Lin & Lin (2011)
Socialization – social interaction	Ryan et al. (2006); Yee (2006); Chou & Tsai (2007); Tychsen et al. (2008); Frostling-Henningsson (2009); Mintel (2009); Lin, Chen, & Kuo (2011)
Excitement	Lucas & Sherry (2004)
Arousal	Lucas & Sherry (2004)
Seeking information and exploration	Chou & Tsai (2007)
Kill time	Chou & Tsai (2007); Mintel (2009)
Fun and enjoyment	Chou & Tsai (2007); Lin & Lin (2011); Lin et al. (2011); De Carvalho & Ishitani (2012); Huang, Backman, Backman, and Moore (2013)
Escapism	Yee (2006); Frostling-Henningsson (2009); Tychsen et al. (2008)
Immersion – discovery – role-playing – customization	Paras & Bizzochi (2005); Yee (2006); Tychsen et al. (2008); Carrigy, Naliuka, Paterson, & Haahr (2010); Engl & Nacke (2012)
Ease of use	Lin et al. (2011); Huang et al. (2013)
Perceived usefulness	Huang et al. (2013)
Extrinsic motivation effect on intrinsic motivation	Lin et al. (2011)
Fantasy	Paras & Bizzochi (2005)
Positive emotions	Huang et al. (2013)
Flow	Huang et al. (2013); Zhou (2012); Engl & Nacke (2012)
Character	Tychsen et al. (2008)

MMOG only; whether it is applicable to today's mobile games is uncertain. Given the differences in mobile games, it is necessary to revisit game players' motivation in a mobile context. Nevertheless, Bartle's (1996) model of player types recognizes the need to understand different players' motivations.

Researchers also suggest that gender, age, experience, and even personality, could influence the motivation for playing. Jansz, Avis, and Vosmeer (2010) find that males rate social interaction, fantasy, and challenge as more important motivations than females. Olson (2010) agrees that for males fun, competition, challenge and excitement, relaxation, and coping with anger are important motives for playing games than for females. Eglesz, Fekete, Kiss, and Izsó (2005) find different motivations in different age groups. Younger people tend to have more sensation-seeking motives, while older people (over 30 years old) tend to try again when they fail. Researchers agree that motivation changes when players become more experienced. Wan and Chiou (2007) find that intrinsic motives are more important to online addictive players, while extrinsic motivation is more important to the non-addictives.

Most research on player motivation is based on traditional games. Little is known about mobile game players, and particularly those GPS-supported mobile game players who may have a different motivation due to the context awareness and mobile positioning characteristics of those games (de Souza e Silva, 2013). A context or environment can alter significantly the way a user interacts with a mobile game which involves movement, unpredictable states, and various physical parameters, like noise and light, limited screen and so on (Rapits, Tselios, & Avouris, 2005). A mobile device's location-aware capabilities allow users to annotate locations, find other people in the vicinity, and access information connected to specific locations (de Souza e Silva, 2013). Socialization becomes more important for mobile players. The concept of Net locality (Gordon & de Souza e Silva, 2011) demonstrates that the player is part of the local space. However, the distractions of traffic (particularly in urban areas) also constrain the players' movements in the game. Context awareness provides players with information that is highly relevant to their current situation or a personalized context, allowing an effective and dynamic way to communicate in the game. Researchers also identified that mobile gaming fosters feelings of community and team play (social motivation) and competition (Li & Counts, 2007; Schønau-Fog, 2011).

Tourism and Gaming

The use of games in the tourism industry may potentially provide great marketing opportunities. Tourism is an experience industry (Pine & Gilmore, 2011) that is increasingly based on co-creating personalizable services. New technologies such as social media, smartphones, and gaming provide technological tools for developing such experiences. Indeed, the travel industry has always been one of the first ones to engage new initiatives (Buhalis & Law, 2008). According to the World Travel Market Report (2011), gamification is a major trend for the coming years in tourism, which will appeal to consumers across all age demographics.

The current use of gaming by the tourism industry can be divided into two types, as follows

(1) Social games (play before you are there), based on social media such as Facebook, which are mainly used for brand awareness, to attract potential customers, and to build up a destination or a company image. Examples can be found in Thailand (Smile Land Game, 2012), Cape Town, South Africa (The Real Time Report, 2012), Ireland (Tourism Ireland, 2011), and Nanjing, China (People, 2013). These games were developed by destination management organizations (DMOs) for destination marketing purposes. Many airlines including KLM, British Airways, and Virgin Atlantic have also developed games to engage consumers in branding and marketing exercises.

(2) Location-based mobile games (play while you are there) are mainly used to encourage more engagement on-site, to enhance tourists' on-site experiences at the destination in a more fun and informative way (Waltz & Ballagas, 2007). However, "a tourist destination is an extremely rich source of information, supplying tourists at each moment with a continuous flow of images, sounds and feelings that cannot be fully simulated by computers" (Linaza et al., 2014, p. 498). Most of the existing tourism destination games are based on the game principles of the classic treasure hunt. For example, REXplorer aims to persuade on-site tourists to explore and enjoy the history of the United Nations Educational, Scientific and Cultural Organization (UNESCO) world heritage city of Regensburg, Germany (Waltz & Ballagas, 2007). The *Amazing City Game* has been developed in Trondheim, Norway, to encourage tourists to enter a knowledge competition tour by solving tasks at different locations (Wu & Wang, 2011). AR is a popular technique used in location-based tourist games to enhance immersive experiences on-site (Mashable, 2011) as it enables a blend between virtual and real environments. (Yovcheva, Buhalis, Gatzidis, & van Elzakker, 2014).

However, these game apps are not always successful. Some fail to engage travelers and often lack fun and sometimes facts about tourist spots. For example, after reviewing 15 mobile advertgames, Celtek (2010) concluded that none of the games gave information about the destination and country except *VeGame* and *Geocaching*. Game developers with a technical background sometimes may not be fully aware of the tourists' need and motivation to play. Therefore, a user-centered approach in game design is critical (Ermi & Mäyrä, 2005; Yovcheva et al., 2014).

A sufficient understanding of tourist players' motives and gaming experiences will be helpful in the design of these games. Although there are theories on game player motivations, they do not specifically address tourists, and thus fail to identify tourists' needs. Research suggests that tourists have information needs which differ from other players (Yovcheva et al., 2014), tourists usually have a limited time at their disposal (Fernandes et al., 2013), and are not familiar with the location. Therefore, when playing games, tasks need to be less ambiguous and less challenging. Why do tourists play games, when do they play, what type of games do they prefer, what do they expect from game-based marketing, are critical aspects of game design.

Gamification in Tourism Marketing

Game-based marketing offers a potentially new type of marketing opportunity in tourism. Chaffery and Ellis-Chadwick (2012) recognize that gamification and mobile marketing are important trends of the future of marketing. Digital technology is reshaping the entire marketing mix (Jobber, 2009). In terms of game-based marketing, it adds more fun and personal experience to marketing the product through virtual experiential marketing (Middleton, Fyall, & Morgan, 2009, p. 260). Zichermann and Linder (2010) argue that games are about pleasure, and pleasure is the new marketing element, an extremely powerful dimension of marketing. Games therefore can provide a new and powerful way of interaction and engagement in a fun and rewarding way.

The importance of using experiential information in promoting stimuli for tourism marketing has been recognized by many academics (Huang et al., 2013). Williams (2006) recommends that the use of an immersive virtual environment as a new approach to promote tourism sites offers destination marketers an opportunity to create informative and entertaining settings for successful interaction and communication between the destination and the tourists (Bogdanovych et al.,

2007). Berger et al. (2007) note that technologies such as virtual reality allow potential tourists to collect travel information and experience the 3-D representation of a destination (Hay, 2008). The use of games offers a variety of benefits for tourism marketing, and can increase brand awareness, attract potential customers, enhance tourists' on-site experiences, and increase engagement.

Game design can be based on real environments, for example, tourist attractions (as in the case of Thailand and China). It provides potential visitors with an informative and entertaining setting. Games are usually presented with a virtual reality or AR 3-D technology, providing an immersive and engaging experience with the virtual and the real destination (Huang et al., 2013; Yovcheva et al., 2014).

Games with an advertising purpose, also known as advertgames, are an important new type of marketing tool that could offer entertainment to game players in order to make an emotional connection between the game and the brand. Celtek (2010) concludes that the advantages of using advertgames are that they are less annoying and more personalized.

In addition, gaming provides a good opportunity to build an online community as often a sense of community is identified (Fong & Frost, 2009). Buhalis and Law (2008) recognized that virtual communities could have an influence on brand awareness, therefore suggesting they should be used as way to better understand customers as well as compensate for negative word-of-mouth. Wang, Zhang, Choi, and D'Eredita (2002) also agree that the brand-building associated with virtual communities can lead to brand awareness and brand loyalty.

The tourism industry provides multidimensional and multifaceted experiences (Kim, Ritchie, & Mccormick, 2012; Neuhofer, Buhalis, & Ladkin, 2012). Researchers suggest that leisure experiences are about feeling, fantasy and fun (Holbrook & Hirschman, 1982), escape and relaxation (Beard & Ragheb, 1983), entertainment (Farber & Hall, 2007; Pine & Gilmore, 1999), and novelty and surprise (Duman & Mattila, 2005). The research on tourist experiences could benefit from gaming research. The enjoyment of playing (Klimmt, 2003) and the desire to continue playing to challenge one's own abilities (Brown & Vaughn, 2011); the different types of emotion, such as hope, fear, excitement (Zichermann & Cunningham, 2011); the experiences of fantasy, fun, and challenges all contribute to a deep engagement and the addiction to game play, and engaging with tourism organizations and destinations.

Researchers argue that with the growing up of a new generation, "Generation G, who was born after 1998, whose principle form of entertainment is games and who is the first truly mobile and social generation" (Zichermann & Linder, 2010, p. 163), future marketing faces a new challenge to satisfy this mobile and social generation and to dynamically co-create products and services.

Tourists' Leisure Motivations on Holiday

Understanding the holiday motivation of tourists and their requirements regarding tourism products and services is critical. In the field of tourism, studies of tourist holiday motivation have been carried out for a long time (Hsu, Cai, & Li, 2010). Maslow (1943) suggests that people start with a basic low level of the physiological need for safety, belonging and love, and esteem and self-actualization. Dann (1977) and Crompton (1979) divide motivations into push and pull factors; Beard and Ragheb (1983) suggest four aspects of motivation: intellectual, social, self-challenge, and stimulus-avoidance. Iso-Ahola's (1982) motivations include escaping and seeking; McIntosh, Goeldner, and Ritchie (1995) suggest physical, cultural, interpersonal motivations, and status and prestige motivations. Holiday motivation referred to in this paper is primarily applicable to leisure travelers, as business travelers often have no choice of destinations or activities which are determined by meetings, conferences, and business agendas. However, even business travelers with a few hours to spare may use a game (such as *Treasure Hunt*) to explore a destination in the limited time available or they can play a game before traveling to familiarize themselves with the destination.

Researchers agree that the motivation to play games is multidimensional. It can be influenced by many factors, such as gender, age, life stage,

FIGURE 1. Motivation of Mobile Gaming Usage by Different User Group

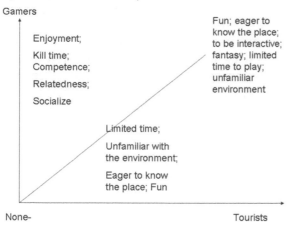

and previous travel experiences (Jang & Cai, 2002; Jönsson & Devonish, 2008; Pearce & Lee, 2005; Reisinger & Mavondo, 2005). From the above literature, it is obvious there are some overlapping dimensions between a tourist's motivation to travel and a game player's motivation to play games. However, whether these general motivations of game players apply to tourist game players is uncertain. In order to understand tourist players' experiences, it is essential to explore tourist game players' motivations. Figure 1 illustrates the uniqueness of tourists' motivations in using mobile games in comparison with non-tourists based on previous literature

METHODOLOGY

This research is explorative as it investigates a new and emerging area. It aims to explore how gaming can be used in tourism marketing and how consumers can benefit from gaming whilst traveling. Since this is a new area it needs to be explored in depth and thus qualitative research paradigms are followed. Focus groups have been widely used in social sciences and applied research (Puchta & Potter, 2004). As a qualitative research method, focus groups emphasize group discussions and group interactions, as well as share and compare individual experiences among the participants (Marshall &

Rossman, 2006). The method is usually used for topics that are not well understood to discover new insights. This paper aims to explore the new topic of tourists' opinions of and experiences with game-based marketing, its explorative nature made focus groups a suitable method for this study. As an exploratory study on the new emerging area of gaming and tourism, representation of the sample as part of the population is not a major concern as the method aims to explore the dimensions and create constructs rather than measure variables and representation, and a larger scale of quantitative sample will be conducted at the next stage of this project.

Games are extremely popular among students. In this research, a student sample was chosen based on the following considerations:

(1) students are advanced users in technology and they are early adopters of technology (Williams, Yee & Caplan's, 2008); Nelson (2006) mentions that college students are more likely to be innovators or early adopters of new information technologies than the general population. Arif and Aslam (2014) also mention that university students are early adopters compared with other demographic groups;

(2) students are also main game players as suggested by many game researchers. Griffiths, Davies, and Chappell's (2004) study shows that two thirds of game players are under 31 years old, and 29% of game players are current university students studying for an undergraduate degree;

(3) games are extremely popular among students. Student samples have often been used by game researchers (Doughty & O'Coill, 2005; Eglesz et al., 2005; Lucas & Sherry, 2004);

(4) today's students are the professional classes of tomorrow so an understanding of their opinions is likely to give some indication of the kind of marketing offers and messages that will be needed to attract them in the future (Xu & Morgan, 2009). Richards and Wilson (2003) reported that the 15–25 year-old

age group accounts for 20% of all tourism journeys and that 140 million young people travel every year.

The study was carried out in Nanjing University, China. China is one of the largest mobile users in the world, and marketers estimate that there are 1 billion mobile users in China alone (Emarketer, 2013). Nanjing University is a comprehensive university which includes 86 different majors. It covers undergraduates, postgraduates, and PhD students. Students are well equipped with mobile devices. A message to recruit participants was posted on the university intranet for two weeks. In order to participate in the focus group, the respondents had to meet the following criteria: (1) currently uses a smartphone; (2) plays PC games or mobile games at least twice a week; (3) has taken at least one holiday trip during the last 12 months. Finally, 26 students who met the above criteria volunteered. These 26 students were then divided into groups based on their year of study. As there are only two students from the third-year undergraduate program, they were combined with second-year students to form a bigger group; this group contains seven students. Profiles of the group participants can be found in Table 2. Four focus groups were conducted, lasting between 1 and 1.5 hours. Each focus group was conducted in a quiet meeting room on campus to avoid any disturbance. One of the authors acted as a moderator in all groups. A research assistant was employed to document group interaction, including non-verbal communication (Krüger, 1998). At the end of each session, the researcher and the assistant exchanged their ideas on group interaction.

At the beginning of the focus group, the interviewer explained the purpose of the research, and each respondent was asked to sign a consent form of confidentiality and anonymity (Creswell, 2008). Each focus group was recorded using a digital voice recorder. Interviews were transcribed verbatim. Data was analyzed using thematic analysis (Marshall & Rossman, 2006). During the interview, a short video of *Smile Land Thailand* was shown (material was downloaded from YouTube; retrieved from https://www.youtube.com/watch?v=rhPNzUUndWw), and respondents were asked about their general use of gaming, gaming activity on holiday, motivation to play games, and whether they would play a specific tourism game. The respondents' age ranged from 18 to 28 years, covering undergraduate and postgraduate research students (see "Profile of Respondents" in Table 2). Interaction between the respondents in the groups showed that they helped each other to generate discussion. No major disagreements were discovered in the discussion.

RESULTS AND DISCUSSION

It was established that the general use of smartphones was quite extensive and the role of gaming was quite important. Each group was asked about the general usage of their smartphones. Popular themes among the students include making phone calls, sending messages, information search, social networking, and other entertainment (music, photos, reading novels, playing games), although individual usage and preferences varied. Surprisingly, on average, the most popular usage of smartphones

TABLE 2. Profile of Respondents

	Group A	Group B	Group C	Group D
Year	UG 1	UG 2 and 3	UG 4	PG and PhD
Male	4	4	4	3
Female	2	3	2	4
Age (years)	18–19	19–22	20–22	20–28
Marital status	All single	All single	All single	All single except one married without children

Notes. UG: undergraduate; PG: postgraduate.

among the students is for social networking and information search rather than the traditional usage of communication functions (such as phone calls, messages). The popularity of social networking on smartphones has also been proved in other research (Wang & Fesenmaier, 2013). In daily use, gaming was mentioned by many students as an entertainment function by both males and females in each group, reflecting the popularity of gaming among young people (Zichermann & Linder, 2010).

Timing is critical and the research aimed to answer the question of when do we play a game on holiday. The groups agreed that people play games mainly before the trip, sometimes during the journey, and maybe after the trip. Most people agreed that they used mobile phones to check information about the destination before the trip and they confirmed that if a game can deliver this information they would have a try. This suggests a possibility of using games as brand awareness before the trip. However, they explained that when they are actually at the destination, they prefer to enjoy the real world rather than virtual the world. Nevertheless, most of the groups showed an interest in the idea of location-based mobile games.

> *I like playing games, but when I am on holiday, I am busy looking around, enjoying the scenery and local food, I do not have time to play games. (Group D)*

> *… After a day's tour, you just feel so tired, you do not want to play games … (Group A)*

> *A location-based game is different, it tells you where you are and gives you some tasks at the destination. It's interesting as it links with your real environment. It is fun. (Group B)*

All groups agreed that they often played a game on the way to the destination, on a train or flight, or waiting in the airport, and the main reason for that is to kill time. This proves previous research on gaming kills time (Chou & Tsai, 2007; Mintel, 2009).

Increasingly people play games during holidays and in various locations. Perhaps context

determines what types of games players prefer to play on holiday? All groups agreed that while on holiday, due to the constraints of mobile phones (slow internet speed, data roaming, small screen, etc.), they prefer simple, relaxed, not too challenging games. However, in each group, there seems to be a difference between genders. Boys prefer action and strategy games, while girls prefer brain and leisure games. This is similar to Jansz et al.'s (2010) research on traditional games.

When considering the reasons to play games on holiday respondents mentioned playing games is mainly to kill time on the way to the destination.

> *You can play games on the train, plane on the coach. Because you are bored, and you have nothing to do, this is a good way to kill time, particularly when you are travelling alone. (Group C)*

> *Sometimes I arrive too early at the train station, or sometimes my flight is delayed, I usually play games (or listen to music) on my mobile to kill the long waiting time. (Group B)*

All groups agreed that when arriving at the destination, they prefer sightseeing rather than games. Some groups added that the only opportunity to play games at the destination is when they come back to the hotel in the evening, when they can play games again.

> *Some games give you tasks to do everyday; therefore, you need to finish it. And the only time to do it when actually at the destination is when you are in bed in the hotel before you go to sleep. (Group A)*

There are several motivations to play a tourism-related game. Each group was given a video of the *Smile Land Thailand* marketing campaign of their mobile game (retrieved from https://www.youtube.com/watch?v=rhPNzUUndWw), and asked about whether they would play this kind of game, and what might motive them to play. Themes of motivation for playing a tourism game differs from previously mentioned motivations of game players but reflects more the needs of tourists as identified in the following motivations:

Curiosity

Curiosity emerged as the most popular theme. Several groups mentioned that as they have never played something like this before, the idea of "a tourist game" attracts them, and they would definitely have a try.

> As this is a new thing, I have never heard of it, and have never played it, I would like to have a try to see what it looks like. So, curiosity would be my first motivation. As this is a specific tourism context, I would like to see what I can do there in Thailand, shopping, food, etc. What does the Royal Palace look like, you know, that sort of tourist stuff. Explore .... (Group C)

Comments reflect curiosity as the first stage of starting a tourist game, the innovative idea of marketing through a game attracts them to play. This was not mentioned by any previous literature on game playing motivation.

Exploration

The second most popular theme is exploration. Groups mentioned that the main motivation would be to see the destination in a virtual world, to gather some information about the destination.

> ... a good way to get to know some practical information about the destination, particularly the small attractions, rather than popular, hot spot attractions. (Group A)

> '... practical information for tourists and time saving ... you know all about the destination through a game.' (Group D)

Although this theme reflects more on the tourist motivation to explore the destination, the fun element of gaming cannot be ignored. Groups mentioned that there are lots of ways to get to know the destination, but playing a game and getting to know the destination is more fun. Compared with other traditional ways of getting to know a destination (travel agents, books, internet, etc.), playing a specific destination-related game is more fun. Although whether the information provided in the game is accurate and updated is still debatable, nevertheless, the fun element of exploratory play has been highlighted by the participants. Exploratory play includes a fun element in which participants seek entertainment from the game; this again proves Williams' (2006) comment that gaming as a new approach provides an entertaining setting for tourists.

Virtual Experiences: a Mixed Feeling of Reality and Virtual Reality

This primarily reflects virtual and AR games.

> When you play this kind of game, if you have already been to the destination, you will have a feeling of real and virtual, this is a wonderful feeling and exciting experience. And if you visit the destination after you played the game, you will also remember how you played in the game, you might wonder, am I in the virtual world or real world (laughs). I really look forward to playing this game as I have been to some places in Thailand. (Group D)

Comments confirm the potential influence such games could have on enhancing tourists' experiences. This echoes various researchers that gaming can contribute to tourist experiences. Waltz and Ballagas (2007) suggest that gaming can be used to inspire, educate, and train tourists.

Socializing

Socializing refers to getting to know people who might also want to go to the destination or local people who live at the destination. This may contribute to co-creating tourism products with fellow travelers or local residents. It was also a popular theme, particularly mentioned by females in the group.

> *If they provide a platform to allow game players to communicate with each other, you might be able to meet some people to go to the destination together. Saying buying a group ticket to get into the attraction or something. (Group A)*

> *I think it would be good to get to know something about the local people there, to ask them (local residents in the game) questions, to see their dress code, their local food. Sometimes on holiday, particularly if it is a package holiday, you don't have much opportunity to ask the local people, as everything has been arranged for you. (Group B)*

Here, socialization includes socializing with potential tourists and online with local residents. The first type of socializing may result in exchanging ideas, perhaps meeting at the destination, travel in company, sharing costs, while the second type of interaction will result in learning more about the destination and the local community. The theme of socializing reflects the desire to establish new or maintain existing social relationships, it supports Lin and Lin's (2011) opinion that the online community is important as a platform for socializing in games. Meanwhile, socialization is also an important dimension as a tourist holiday motivation as suggested by many researchers (Beard & Ragheb, 1983; McIntosh et al., 1995). Therefore, this dimension of socialization reflects both tourists' and game players' motivation and can lead to the co-creation of tourist experiences.

Fun: a Fun Way to Get to Know the Destination

Gaming can also add pure fun to the travel experience as it animates the travel experience and enables users to engage with the destination in an interactive way. This may be a better way to show the different elements of the destination and to animate certain aspects.

> *Unlike reading a guidebook or search online information and filter this information for a specific destination, I think it is fun to play a game and get to know the destination. Very useful. (Group C)*

> *If it is well designed, it would be fun as well. As everyone who plays a game is attracted by the fun element of gaming. Otherwise, people would quit quickly after a few tries. (Group C)*

> *It is a better way to show a destination to friends. Traditionally you sent photos to your friend, now I invite you to play the game and show you exactly where I have been, what it looks like. You know, it is fun. (Group D)*

> *Years later, when I am older, I can show it to my son that I have been to the places in your game … (Group D)*

Comments suggest that fun is a fundamental dimension of game playing motivation. This echoes Zichermann and Linder's (2010) opinion that pleasure can be a powerful dimension of marketing. It also reflects fun as a useful element in virtual experimental marketing (Middleton et al., 2009). This theme was highlighted by both male and female respondents.

Challenge and Achievement

Gaming also includes challenge and achievement, and these elements were also mentioned by a few students. A tourism game may include a challenge such as visiting a number of attractions in a limited period of time or identifying a number of interlinked monuments. As a reward to mark achievement, games may collect points or badges, or some other rewards. The level of difficulty may vary and the challenge should lead to a reward for the player achievement.

> *You might start with basic information search, but in the end, it is still a game. I*

guess most people who play games are like me, looking for some kind of achievement. Yes, if there is some challenge there, not to be so easily conquered then I will be interested. Otherwise, you play a few times before you go to the destination, then you will never come back to play again. (Group D).

Comments suggest that the dimensions of challenge and achievement of traditional games also apply here, but are not as popular as other dimensions. Challenge and achievement, together with competition, are intrinsic motivations. They support the flow of the game, and are considered fundamental motivations in traditional game play (Deci & Ryan, 1985; Li & Counts, 2007; Lucas & Sherry, 2004; Ryan et al., 2006; Yee, 2006).

Figure 2 summarizes the main motivation of playing a tourism game. As illustrated, the basic motivation for playing a tourism game is curiosity. This can be developed into a cutting-edge way of tourism marketing where tourism organizations engage players and support them to explore tourism products and destinations. Exploring the destination is also a popular theme where players are keen to virtually explore a destination before arrival but also use AR games to add information and fun to their real life experience during their travel experience. These motivations might co-exist at the same time, as gaming motivation can be multidimensional. The popular sensation-seeking motivation in game players (see Table 1) is

not a popular choice here. Rather the intellectual motivations of a tourist (Beard & Ragheb 1983), to learn, explore, and discover new things, were highlighted in the findings, reflecting Iso-Ahola's (1982) seeking-dimension of tourists' motivations. Tourism games can be very purposive, as tourist game players want to know more about the destination. The socialization motivation reflects the possible encounter between players and fellow players or tourists as well as with local residents. This can lead to the co-creation of tourism experiences with local residents and also among tourists themselves. The intrinsic motivation (fun and fantasy, challenge and achievement) seem to support the flow of the game. When players become more experienced they look for more fun and challenges. This has been verified in both situations, namely playing a general game and playing tourism games. Overall, the respondents identified clear potential in games as a way of engaging with tourism organizations and destinations and suggested that if they are designed properly they can clearly enhance their tourism experience before, during, and after their visit.

CONCLUSION

Being one of the world's largest and most pervasive industries, the travel and tourism sector is as exposed as any other to the forces of change that are at work in the rapid developments in the information and communication technologies (ICT) arena (Buhalis, 2003; Buhalis & Law, 2008). Destinations around the world are investing more in how to use ICT in destination management and marketing. Gaming represents one of the most promising ICT technologies that offer benefits in various areas such as entertainment, education (interpretation), and the co-creation of tourism experiences. Gaming can enhance tourists' interest in the destination, provide experiences and knowledge which otherwise are not available, thus co-creating a personal experience during the visit. Engaging other players and locals can enhance this experience even more and influence how

FIGURE 2. Motivation to Play Tourism Games

people interact with destinations on a large scale.

Gaming motivation has always been an important topic for research. Understanding the game playing motivation can be useful in design-specific games. This study makes an important contribution by identifying gaming tourists' motivations. The main motivation to play a tourism game is to gain practical information about the destination before, during, and after the visit, and to socialize with other people. The feeling of playing games in a virtual and at the same time in a real environment (fantasy and fun) is also important. The usual motivation of playing games such as killing time (Chou & Tsai, 2007; Mintel, 2012) is only important in this case during the transit period, as many tourists who play games seek purposive information, to prepare for the holiday, or to enhance their experience on location. The motivations identified in this study reflect a mixture of tourists' needs and motivation (Beard & Ragheb, 1983; Crompton, 1979; Dann, 1977). They suggest that tourist players might start with a basic information-seeking purpose but when they become more experienced in the game, they may seek more challenges and achievements, reflecting some of the intrinsic motivations of game play, thus supporting Wan and Chiou's (2007) study.

It is evident that gaming can create a new industry paradigm by engaging tourists in dynamic, personalized, and contextualized experiences. Understanding the tourism players' motivations is critical for both tourism marketers and game designers, as this can help them develop suitable games and experiences using cutting-edge technologies.

Gaming can engage tourists in a fun, informative, and memorable way through their entire travel experience before, during, and after the trip.

Before traveling, gaming can offer an innovative way of marketing a destination and not only attract many potential tourists but also enable them to engage with the destination at a deeper level. Game-based marketing has great potential to attract tourists' attention and to increase brand awareness. As players are looking for information about the destination, gaming can allow them to explore specialized aspects and assist them to develop their prospective experience. Therefore, the purposive feeding of destination information through highly interactive and customizable games is very important. Marketers can design their games based on specific attractions and facilities (Huang et al., 2013), particularly those of the lesser known spots. They can also design games to allow players to explore special interests such as archaeology, birdwatching, or gastronomy, in a way to prepare for a more rewarding visit. This new marketing method may provide a great opportunity for small tourism destinations and businesses as well as lesser known spots as it is an innovative and relatively inexpensive way of marketing.

During the trip, games can be used to kill time in the transit area. They can also add more fun to the journey and enhance tourist onsite experiences. Particularly location-based games and AR games can encourage tourist players to interact with the surrounding physical environment, to learn more facts about the spot, to tailor their visit to their interests, and to enrich a more dynamic and real experience (Waltz & Ballagas, 2007). Gaming may give tourist players a real, personalized, fun and fantasy experience by making them feel that they are actually in the game themselves, rather than being a separate, exterior entity. Games can also help tourists to develop an emotional attachment through immersion in the destination (Klopfer & Squire, 2008). The results highlight the opportunity of socializing with both other tourist players and local resident players. Hence games can emerge as online platforms to help establish new or maintain existing social relationships (Chou & Tsai, 2007) and support value co-creation. This element of socializing is a key dimension of tourist motivation, as suggested by many researchers (Beard & Ragheb, 1983; Iso-Ahola, 1982).

After the trip, games are mainly used to recall the journey and show off to other people. They can also support players to further engage with the destination and expand elements in depth. However, the attractiveness of game playing can always cause players to continue playing and engage further with tourism organizations and destinations. Game players usually look for challenges and pursue a sense of achievement in a virtual world. A well-designed game can always cause players to continue playing and draws them into an emotional immersion in the virtual world. A number of challenges can also intrigue them to continue playing in order to achieve certain benefits and recognition. Rewards in the form of free holidays, meals, and entry to attractions can provide the motivation and the challenge to continue the player involvement and stimulate repeat visits. Juul (2003) and Lucas and Sherry (2004) suggest that intrinsic motivation contributes to the flow of the game. Rewards and points are linked to extrinsic motivations of game play, while social connection and challenge are linked with intrinsic motivation. In a tourism mobile game, virtual rewards can be transferred to real world rewards, such as coupons for the shopping center, loyalty cards for the restaurant, free entrance of the theme park, and so on. The context awareness (such as personal preferences regarding sights, food, etc.) in the game allows destination marketers to deliver a highly personalized experience to address the individual tourist's motivation. After-trip play could also contribute to tourism marketing by engaging gamers and making them ambassadors for the tourism organization and destination. As tourists have already been to the destination, the mixed feeling of reality and fantasy when recalling the trip can enhance tourists' satisfaction, keep the destination in their memory, and encourage them to recommend it to other people.

Motivations for game playing have always been an important topic for research. By understanding these motivations, game companies develop games based on specific demands. The findings of this study suggest that a UCD approach is important when designing games. Schell (2008) suggests that one of the basic elements in game design is the "goals" – our findings regarding the motivations of tourist game players directly contribute to this element. For tourism-specific games it is crucial to feed tourist players accurate information about the destination to satisfy the players' initial motivation, namely purposive information-seeking. With clear "goals" in mind the game designers are more likely able to produce a game which is attractive to the tourist players and educative.

When designing a specific tourism game, destination marketers and designers should work closely with each other, and consider carefully the above mentioned specific motivations for playing a tourist game. They should also explore the latest technological developments in both gaming and smart mobile devices to ensure that all capabilities are utilized to maximize the interactivity and engagement. Only when tourist players' motivation is fully understood by game designers and the informational and experiential motivations supported by tourism marketers, can a game become attractive and desirable to tourist players.

This research is an exploratory study into the motivations of players and the opportunity to use games for tourism marketing. It uses a qualitative method to explore students players' opinions. As the research was undertaken before the demonstrated game was officially available, this is a limitation in our research. As suggested, there are many factors that might influence game play motivation, which include both external and internal factors. Future research could use the results of this research to develop constructs to be surveyed, test the conceptual model quantitatively, and identify which of these key factors play a more important role for each market segment affected. A quantitative method could also be used to test the gender, age, and cultural differences between tourist game players. In this study, the focus group was used to explore students' opinion of the game; future research could also use an experimental method to investigate tourists' experiences after game playing, for example, their learning about the destination and how that enhances their motivation to visit. Future research can also concentrate on location-based and augmented location games for gamers who are playing games whilst at the destination. The study offers a significant contribution to understanding how gaming can contribute to tourism marketing before, during, and after tourists' visit.

FUNDING

This work is partly supported by Fusion Fund [NX0392], Bournemouth University, UK; Fundamental Research Funds for the Central Universities, Southeast University [2242015R30020], China and Chinese National Nature Science Foundation [41371161].

REFERENCES

Arif, I., & Aslam, W. (2014, August). Students' dependence on smart-phones and its effect on purchase behavior. MPRA paper No. 58919.

Bartle, R. A. (1996). *Hearts, clubs, diamonds, spades*: *Players who suit MUDs*. Retrieved from http://www.mud.co.uk/richard/hcds.htm

Beard, J., & Ragheb, M. G. (1983). Measuring leisure motivation. *Journal of Leisure Research, 15*(3), 219–228.

Benford, S. (2012). Future location-based experiences JISC technology and standards. *Watch, 1–17*. Retrieved December 11, 2013, from http://www.jisc.ac.uk/media/documents/techwatch/jisctsw_05_01.pdf

Benford, S., Magerkurth, C., & Ljungstrand, P. (2005). Bridging the physical and digital in pervasive gaming. *Communications of the ACM, 48*(3), 54–57. doi:10.1145/1047671

Berger, H., Dittenbach, M., Merkl, D., Bogdanovych, A., Simoff, S., & Sierra, C. (2007). Opening new dimensions for e-tourism. *Journal of the Reality Society, 11* (2–3), 75–87.

Blum, L., Wetzel, R., Mccall, R., Oppermann, L., & Broll, W. (2012). The final timewarp: Using form and content to support player experience and presence when designing location-aware mobile augmented reality games. In *Proceedings of the designing interactive systems conference* (pp. 711–720).

Bogdanovych, A., Esteva, N., Gu, M., Simoff, S., Maher, M. L., & Smith, G. (2007, January 24–26). *The role of online travel agents in the experience economy*. Proceedings of the 14th international conference on information technology in tourism ENTER, Ljubljana, Slovenia.

Bogost, I. (2007). *Persuasive games: The expressive power of videogames*. Cambridge, MA: MIT Press.

Boyle, E. A., Connolly, T. M., Hainey, T., & Boyle, J. M. (2012). Engagement in digital entertainment games: A systematic review. *Computers in Human Behavior, 28*, 771–780. doi:10.1016/j.chb.2011.11.020

Brown, V. R., & Vaughn, E. D. (2011). The writing on the (Facebook) wall: The use of social networking sites in hiring decisions. *Journal of Business and Psychology, 26*(2), 219–225. doi:10.1007/s10869-011-9221-x

Buhalis, D. (2003). *eTourism: Information technology for strategic tourism management*. London: Pearson (Financial Times/Prentice Hall).

Buhalis, D., & Law, R. (2008). Progress in information technology and tourism management: 20 years on and 10 years after the Internet—The state of eTourism research. *Tourism Management, 29*, 609–623. doi:10.1016/j.tourman.2008.01.005

Carrigy, T., Naliuka, K., Paterson, N., & Haahr, M. (2010). Design and evaluation of player experience of a location-based mobile game. In *Proceedings of the 6th Nordic conference on human-computer interaction: Extending boundaries*. Reykjavik: ACM.

Celtek, E. (2010). Mobile advergames in tourism marketing. *Journal of Vacation Marketing, 16*, 267–281. doi:10.1177/1356766710380882

Chaffery, D., & Ellis-Chadwick, F. (2012). *Digital marketing, strategy, implementation and practice* (5th ed.). Harlow, Essex: Pearson.

Chou, C., & Tsai, M.-J. (2007). Gender differences in Taiwan high school students' computer game playing. *Computers in Human Behavior, 23*, 812–824. doi:10.1016/j.chb.2004.11.011

Creswell, J. W. (2008). *Research design: Qualitative, quantitative, and mixed methods approaches*. London: Sage.

Crompton, J. (1979). Motivations for pleasure vacation. *Annals of Tourism Research, 6*(4), 408–424. doi:10.1016/0160-7383(79)90004-5

Dann, G. (1977). Anomie, ego-enhancement and tourism. *Annals of Tourism Research, 4*(4), 184–194. doi:10.1016/0160-7383(77)90037-8

De Carvalho, R., & Ishitani, L. (2012). *Motivational factors for mobile serious games for elderly users*. Paper presented at the Proceedings of XI SB Games 2012, Brasilia, Brazil.

de Souza e Silva, A. (2013). Location-aware mobile technologies: Historical, social and spatial approaches. *Mobile Media & Communication, 1*(1), 116–121. doi:10.1177/2050157912459492

Deci, E. L., & Ryan, R. M. (1985). *Intrinsic motivation and self-determination in human behavior*. New York, NY: Plenum Publishing.

Doughty, M., & O'Coill, C. (2005, February 23–25). Collaborative software environments and participatory design. In *Proceedings of IADIS international conference on web based communities* (pp. 303–306). Algarve: IADIS.

Duman, T., & Mattila, A. S. (2005). The role of affective factors on perceived cruise vacation value. *Tourism Management, 26*, 311–323. doi:10.1016/j.tourman.2003.11.014

Eglesz, D., Fekete, I., Kiss, O. E., & Izsó, L. (2005). Computer games are fun? On professional games and players' motivations. *Educational Media International, 42*(2), 117–124. doi:10.1080/09523980500060274

Emarketer. (2013). Asia-Pacific Reaches Whopping 2.5 Billion Mobile Phone Users. Retrieved November 27, 2013, from http://www.emarketer.com/Article/Asia-Pacific-Reaches-Whopping-25-Billion-Mobile-Phone-Users/1010247

Engl, S., & Nacke, L. E. (2012). Contextual influences on mobile player experience – A game user experience model. *Entertainment Computing, 4*(1), 83–91.

Ermi, L., & Mäyrä, F. (2005). Player-centred game design: Experiences in using scenario study to inform mobile game design. *The International Journal of Computer Game Research, 5*(1). Retrieved May 3, 2015, from http://www.researchgate.net/profile/Frans_Maeyrae/publication/220200719_Player-Centred_Game_Design_Experiences_in_Using_Scenario_Study_to_Inform_Mobile_Game_Design/links/09e4150c5499d39f10000000.pdf

Farber, M. E., & Hall, T. E. (2007). Emotion and environment: Visitors extraordinary experiences along the Dalton highway in Alaska. *Journal of Leisure Research, 39*(2), 248–270.

Fernandes, R. P. A., Almeida, J. E., & Rosseti, R. J. F. (2013). A collaborative tourist system using Serious Games. *Advances in Intelligent Systems and Computing, 206*, 725–734.

Fong, P., & Frost, P. M. (2009). The social benefits of computer games. In *Proceedings of the 44th Annual APS conference* (pp. 62–65). Melbourne: The Australian Psychological Society Ltd.

Frostling-Henningsson, M. (2009). First-person shooter games as a way of connecting to people: 'Brothers in Blood'. *CyberPsychology & Behavior (numera CyberPsychology, Behavior, and Social Networking), 12*(5), 557–562.

Gentes, A., Guyot-Mbodji, A., & Demeure, I. (2010). Gaming on the move: Urban experience as a new paradigm for mobile pervasive game design. *Multimedia Systems, 16*, 43–55. doi:10.1007/s00530-009-0172-2

Goh, D. H., Ang, R. P., Lee, C. S., & Chua, A. Y. K. (2011). Fight or unite: Investigating game genres for image tagging. *Journal of the American Society for Information Science and Technology, 62*(7), 1311–1324. doi:10.1002/asi.21478

Goossens, C. (2000). Tourism information and pleasure motivation. *Annals of Tourism Research, 27*(2), 301–321. doi:10.1016/S0160-7383(99)00067-5

Gordon, E., & de Souza e Silva, A. (2011). *Net locality: Why location matters in a networked world.* Boston, MA: Blackwell Publishers.

Gretzel, U., Yuan, Y.-L., & Fesenmaier, D. R. (2000). Preparing for the new economy: Advertising strategies and change in destination marketing organizations. *Journal of Travel Research, 39*, 146–156. doi:10.1177/004728750003900204

Griffiths, M. D., Davies, M. N. O., & Chappell, D. (2004). Demographic factors and playing variables in online computer gaming. *Cyber Psychology & Behavior, 7*(4), 479–487. doi:10.1089/cpb.2004.7.479

Grüter, B. (2008, September 1–5). *Studying mobile gaming experience.* Paper presented at the Workshop: Evaluating Player Experiences in Location Aware Games, HCI 2008, Culture, Creativity, Interaction, John Moores University, Liverpool, UK.

Han, D., Jung, T., & Gibson, A. (2014). Dublin AR: Implementing Augmented Reality (AR) in tourism. In Z. Xiang & I. Tussyadiah (Eds.), *Information and communication technologies in tourism 2014* (pp. 511–523). Wien: Springer Computer Science.

Hay, B. (2008). *Fantasy Tourism and Second Life.* In S. Richardson, L. Fredline, A. Patiar & M. Ternel (Eds.), *CAUTHE 2008: Tourism and Hospitality Research, Training and Practice; "Where the 'Bloody Hell' Are We?"* (pp. 345–348). Gold Coast: Griffith University. Retrieved October 13, 2015, from http://search.informit.com.au/documentSummary;dn=970132315896676;res=IELBUS

Hinske, S., Lampe, M., Magerkurth, C., & Röcker, C. (2007). Classifying pervasive games: On pervasive computing and mixed reality. In *Concepts and technologies for pervasive games – A reader for pervasive gaming research* (Vol. 1). Aachen: Shaker Verlag.

Holbrook, M. B., & Hirschman, E. C. (1982). The experiential aspects of consumption: Consumer fantasies, feelings, and fun. *Journal of Consumer Research, 9*(2), 132–139. doi:10.1086/jcr.1982.9.issue-2

Hsu, C. H. C., Cai, L. A., & Li, M. (2010). Expectation, motivation, and attitude: A tourist behavioral model. *Journal of Travel Research, 49*(3), 282–296. doi:10.1177/0047287509349266

Huang, Y., Backman, S. J., Backman, K. F., & Moore, D. (2013). Exploring user acceptance of 3d virtual worlds in travel and tourism marketing. *Tourism Management, 36*, 490–501. doi:10.1016/j.tourman.2012.09.009

Iso-Ahola, S. E. (1982). Toward a social psychological theory of tourism motivation: A rejoinder. *Annals of Tourism Research, 9*, 256–262. doi:10.1016/0160-7383(82)90049-4

Jacob, J. (2011). *A mobile location-based game framework.* Paper presented at the DSIE'11 – 6th Doctoral Symposium on Informatics Engineering, Porto, Portugal.

Jang, S., & Cai, L. A. (2002). Travel motivations and destination choice: A study of British outbound market. *Journal of Travel & Tourism Marketing, 13*(3), 111–133.

Jansz, J., Avis, C., & Vosmeer, M. (2010). Playing The Sims2: An exploration of gender differences in players' motivations and patterns of play. *New Media & Society, 12*(2), 235–251. doi:10.1177/1461444809342267

Jobber, D. (2009). *Principles and practices of marketing* (6th ed.). Columbus, OH: McGraw-Hill Higher Education.

Jönsson, C., & Devonish, D. (2008). Does nationality, gender and age affect travel motivation? A case of visitors to the Caribbean island of Barbados. *Journal of Travel & Tourism Marketing*, 25(3–4), 398–408. doi:10.1080/10548400802508499

Juul, J. (2003). *The game, the player, the world: Looking for a heart of gameness.* Paper presented at the Level Up: Digital games research conference proceedings, Utrecht, Netherlands.

Kim, H., Ritchie, J. R., & Mccormick, B. (2012). Development of a scale to measure memorable tourism experiences. *Journal of Travel Research*, 51(1), 12–25. doi:10.1177/0047287510385467

Klimmt, C. (2003, November). Dimensions and determinants of the enjoyment of playing digital games: A three-level model. In M. Copier & J. Raessens (Eds.), *Level up: Digital games research conference* (Vol. 246, p. 257). Utrecht: Faculty of Arts, Utrecht University.

Klopfer, E., & Squire, K. (2008). Environmental detectives—The development of an augmented reality platform for environmental simulations. *Educational Technology Research and Development*, 56(2), 203–228. doi:10.1007/s11423-007-9037-6

Krüger, R. A. (1998). *Moderating focus group.* Thousand Oaks, CA: Sage.

Li, K. A., & Counts, S. (2007). *Exploring social interaction and attributes of casual multiplayer mobile gaming.* In Proceedings of the 4th International Conference on Mobile Technology, Applications and Systems and the 1st International Symposium on Computer Human Interaction in Mobile Technology, ACM, Singapore.

Lin, T.-M., Chen, S.-C., & Kuo, P.-J. (2011). *Motivations for game-playing on mobile devices: Using smartphone as an example.* In Proceedings of the 6th international conference on E-learning and games, edutainment technologies, Springer Verlag, Taipei, Taiwan.

Lin, Y.-L., & Lin, H.-W. (2011). A study on the goal value for massively multiplayer online role-playing games players. *Computers in Human Behavior*, 27, 2153–2160. doi:10.1016/j.chb.2011.06.009

Linaza, M. T., Gutierrez, A., & Garcia, A. (2014, January 21–24). Pervasive augmented reality games to experience tourism destinations. In Z. Xiang & I. Tussyadiah (Eds.), *Information and communication techonologies in tourism* (pp. 497–510). Wiern: Springer. Proceedings of the International Conference in Dublin.

Lucas, K., & Sherry, J. (2004). Sex differences in video game play: A communication-based explanation. *Communication Research*, 31(5), 499–523. doi:10.1177/0093650204267930

Marshall, C., & Rossman, G. B. (2006). *Designing qualitative research* (4th ed.). California: Sage.

Mashable. (2011). Why location-based gaming is the next killer app. Retrieved June 3, 2013, from http://mashable.com/2011/07/24/location-based-gaming/

Maslow, A. H. (1943). A theory of human motivation. *Psychological Review*, 50(4), 370–396. doi:10.1037/h0054346

McGonigal, J. (2011). *Reality is broken: Why games make us better and how they can change the world.* New York, NY: Vintage.

McIntosh, R. W., Goeldner, C. R., & Ritchie, J. R. B. (1995). *Tourism: Principles, practices, philosophies* (pp. 167–190). Hoboken, NJ: John Wiley & Sons, Inc.

Middleton, V. T. C. (1994). *Marketing in travel and tourism.* Oxford: Butterworth-Heinemann.

Middleton, V. T. C., Fyall, A., & Morgan, M. (2009). *Marketing in travel and tourism* (4th ed.). Oxford, UK: Butterworth-Heinemann.

Mintel (2009, August). Gaming in the interactive world.

Mintel (2012, February). Mobile application gaming. Executive summary report- UK.

Nelson, M. R. (2006). Digital content delivery trends in higher education. *Research Bulletin, Centre for Applied Research*, 25(9). Retrieved April 14, 2015, from https://net.educause.edu/ir/library/pdf/ERB0609.pdf

Neuhofer, B., Buhalis, D., & Ladkin, A. (2012). Conceptualising technology enhanced destination experiences. *Journal of Destination Marketing & Management*, 1(1–2), 36–46. doi:10.1016/j.jdmm.2012.08.001

Oinas-Kukkonen, H., & Harjumaa, M. (2008, February 10–15). *Towards deeper understanding of persuasion in software and information systems.* Proceedings of The First International Conference on Advances in Human-Computer Interaction (ACHI 2008) (pp. 200–205), Sainte Luce. IEEE Computer Society. Retrieved from http://www.iaria.org/conferences2008/ACHI08.html

Olson, C. K. (2010). Children's motivations for video game play in the context of normal development. *Review of General Psychology*, 14(2), 180–187. doi:10.1037/a0018984

Paras, B., & Bizzochi, J. (2005). *Game, motivation, and effective learning: An integrated model for educational game design.* Paper presented at the Proceedings of DiGRA 2005 Conference: Changing Views – Worlds in Play.

Pcarce, P., & Lee, U. (2005). Developing the travel career approach to tourist motivation. *Journal of Travel Research*, 43(3), 226–237. doi:10.1177/0047287504272020

People. (2013, March 17). Retrieved March 18, 2013, from http://js.people.com.cn/html/2013/03/17/214163.html

Pine, B. J., & Gilmore, J. H. (1999). *The experience economy: Work is theatre and every business is a stage.* Boston, MA: HBS Press.

Pine, B. J., & Gilmore, J. H. (2011). *The experience economy*, updated version. Watertown, MA: Harvard Business School.

Puchta, C., & Potter, J. (2004). *Focus group practice.* London: Sage.

Rapits, D., Tselios, N., & Avouris, N. (2005, September 19–22). *Context design for mobile applications for museum, a survey of existing practices* Proceedings of the 7th Conference on Human-Computer Interaction with Mobile Devices and Services, Mobile HCI 2005, Salzburg, Austria. Source: DBLP. doi:10.1145/1085777.1085803

Reisinger, Y., & Mavondo, F. (2005). Travel anxiety and intentions to travel internationally: Implications of travel risk perception. *Journal of Travel Research, 43*(3), 212–225. doi:10.1177/0047287504272017

Richards, G., & Wilson, J. (2003). New horizons in independent youth and student travel. A report for the International Student Travel Confederation (ISTC) and the Association of Tourism and Leisure Education (ATLAS). Amsterdam: International Student Travel Confederation.

Ryan, R. M., Rigby, C. S., & Przybylski, A. (2006). The motivational pull of video games: A self-determination theory approach. *Motivation and Emotion, 30,* 344–360. doi:10.1007/s11031-006-9051-8

Salen, K., & Zimmerman, E. (2004). *Rules of play: Game design fundamentals.* Cambridge, MA: MIT Press.

Schell, J. (2008). *The art of game design, the book of lences.* San Francisco, CA: Morgan Kaufmann.

Schønau-Fog, H. (2011). The player engagement process – An exploration of continuation desire in digital games. *Eludamos: Journal for Computer Game Culture, 6*(1), 53–70.

Smile Land Game. (2012). Retrieved January 12, 2014, from http://www.smilelandgame.com/

Stamboulis, Y., & Skayannis, P. (2003). Innovation strategies and technology for experience-based tourism. *Tourism Management, 24*(1), 35–43. doi:10.1016/S0261-5177(02)00047-X

The Real Time Report. (2012). Retrieved March 1, 2013, from http://therealtimereport.com/2013/02/05/tourism-marketing-how-a-facebook-game-lured-fans-to-cape-town/

Tourism Ireland. (2011). Retrieved March 1, 2013, from http://www.tourismireland.com/Home!/About-Us/Press-Releases/2011/Tourism-Ireland-Launches-Game-on-Facebook—First.aspx)

Tychsen, A., Hitchens, M., & Brolund, T. (2008). Motivations for play in computer role-playing games. In *Proceedings of the 2008 conference on future play: Research, play, share* (pp. 57–64). Toronto, ON: ACM.

Waltz, S. P., & Ballagas, R. (2007, September 24–28). Pervasive persuasive: A rhetorical design approach to a location-based spell-casting game for tourists In *Proceedings of situated play. DiGRA 2007 – The 3rd international digital games research conference* (pp. 489–497). Tokyo.

Wan, C.-S., & Chiou, W.-B. (2007). The motivations of adolescents who are addicted to online games: A cognitive perspective. *Adolescence, 42*(165), 179–197.

Wang, C., Zhang, P., Choi, R., & D'Eredita, M. (2002). Understanding consumers attitude toward advertising. *AMCIS 2002 Proceedings, 158,* 1143–1148.

Wang, D., & Fesenmaier, D. (2013). Transforming the travel experiences: The use of smart phones for travel. In L. Cantoni & X. Zheng (Eds.), *Information and communication technologies in tourism 2013* (pp. 58–69). Berlin: Springer-Verlag.

Williams, A. (2006). Tourism and hospitality marketing: Fantasy, feeling and fun. *International Journal of Contemporary Hospitality Management, 18*(6), 482–495. doi:10.1108/09596110610681520

Williams, D., Yee, N., & Caplan, S. E. (2008). Who plays, how much, and why? Debunking the stereotypical gamer profile. *Journal of Computer-Mediated Communication, 13*(4), 993–1018. doi:10.1111/jcmc.2008.13.issue-4

Wu, B., & Wang, A. I. (2011). A pervasive game to know your city better. In *Proceedings of the 2011 IEEE international games innovation conference* (pp. P117–120). Washington, DC: IEEE Computer Society.

Xu, F., & Morgan, M. (2009). Student travel behavior—A cross cultural comparison. *International Journal of Tourism Research, 11*(3), 255–268. doi:10.1002/jtr.686

Xu, F., Webber, J., & Buhalis, D. (2014, January 21–24). The gamification of tourism. In Z. Xiang & I. Tussyadiah (Eds.), *Information and communication technologies in tourism 2014* (pp. 525–537). Wien: Springer. Proceedings of the International Conference in Dublin.

Yee, N. (2006). Motivations for play in online games. *Cyber Psychology & Behavior, 9*(6), 772–775. doi:10.1089/cpb.2006.9.772

Yovcheva, Z., Buhalis, D., Gatzidis, C., & van Elzakker, C. (2014). Empirical evaluation of smartphone augmented reality browsers in urban tourism destination context. *International Journal of Mobile Human Computer Interaction, 6*(2), 10–31. doi:10.4018/ijmhci.2014040102

Zhou, T. (2012). Understanding the effect of flow on user adoption of mobile games. *Personal and Ubiquitous Computing, 17*(4): 741–748. Springer.

Zichermann, G., & Cunningham, C. (2011). *Gamification by design: Implementing game mechanics in web and mobile apps.* Sebastopol, CA: O'Reilly Media.

Zichermann, G., & Linder, J. (2010). *Game based marketing.* Hoboken, NJ: John Wiley & Sons.

SUBMITTED: November 17, 2014
FINAL REVISION SUBMITTED: August 18, 2015
ACCEPTED: September 8, 2015
REFEREED ANONYMOUSLY

Index

Aaron, T. 41
aerial drone videos 41, 43–44, 46, 48, 50
Agarwal, R. 4
Ahmad, A. N. E. E. S. 69
Al-Jabri, I. M. 7
Amazon 6
amenities 30, 32, 34–37
Andreu, L. 56, 60
anthropomorphism 16–17, 19, 21–23
anticipated emotions 68–71, 73–75
Apaolaza-Ibáñez, V. 68–69, 71
Arif, I. 103
Ariwi, J. 42
Aslam, W. 103
attractive attributes 28–32, 34–35, 37–38
attributes 29–32, 34–38
augmented reality (AR) 97
Avci, N. 56
Avis, C. 100

Babakus, E. 30, 37
Back, K.-J. 30
Bagozzi, R. P. 71
Ballagas, R. 106
Bartle, R. A. 99–100
Beard, J. 102
Beatty, S. E. 21
Becken, S. 56
behavioral intentions 3, 70, 79–80, 82–88; engagement 81
Beldona, S. 30
Benbasat, I. 7
Berger, H. 102
Berry, L. L. 71
Bögeholz, S. 69
Bowen, J. T. 30
Boyle, E. A. 99
Boyle, J. M. 99
Buhalis, D. 28, 102

cellphone applications 35, 37–38
Celtek, E. 101–102
Chaffery, D. 101
Chappell, D. 103
Cheema, A. 6
Chen, C.-H. 42
Chen, J. V. 5
Chen, L. C. 28
Chen, W. Y. 30, 37
Chen, Z. 41
Chiou, W.-B. 100, 109

Choi, J. K. 68–69, 71
Choi, R. 102
Choi, T. Y. 30
Chu, R. K. S. 30
Cifter, N. 56
Cohen, J. 10
community 42, 46, 55, 58, 62–64, 100, 102
complexity 4–6, 9, 11–12, 24
Connolly, T. M. 99
consumer drone market 40
consumers 3–6, 8, 10–12, 16, 19, 22, 38, 40, 42–44, 50, 67–70, 73–75, 100, 103
Craig, A. B. 81
Cranage, D. A. 28
Crespí-Cladera, R. 29
Crompton, J. 102
Cruz, P. 7
Cryder, C. E. 6
curiosity 70, 106, 108
customer dissatisfaction 30–31, 36
customer satisfaction 30–32, 35–36, 38

Dann, G. 102
data collection 71, 75
Dautenhahn, K. 18–19
Davies, M. N. O. 103
DeFranco, A. 3
DeMicco, F. J. 30
demographic profile 7, 57
dependent variables 85–86
D'Eredita, M. 102
destination 41–44, 46, 48–50, 55–56, 59, 64, 79–80, 82–88, 90, 97, 100–102, 105–110
destination marketing 40–43, 46, 48, 50
destination marketing organizations (DMOs) 41–43, 46, 49–50, 55, 100
Dev, C. 29
Dinhopl, A. 41
Dolnicar, S. 30
Donaire, J. 56, 60
Donovan, R. 80
drone food delivery services 67–69, 71–75
drones 40–41, 43–46, 48–50, 67–68, 71, 75; users 49
drone videos 41–46, 49–50; characteristics 44
Dube, L. 30

eco-friendly services 68
Eglesz, D. 100
Ellis-Chadwick, F. 101
embodied devices 81–83, 88, 90

Emenheiser, D. A. 29
emotions 17, 20, 68–75, 88, 102
environmental protection 67–68, 75

factor analysis 8, 29, 31, 34–35, 37
Fang, K. 4
Fawzy, A. 30
Fekete, I. 100
Flavián, C. 80
Fong, T. 19, 23
food 30, 57, 59–61, 64, 67–68, 75, 106, 110
Frost, W. 64

Gali, N. 56, 60
game-based marketing 98, 101, 103, 109
game players 96, 99, 102–103, 105–108, 110
gamification 96–97, 100–101
gaming concept 96–100, 102–110
gaming motivation 98, 108–109
Geographical Positioning System (GPS) 98
geographic space 56, 64
geomorphology 56
Giger, J. C. 70
Goeldner, C. R. 102
Goodman, J. K. 6
Gretzel, U. 41
Griffin, T. 82
Griffiths, M. D. 103
Grüter, B. 98

Hainey, T. 99
Han, H. 70–71
Hardgrave, B. C. 4–5
Hardy, A. 57
Hartmann, P. 68–69, 71
Hasan, B. 5
Hay, B. 41
Hayes, A. F. 86
Hinterhuber, H. H. 31–32
Hlavacs, H. 41
Hochmair, H. H. 44
hospitality marketing considerations 21
hotel attributes 28–31, 34–35, 37–38; Kano analysis of 35
hotel development strategies 38
hotel technological innovation 29
Hu, H. H. S. 69
Hua, N. 28
Hudson, S. 3
human likeness 16, 20–21
human robot interaction (HRI) 17–20, 22–23
Hwang, J. 68–71

immersion 81–84, 86–88, 109
indifferent attributes 29–32, 34, 36–38
innovation 4–6, 10–11, 28, 41
Iso-Ahola, S. E. 102, 108
Izsó, L. 100

Jansz, J. 100, 105
Jogaratnam, G. 29, 31
Johnson, P. A. 42
Jung, H. 70
Jung, T. 82
Juul, J. 98, 110

Kaiser–Mayer–Olkin (KMO) value 34
Kang, M. 42
Kano, N. 29–30
Kano analysis 32, 36
Kano model 28–32, 37–38
Kano two-dimensional quality model 31
Karahanna, E. 7
Kim, C. 7
Kim, J. 3, 7, 70
Kim, M. J. 82
Kim, S. 68
Kim, W. 71
Kim, Y.-S. 30
Kiss, O. E. 100
Klaus, P. 42
Klopfer, E. 98
Koç, B. 42
Kokkinou, A. 28
Korea 68, 71–73, 75
Kozak, M. 56
Krishna, A. 81
Kuo, C. M. 28

Lam, C. Y. 30
Laukkanen, T. 7
Law, R. 28–29, 31, 41, 102
Lee, C. K. 70, 82
Lee, I. 7
Lee, J. 30, 37
Lee, M. J. 70
Lee, S. 70
Lee, Y. H. 4–5
leisure motivations 102
Lema, J. D. 29, 31
Leung, R. 28
Lim, Y. 50
Lin, H.-W. 107
Lin, Y.-L. 107
Linder, J. 101
Liu, S. Q. 3
Lu, Y. 41
Lucas, K. 110
Lumsden, S. A. 30
Luoh, H. F. 30
Lyu, S. O. 71

Magnien, N. 42
Manochehri, N. 7
Martínez-Ros, E. 29
Maslow, A. H. 102
Mattila, A. S. 3
Matzler, K. 31–32
McGonigal, J. 98
McIntosh, R. W. 102
McKercher, B. 56
Mechanical Turk (MTurk) 6
Mediation effects 82, 86
Mehrabian, A. 80
Mendes-Filho, L. 42
Meng, B. 70–71
mental space 56, 64
Middleton, V. T. C. 97
Mirk, D. 41
Mirusmonov, M. 7

mobile games 96–98, 100, 103–105
mobile phones 18–19, 80, 84–88, 105
model of goal-directed behavior (MGB) 69–70
Moore, G. C. 7
Morosan, C. 3
motivations 3, 41, 46, 50, 83, 98–105, 107–110
Muñoz, P. 7
must-have attributes 30

negative anticipated emotions 69–75
Nelson, M. R. 103
Nguyen, B. 42
Nourbakhsh, I. 19

observability 4–6, 9, 11
Olson, C. K. 100
one-dimensional attributes 29–30, 32, 35, 37
Orfila-Sintes, F. 29

Parasuraman, A. 71
Park, E. 56
Park, J. 68
Park, Y. 5
partial least squares path modeling (PLS-PM) 8
passive tourism videos 86, 88
Pawitra, T. A. 31
personal digital assistants (PDAs) 98
personal service robots 17, 23
Perugini, M. 71
Pesonen, J. 3
Petrick, J. F. 70
Phetkaew, P. 30
Piçarra, N. 70
Plaschka, G. 29
PLS-PM 8, 10
Podsakoff, P. M. 9
positive anticipated emotion 69–70, 72–73
potential customers 79, 90, 100, 102
potential tourists 82–83, 87–88, 90, 102, 107, 109
Prasad, J. 4

Qu, H. 30

Raab, C. 30
Ragheb, M. G. 102
Rahman, M. A. 41
reality 106
Reisinger, Y. 70
relative advantage (RA) 4, 6, 9–11
Renaghan, L. M. 30
research 3, 12, 22–24, 40–44, 46, 50, 67, 71, 73, 75, 87–91,
     98, 100–105, 109–110
reverse attributes 29–30
rewards 107, 110
Reynolds, K. E. 21
Rhee, H. T. 30, 37
Richards, G. 103
Ritchie, J. R. B. 102
robots 16–24; capabilities 20, 22; design 19–20, 22;
     development 17; managing 22; personality 23;
     services 16–24, 35
Rogers, E. M. 4
Rossiter, J. 80
Russell, J. A. 80

Ryan, B. 30
Ryan, R. M. 99

Schell, J. 110
Schuett, M. A. 42
senses 80–81, 87–88
sensory cues 82, 88
sensory stimulation 80–84, 86–88; immersion 81
Seraku, N. 29
service quality 18, 29–30, 32, 35–37
service robots 16–19, 21–24
Shanka, T. 30, 37
shared aerial drone videos 40, 42, 48, 50
Sherman, W. R. 81
Sherry, J. 110
Shih, J. F. 30
Shih, Y. Y. 4
Shoemaker, S. 30
Sieber, R. E. 42
Singer, M. J. 80
smartphones 12, 20, 28, 32, 34–38, 40, 96, 98, 100,
     104–105
So, K. K. F. 3
social influence 4–7, 9, 11–12, 19, 21, 97
social space 56, 62, 64
Sohail, M. S. 7
Song, H. 70
Sönmez, S. 42
space 56, 62, 64
spatial analysis 44–45
Squire, K. 98
stimulus-organism-response (S-O-R)
     paradigm 80
Stolaroff, J. K. 68, 71
Straub, D. W. 7
Suh, K. 68
Sundarraj, R. 7

tablets 28, 40, 84, 96, 98
Takahashi, F. 29
Tan, K. C. 31
Tan, M. 7
Tanford, S. 30
Tas, R. F. 29
Tasmania 55–57, 59
Taylor, R. 30, 37
Taylor, S. 7
technological embodiment 79–91
technological innovation 28–29, 31, 34, 37–38
technology acceptance model (TAM) 3–5, 10–11
Teo, T. S. 7
Thyagaraj, K. S. 69
Todd, P. 7
Torres, E. 28
tourism game 104, 107–110
tourism organizations 97, 102, 108, 110
tourist players 98, 101, 103, 109–110
Tseng, C. Y. 28
Tsuji, S. 29
Tussyadiah, I. P. 3, 82

Uber mobile application 3–8, 10–12
Uber users 6
Uncanny Valley 17, 20–24

unmanned aerial vehicle (UAV) 40
Uşaklı, A. 42

values 4, 8, 10, 30, 34–36, 69, 72, 79, 85
Van Doorn, J. 22
Verma, R. 29
Victorino, L. 29
Vieregge, M. 30
virtual experiences 41, 81–82, 106
virtual reality 106; devices 79
visitors 42, 57, 59–60, 62, 64
Vosmeer, M. 100

Wall, G. 56, 60
Waltz, S. P. 106
Wan, C.-S. 100, 109
Wang, C. 102
Wang, D. 56
Wang, K. C. 30
Wei, W. 28

Williams, A. 101, 106
Wilson, J. 56, 103
Witmer, B. G. 80
Wong, K. F. 30
World Travel Market Report 100
Wu, M.-S. 42
Wuest, B. E. S. 29

Xu, H. L. 70

Yang, S.-B. 30, 37
Yavas, U. 30, 37
You, Y. S. 30
Youtube meta-data analysis 44

Zeithaml, V. A. 71
Zhang, P. 102
Zhu, G. 3
Zichermann, G. 101
Zielstra, D. 44